GOMPA OR BUDDHIST MONASTERY. G.
RIVER, RIVERLET OR STREAM. Chhu
LAKE. Tso
PEAK. △ **LA OR PASS.**
HOT WATER SPRING + **AUTHOR'S ROUTES.**
VILLAGE. o **CAMPING GROUND.** ●

ŌM

Specially drawn by **SWAMI PRANAVANANDA.**
To illustrate his "Kailās Yātra". Original on 18.1.1929 F.R.G.S.
Revised on 18. 2. 1947.
(5TH EDITION)
Scale 1 Inch to 4 Miles.

NEPAL

Karbu
Karbu La
Horkong
Phijul
Namardung La
TO THE SOURCE OF THE BRAHMAPUTRA
Tomomopo
Tag Tsangpo
Tora
Tashigomba
Ambu phuk
Chhuphuk
Notokur
YERNGO. Chhuten Nyombat
Purupa V. or Dayul
Nima Pendi
Riljung
Riljen Chhu
Jakpolung
Tokyul
THUGOLHO G
△ 22650
Namreldi
Thampara
Selung
Hurdung
Gogta
Rezang
SHUSHUPTSO
Lanka Donkhang
TRUSSEL.G
Dachato
14.900
Thallabhung La
Gurla La
16200
(Gori Udyar)
Gurla Phuk
GURLA MĀNDHĀTA (MEMO NANI)
△ 25355
△ 22160
Mangza Gurla Chhu
Baldak
Sekang
15000
Ringung Chhu
14400 Garu Chhu
Dungmar
Purbu
Toyo
Gary
Ronam
Lee
Doho
ChhemoChhorten
Dange chen
G
N A R P U
TAKLAKOT
1300 G
SIMBILING. G.
Mogrum
Shukung
Pala
16750
Lipu Lekh. P.
Doh Chhu
Yangse Chhu
Delaling Chhu
Helini Chhu
Takkar
Chhibra La
Dang La
Phu
Chhurku
MapChhu or KarnaliR.
Mapcha Chungo
KARDUNG
Ur-La 13300
Horkong
TO GYANIMA
TO GYANIMA

THE SACRED MOUNTAIN

THE
SACRED MOUNTAIN

Travellers and Pilgrims at Mount Kailas in
Western Tibet, and the Great Universal
Symbol of the Sacred Mountain

John Snelling

Foreword by
Christmas Humphreys

East West Publications
London and The Hague

For Jean Warren

First published 1983

East West Publications (UK) Limited
Jubilee House, Chapel Road,
Hounslow, Middlesex TW3 1TX

Copyright © John Snelling 1983

Snelling, John
  The sacred mountain.
  1. Kailas, Mount (Tibet)
  2. Mountains (in religion, folk-lore, etc.) –
  Tibet
  I. Title
  291.2'12   BL447
ISBN 0 85692 111 4

Printed and bound in Great Britain at
The Camelot Press Ltd, Southampton

CONTENTS

Contents

ACKNOWLEDGEMENTS

TO THE FOLLOWING:

Messrs. Macmillan, for permission to quote from *Transhimalaya* by Sven Hedin

Theosophical Publishing House, for permission to quote from *Three Years in Tibet* by Ekai Kawaguchi

Messrs. Faber and Faber, for permission to quote from *The Holy Mountain* by Bhagwan Shri Hamsa and from *Tibetan Adventure* by Herbert Tichy

Messrs. Frederick Warne, for permission to quote from *In Search of the Mahatmas of Tibet* by Edwin G. Schary

Messrs. Edward Arnold, for permission to quote from *In the Forests of Upper India* by Thos. W. Webber and from *Western Tibet and the British Borderland* by Charles A. Sherring

Messrs. Heinemann, for permission to quote from *In the Forbidden Land* by A. H. Savage Landor

Mrs. Margaret Shinnie, for permission to quote from articles by Captain H. U. Smith, Major C. H. D. Ryder and Hugh Ruttledge, originally published in *The Geographical Journal*

Edward Pyatt, Esq., for permission to quote from articles by Major T. S. Blakeney and Colonel R. C. Wilson, originally published in *The Alpine Journal*

Lama Anagarika Govinda, for permission to quote from his book, *The Way of the White Clouds*

Messrs. A. P. Watt Ltd., for permission to quote from the poem 'Meru' by William Butler Yeats

Acknowledgements

TO THE FOLLOWING FOR KINDLY PROVIDING PICTURES, PHOTOGRAPHS OR MAPS, AND GIVING PERMISSION TO REPRODUCE THEM:
Major David Ruttledge, C. B. Kapur, Esq., Mrs. Vera Sherring, Mrs. Charmian Longstaff, Marcelle Hanselaar, The Buddhist Society, Library of Tibetan Works and Archives (Dharamsala), India Office Records and Library, Royal Geographical Society, Shri Uma Prasad Mookerjee (Calcutta), Dr. Sálim Ali (Bombay), Government of India Tourist Office, Chris Piper, Dr. Giovanna Galluppi Vallauri of I.S.M.E.O. (Rome), John Swain, Esq., H. Harrer, Esq.

AND TO THE FOLLOWING FOR OTHERWISE HELPING OR LENDING ENCOURAGEMENT:
Lama Anagarika Govinda, Herbert Tichy, Esq., John Knight, Esq. of the B.B.C. (who produced the Radio 4 programme, *Pilgrimage to the Sacred Kailas*, broadcast in August 1980), C. B. Kapur, Esq., Miss Martha Patrick, Dr. Irmgard Schloegl, Mr. Christmas Humphreys, Phiroz Mehta, Esq., Dr. Carmen Blacker, Edward Henning, Esq., M. Hookham, Esq., S. Hodge, Esq., John Blofeld, Esq., John Hearsey, Esq., Alpo Ratia, Esq., Shri Uma Prasad Mookerjee of Calcutta, Dr. Sálim Ali of Bombay, Messrs. Gyatsho Tshering (Director) and Samphel of the Library of Tibetan Works and Archives (Dharamsala), Mr. Werner Leonhard, Mrs. Jean Warren, Dr. G. Alder, Geoffrey Marshall-Taylor, Esq., and my wife.

FOREWORD

by Christmas Humphreys

When I was at school at Malvern, some sixty-odd years ago, the boys were turned out twice a week for a long walk round the countryside. But I, with a boon companion, would run from the College and race up the Beacon, the highest point in the Malvern Hills, through gorse and bracken, over rocks and holes, in a 900-foot scramble. At the summit, we would lie on our backs, with nothing above us but the sky and, when we stood up, a glorious view of seven counties.

This, I am sure, was more than a joyous form of exercise. Something happened in us beyond a mere climb for sturdy limbs. Already the mountain as such was calling us, and ever since, in the Alps, or later in the Himalayas, it was the non-stop scramble upwards of the heart and mind which I for one was seeking, and later found in the field of Buddhism.

And here is a book about the same phenomenon, beautifully produced and illustrated, and from an unexpected source. Mr. John Snelling, who has honoured me by asking for this Foreword, is the General Secretary of the Buddhist Society, London, and Editor of its journal, *The Middle Way*, a most sedentary pair of occupations. But ten years ago he made the Everest Trek from Kathmandu and in due course climbed to some 19,000 feet, which is higher than any mountain in Europe. This is an arduous and hazardous journey, and the clearly distinguishable stages of it were for him 'a series of hierarchic levels that suggested the graduated stages in the progress of the soul on the spiritual journey as described in traditional religious texts, both Eastern and Western'. He learnt the meaning of the mountains to both heart and feet, and much of Buddhism along the way. For these are truly *the* Hills, and those who travel in them are never the same afterwards. Even a single view, deeply seen and absorbed, can change one's inner being, as I found myself when I stood with Bhante Sangharakshita twenty years ago on a hill in Gangtok, Sikkim, and gazed on Kanchenjunga, forty miles away, and its sunlit peaks, which rise to some 28,000 feet above sea level.

It is therefore not surprising that many religions have sacred mountains at the heart of their cosmology, and Buddhism, a child of India, early accepted Mount Meru as the invisible yet ineffable Centre of all. It stands, as Mr. Snelling puts it, 'as heart and hub of a complex multidimensional system embracing both the spiritual and material realms', and he describes its symbolism in detail. But where is it to be found, for who is content with a cosmological symbol when sufficient search may reveal the physical fact? Seekers ranged the Himalayas for centuries, but eventually the mantle of Meru fell upon the crowning peak of a range in Western Tibet, a peak known as Kailas, which is some 22,000 feet high.

Only a very few Western explorers and pilgrims have seen this remote and remarkable peak, and written of its wonderful symmetry and compelling spiritual presence. Giuseppe Tucci was there in 1935 and, in 1948, Lama Govinda, well known to us at the Buddhist Society in London, who talks of the 'joyful tension' felt by pilgrims as, after the rigours of the gruelling outward journey across the full width of the Himalayas, they begin the long circumambulation around the mountain which has been trodden by generations of devotees. I understand that for the time being, the Chinese, nowadays in political command of Tibet, will only allow access to the sacred mountain via Ladakh, and then to serious pilgrims only, travelling on foot. There may be merit in this decision, for the mountain is a supremely holy one, and difficulty of access protects its sanctity from the less pleasant aspects of tourism.

For millions this is Mount Meru made visible. From its environs rise four of the great rivers of India, with traditional names very similar to those accorded in ancient texts to the four rivers that rise from Meru. The mountain is venerated by the followers of four great religions, not only by Hindus and Buddhists but also by Jains and the indigenous Tibetan Böns. In its religious heyday, Kailas was crowded with monasteries and shrines, which lined the sacred peregrination route around it. Not even Olympus, or Fuji in Japan, can equal this ecstatic veneration.

To all who made pilgrimage to it, Kailas was the veritable Centre, both of the earth and of the universe and, more importantly, 'that conceptual point where sacred reality impinges upon profane reality, where time and eternity meet, and where all dualities are resolved'.

In his conclusion, where he attempts to unravel something of the great mystery that lies at the heart of the great symbol of the sacred mountain, Mr. Snelling reaches to China and quotes Hui Neng, the sixth Patriarch of the Zen Buddhist school: 'The idea of a self and of a being is Mount Meru . . . When you get rid of the idea of a self and of a being, Mount Meru will topple.' And so too, Mr. Snelling argues, Mount Kailas will topple, not necessarily the physical mountain (though that too, like all compounded things, must pass) but rather the mythical mountain lodged in the mind of the devotee, complete with its dense mantling of mind-made projections.

And what remains after that mighty falling? It would be improper to say anything further here, for if the end of a great pilgrimage could be so readily reached then there would be no virtue in the pilgrimage itself, and the sages all assure us that there is *every* virtue in the pilgrimage itself. (It is said in Buddhism to be better to travel well than to arrive.)

What lies ahead of the reader is a kind of literary pilgrimage to the sacred mountain, mainly conducted through an investigation of what was arguably the greatest of them all, Mount Kailas, in well-chosen words and magnificent pictures. It is replete with adventure, and many curious and absorbing things besides. Hopefully too, along the way, something of the power and magic of the sacred mountain will emerge from the pages and touch the heart of the reader.

PASSES

1 TINKAR
2 LIPU LEKH
3 MANGSHANG
4 LAMPKIYA DHURA
5 KUNGRI BINGRI
   JAYANTI AND
   UNTADHURA
6 NITI
7 MANA

CHAPTER ONE

Himalaya

In 1971, I saw the Himalayas for the first time and like many before me was deeply affected. It was during the rainy season and I had gone up to the hill station of Mussoorie to escape the oppressive heat and humidity of the Indian plains. For weeks, dense monsoon clouds boiled out of the lower valleys, completely obscuring the surrounding mountain landscape. Then one evening I happened to go up to a rocky bluff a little above the new Buddhist temple, built in a small Tibetan refugee community, and I found the world transformed. The usual mantle of cloud had suddenly and completely dissipated, and all around stretched a world whose vastness and beauty could not till then have been imagined. A dramatic sunset was also under way, and the sky looked as though the contents of a crucible of molten metals had been flamboyantly splashed across it. . . . And then, quite unexpectedly, I became aware of the jagged ribbon of the snow mountains. A hundred miles away on the utmost rim of the horizon, they were reflecting the rose light of the setting sun with icy brilliance. They were tiny – but magnificent.

Later, in Nepal, I made the Everest Trek, which had the feel of a religious pilgrimage about it; the earthen trail cut across the grain of the land with innumerable arduous ascents and descents, which, coupled to ancilliary hardships and hazards (like hunger, leeches and dysentery) all added up to a pretty substantial dose of salutary suffering for the two of us making the journey. Furthermore, in so far as we progressed from lush, green, terraced lowlands to barren rocky wastes at the heights, passed through cloud forest, topped the treeline and ventured beyond the critical 15,000 foot altitude level where the oxygen becomes thin in the air, this was also a journey that had a number of clearly-distinguishable stages; it involved passing through a series of hierarchic levels that suggested the graduated stages in the progress of the soul on the spiritual journey as described in traditional religious texts, both Eastern and Western.

There were even foretastes of the ultimate goal, in the form of glimpses of the snow peaks from the occasional high pass, that inspired us onward when our spirits flagged. And there were those soul-destroying phases when we just plodded on

1. *A Buddhist* stupa

through endless, meaningless rain and mud, and felt we would never reach journey's end.

There was also copious evidence of Buddhism all along our route. *Stupas*★ and *mani*† walls dotted the entire length of the trail; enormous *mantras*‡ were carved on the wayside rocks; prayer flags raked the wind along the heights; and there were *gompa*§ to stay at or visit in every village. Entering one cautiously, I found myself in almost total darkness. Then, as my eyes became habituated to the gloom (made more gloomy by everything being encrusted with the soot of butter-lamps), I was drawn to the far end by the dull glint of copper and gold. There I found a small shrine covered with the usual votive

2. *The* mantra, OM MANI PADME HUM

objects. . . . Suddenly I was overtaken by a disconcerting sense of being watched. On checking, I found nothing to right, left or behind. Looking above, however, I discovered that I was being surveyed by an enormous gilded Buddha which occupied the interior of a commodious shaft cut up high behind the shrine. The Buddha was smiling, as though at my discomfort – a good-humoured smile to which I had to respond. . . . On another occasion we sat till deep into the

★ A type of Buddhist monument (see *Fig. 1*).
† Walls composed of stones upon which the sacred formula *Om Mani Padme Hum* has been carved (see *Fig. 2*).
‡ Religious formula, e.g. *Om Mani Padme Hum* (see *Fig. 2*).
§ Buddhist monastery or temple.

night with a bevy of *tsampa**-eating, *chung*†-drinking Sherpa villagers while two lamas – one small, stout and bald; the other gaunt, with long skeins of hair wound around his head – droned the sacred texts by the hour. As the night wore on, the benign and wrathful deities painted in vivid lacquers on the walls seemed to come alive and dance in the unstable hurricane-lamplight, sending me finally out into the alien night, strangely haunted then and for long afterwards by that potent iconography.

After about a week of seesawing between cloud-hidden heights and lugubrious valley depths, we came to a particularly precipitous ascent. We started in the bowels of a deep gorge, passed up into cloud, and finally emerged into a new world of pure light, ultramarine sky and dazzling snow mountains. It ·was arrival – and it had happened, like the encounter with the hidden Buddha, suddenly and dramatically. Nearby was the notable Sherpa centre of Namche Bazaar.

Thereafter we delved on deeper among the bright peaks, finally venturing past the last human habitations to the sequestered heights where movement became difficult in the rarefied air, but where colours, undiminished by the usual atmospheric detritus, reached the eye with a primary intensity that lent the landscape a savage beauty from shimmering dawn till about mid-afternoon, when invariably the substantial world dissolved into a numinous mist. My companion and I lost the true trail in such a mist somewhere up in the Solu Khumbu region, not far from Everest. Completely disorientated, we wandered for hours in a mountain wasteland of moraine and scree, while the air rang with the threatening roar of distant waters plunging into unseen chasms.

As though by grace, in the last flicker of twilight we stumbled upon two isolated yakman's huts in a remote pasture-land amid the peaks, and took shelter for the night. It was, we knew, only a temporary reprieve. We were in deep trouble, for which we alone were to blame. We had in *hubris*

---

* A doughy dish made from roasted barley meal, sometimes mixed with butter tea.

† A pungent alcoholic brew made by Tibetans.

trespassed upon the preserve of the gods, where human beings rightly should not go. With little food, and without either guide or compass, we had no certainty of ever finding our way out of that high labyrinth. Neither of us spoke that night. Sleep, when it came, was thin and fitful. Strangely, however, the possibility of death in the near future from starvation or exposure had, in the final analysis, a liberating effect.

All the mental and emotional baggage that entrammels us for most of our lives seemed to drop away during the hours of darkness, leaving us somehow clearer and freer and more in touch with the world. In short, close to death, we felt, paradoxically, very close to life.

We began to dehydrate in the thin air and I had to get up several times during the course of the night to go outside and slake my rampant thirst at a nearby stream. The veil of mist had miraculously lifted during the intervening hours of darkness; the night was clear and bright with flashing starlight. The great ice mountains, crowding huge and remarkably close all around, were picking up that light and reflecting it. They looked like great crystal cities of the future charged with vast protean energies. . . . And again, next morning, when we two potentially doomed men threw open the door of our little temporary shelter, we walked into a world bathed in brilliant sunshine – a world as fresh and as palpably god-given as on the first morning of creation.

In the event, *Nirvana* was not for us on that occasion; nor did we perish in some uninhabited valley in the no-man's-land between Tibet and Nepal. Within about an hour of setting out, we recognized far below us the sky-blue lake which we had seen the previous afternoon. Then all was made clear. In the mist we had done the classic thing and blindly wandered in an almost perfect circle. The hut where we had spent the night was in fact hardly a stone's throw from the moraine dump where we had originally gone astray. In a very short time, and with intense relief, we were soon following the main trail on up beside the cyclopean debris of the Khumbu glacier. When we met two Sherpas, we did not hesitate to engage them to guide us to Base Camp on Everest and back. We were in no mood for any more mischances.

Finally, next day, to stand in brilliant morning and see the world's highest mountains parading themselves in magnificent panoply to the farmost rim of the horizon. It was yet another demonstration of the infinite scope and beauty of things, which may so easily pass unnoticed as we pursue our blinkered concerns in the narrow confines of the cities of the plains. Would we, however, have been so sensitive to it all without the hard training of the difficult overland haul? The hunger, the blisters, the frustrations, the discomforts, and finally the culminating brush with mortality, had all helped to grind away a little of our usual arrogance and make us more humble and open – and consequently able to see the world a little more clearly.

However, it was just a taste – a little piece of paradise on account. Although we toyed with the idea of finding a cave and taking to the *yogic* life up there, it was not a viable possibility. We knew that we would soon be back among the cities of the plains, where we would have to struggle very hard to retain even a little of the clarity of vision that had been afforded us at the heights. The first spiritual insights may be given; the rest have to be sought through work.

Several weeks later, recrossing the Indian–Nepalese border at Raxaul, I was treated to a final parting glimpse of the Himalayas. It was a vivid evening and good to be back on the teeming, dusty plains, but those great mountains, disposed in full array and magnificence across the northern horizon, were again radiating the rich rose light of the setting sun.

Recalling this evocative scene at a later date, when the world had contracted to a tight knot, bereft of movement and magic, and when even the quality of light seemed to be deteriorating, I suddenly realized that total spiritual hopelessness – *damnation*, if you like – cannot be possible in a universe that affords sights of such beauty to its inmates; that whatever has charge of the disposal of things must be fundamentally benign and forgiving. That was a very great relief – and something that also has strong associations with Buddhism, for not so far from Raxaul, at Lumbini, just a few miles away across the Indo-Nepalese frontier, Gautama the Buddha was born, and such sights must have been familiar and influential to him. It may be a subjective thing, but the beauty of those mountains at sunset images very powerfully the intrinsic beauty of the religious way that the Buddha initiated – a way that itself leads from the morass of our human sufferings and problems to a true wholeness and harmony with that which *is*.

It is understandable that those who have inhabited the plains of India should have, from time immemorial, been similarly affected by those great mountains. The late Professor Junrirō Takakusu, the eminent Japanese Buddhist scholar, has described the process whereby the invading light-skinned Aryans, who began to enter the subcontinent sometime during the second millennium B.C., at first pushed southwards in their march of victory – until they reached the tropical zone:

> Then, because of the severe heat, they chose to select their abode among the cool forests of the Black Mountains, which form the smaller range at the foot of the great Himalaya. Gradually they came to regard the forest as their ideal abode, and in time they acquired the habit of meditating with the great Himalaya as the object of their thoughts, for there was Himalaya, eternally magnificent, eternally unapproachable. During mornings and evenings the snows would glow in changing splendour as the rays of the sun struck them; in winter the glaciers in the valleys were frozen solid; but in summer the glaciers flowed along the winding valleys like giants coming to life after a year's sleep,
>
> (J. Takakusu, *Essentials of Buddhist Philosophy*)

On occasion, the Indians seem to have looked upon the Himalaya, the 'Abode of Snow', as a single, many-peaked mountain, personified as the god Himavat. A daughter of the mountain, by name Parvati Haimavati or Uma Devi, became the consort of the great Lord Shiva himself. Legend describes her playfully covering her Lord's eyes as he sat in meditation on a peak of Himalaya. Instantly all light and life were extinguished in the universe until, out of compassion for all beings, the god opened his third eye, which blazed like a new sun. So intense was its blazing that it scorched the mountains and forests of Himavat to oblivion. Only when he saw that the daughter of the mountain was properly contrite did he relent and restore her father to his former estate.

Many other legends relating to Lord Shiva and the goddess have the Himalaya for their setting. For instance, Dr. Tom Longstaff, the distinguished mountaineer, records an incident where a party of travellers were destroyed by an avalanche which local belief maintained had been hurled from the top of Trisul by Shiva himself, 'who was incensed at their approach to his veiled bride (Nanda Ghungti).' Indeed, one of his names is *Girisa*: 'Lord of the Hills'.

Nor is Lord Shiva alone in this. Hindu mythology records many gods having their abode in Himavat, together with all kinds of semi-divine and demoniac beings such as *rakshas* (demons) and *gandharvas* (celestial musicians). In these mountains the sacred river Ganges, personified as Ganga, another of Himavat's daughters, has its principal source. Here too are situated great shrines: Badrinath, consecrated to Vishnu; and Kedarnath, consecrated to Shiva, where once devotees hurled themselves bodily from the brink of an adjacent precipice – a reminder of the terrible aspect of the great god. In another of his aspects Lord Shiva is the Great Ascetic, and innumerable *yogis* and *rishis* are reputed to dwell in remote caves in the Himalayan fastnesses, performing their austerities. Withal, the virtues of Himalaya are supreme. To merely think of it is to gain vast merit, to see it is to have one's sins expunged as dew is evaporated by the morning sun.

Nor when Europeans came to India did they go untouched either. No less a luminary of the British Raj than Sir Francis Younghusband recognized the fact that the mountains possess a unique capacity to affect the religious susceptibility in man and he wished this consciously exploited in order to awaken people to the truths of religion.

Efforts should be made both in India and England to lead expeditions to the Himalayas to find the best view-points of the mountains and make them known to the outside world. When these best spots would be discovered, they would be turned into and preserved as places of pilgrimage.

(quoted in: Swami Pranavananda,
Exploration in Tibet, 1st edition)

During my time in northern India, as well as during the Everest Trek, I certainly felt deeply affected by this power. I also experienced the way in which a particular mountain can become charged with an almost inexorable magnet-like force capable of drawing one to it, like a fish hooked on a line, over miles and miles of the most inhospitable terrain. Certainly Everest became a sacred mountain for my companion and myself – as indeed it is for those who live in its environs, by whom it is called *Chomolungma*: 'Mother Goddess of the Snows'.★ Strangely this religious magnetism was apparent despite the fact that the mountain was invisible to us for virtually the whole of our journey, or perhaps the effect was heightened by our goal being obscured. Even when we were very close, looking across at it from the best vantage point – atop a 19,000 foot pile of rocks called Kalar Patar – it deigned to reveal only a portion of its summit. The rest of the great mountain remained withdrawn in seclusion behind its entourage of attendant peaks. What we could see of it was surprisingly snow-free and regular – reminiscent of the top of the Great Pyramid of Gizeh. As solid and imperturbable as a great sage in deep meditation, it stood gloriously unmoved by the hurricane blast of the high-altitude winds that ripped a steady jet-stream plume of whiteness from its apex.

And what of those men who have attempted to climb this great mountain? One of the most sensitive responses by a mountaineer that I have come across is by the late G. H. Leigh-Mallory. He describes how Everest appeared to him more than fifty years ago as he approached it from the Tibetan side. Looking from a distance of about ten miles, at the bottom of the Rongbuk glacier:

> At the end of the valley, Everest rises not so much a peak as a prodigious mountain mass. There is no complication to the eye. The highest of the world's mountains, it seems, has to make but a single gesture of magnificence to be lord of all, vast in unchal-lenged and isolated supremacy. To the discerning eye other

★ According to H. Hoffmann (*Religions of Tibet*), 'The White Goddess of Heaven' (gNam-lha dkar-mo) also lives in the neighbour-hood of Everest, together with five 'Sisters of Long Life', each of whom is endowed with a special pool of different-coloured water.

mountains are visible, giants between 23000 and 26000 feet high. Not one of their slendered heads even reaches their chief's shoulder; beside Everest they escape notice – such is the preeminence of the greatest. . . .

(quoted in: M. Ward (ed.), *The Mountaineer's Companion*)

In 1924, Mallory and his climbing partner Irvine were lost at over 28,000 feet while trying to scale this 'prodigious white fang excrescent in the jaw of the world'. As the search for the two climbers proceeded in vain, their colleague N. E. Odell reflected:

What right had we to venture thus far into the holy presence of the Supreme Goddess, or, much more, sling at her our blasphemous challenges to 'sting her very nose-tip'? If it was indeed the sacred ground of Chomolungma, Goddess Mother of the Mountain Snows, had we violated it – was I now violating it? Had we approached her with due reverence and singleness of heart and purpose? And yet, as I gazed again another mood appeared to creep over her haunting features. There seemed to be something alluring in that towering presence. I was almost fascinated. I realized that no mere mountaineer alone could but be fascinated, that he who approached close must be led on and, oblivious of all obstacles, seek to reach that most sacred and highest place of all.

(*Ibid.*)

Odell's tone is humble, even devout; he is obviously aware of the *hubris* inherent in man's desire to conquer great mountain peaks. This conquering spirit is very much a modern and a Western phenomenon; other peoples do not on the whole display much preoccupation with anything so inevitably bound to lead to unnecessary discomfort and danger. Indeed, sensitive as they often are to the spiritual aspect of mountains, a desire to scale them would in their eyes be often tantamount to outright sacrilege. Of course, in recent years the inexorable spread of Western ideas and influences, wedded to the power of Western money, have done a great deal to moderate such scruples. Nevertheless, it was religious considerations that caused the Nepalese authorities to place the Fish-tail peak, Muchapuchare, out of bounds to climbers; and when, in 1956,

Dr. Charles Evans led a British expedition to the world's third highest mountain, Kanchenjunga, which straddles the Nepal-Sikkim frontier, out of respect for Sikkimese beliefs, his party left the top and its neighbourhood untouched, venturing no further up the mountain than was necessary to prove that its summit *could* be reached. Kanchenjunga, 'Five Treasures of the Great Snow', so-called on account of its five majestic peaks, is personified as the highest god of the Himalayan state of Sikkim, and elaborate sword and mask dances are held to celebrate the god's feast in monasteries throughout the land.

Returning eventually from my travels to native ground in Britain, I worked on a B.B.C. radio programme about the religious connotations of mountains. Research revealed the surface of the earth to be liberally sprinkled with spiritually significant peaks: Fuji, Ontake, Wu Tai, Omei, Chiu Hua, P'u T'o, Adam's Peak, Arunachala, Abu, Chomolhari, Demavend, Ararat, Sinai, Moriah, Hira, Kilimanjaro, Athos, Olympus, Helicon, Parnassus, Popocatapetl, Shasta. . . . The list was apparently endless. Even in Britain we have our relatively modest but nevertheless spiritually evocative Glastonbury Tor, our enigmatic Silbury Hill, our various St. Michael's Mounts, not to mention many another mountain, hill, tumulus or tump clearly touched in some measure by the same magic.

One mountain, however, stood high above the rest, a sacred mountain overtopping the ranges of lesser sacred mountains, their epitome and apogee. This mountain was called *Kailas*. The present volume is principally concerned with Mount Kailas. Firstly, its spiritual and mythological associations are examined in some detail, together with their historical, religious, political and geographical contexts. The possibility of identifying Mount Kailas with Mount Meru, the *axis mundi* of many classical Eastern cosmologies, is also discussed. Then the narratives and reports of the relatively few Western travellers and explorers who managed to reach the remote Kailas are outlined with a view to discovering how the mountain impressed them, their purposes for going there and the adventures they experienced in doing so. This section of the book in fact represents a brief survey of the exploration of the part of Western Tibet in which Kailas is situated. Next, the accounts of the pilgrims, the men who travelled to Kailas primarily for spiritual purposes, are outlined with a view to discovering both how the sacred mountain and the long, difficult and dangerous pilgrimage to it affected *them*, especially, of course, from the spiritual point of view. Finally, the other sacred mountains of the world are reviewed, together with the ancilliary kinds of religious and semi-religious associations with which mountains have been invested, and then an attempt is made to define the highest, fullest manifestations of the notion of the sacred mountain. The central thesis of the work is that sacred mountains – that is, mountains that are held in profound religious awe – participate in a universal symbol of archetypal power. In examining in depth the material relating to what was once arguably the greatest of them, it is hoped that it might be possible to unravel the great mystery that this symbol enshrines.

CHAPTER TWO

Mount Kailas and its Sacred Lakes

Had an enterprising cartographer ever been moved to draw a religious map of Asia, many of the thin red lines tracing the principal pilgrim routes would have been shown to converge on a remote and remarkable part of Western Tibet. Here, a little to the north of India, across the jagged rampart of the Great Himalaya, there is a sacred mountain called *Kailas*. For more than two millennia the faithful made the arduous journey there: from all parts of India; from the Himalayan kingdoms of Sikkim, Bhutan, Nepal, Ladakh and Kashmir; from every quarter of the forbidden land of Tibet; and from far into the mysterious hinterland of Central Asia – and perhaps even from beyond.

The above held true until a little over twenty years ago. Up to then, Tibet had for centuries been isolated both by its own sequestered situation on the Roof of the World and by the inwardly-directed religious preoccupations of a sizeable proportion of its population. Though bona fide pilgrims were always tolerated, foreigners were diligently debarred from crossing its frontiers, and no attempt was made by the government to have anything approaching normal relations with either its immediate neighbours or with the international community in general. By default, therefore, Tibet's political status went undefined and unguaranteed, and there was little that the Tibetans could do when, in the middle years of the present century, the Chinese, having carried through their own Marxist revolution, began to revive old claims that Tibet was an integral part of China and to advance these claims by force. In 1959, the monk-ruler of Tibet, His Holiness the Dalai Lama, fled to exile in India. Thereafter, the Chinese completed their takeover, and closed the borders of Tibet more inexorably than ever before to secular and religious traffic alike.

Political régimes, however temporarily powerful, cannot as a rule remove great mountains; so Kailas must remain. We know that it is no longer visited by non-Tibetan pilgrims, and it is unlikely that many Tibetan pilgrims are able to visit it:

> In Tibet the Tibetans are too busy we presume to think about pilgrimage; moreover, even if Tibetans do wish to go on a pilgrimage to this area they cannot because travel and movement within Tibet is extremely restricted. It is possible that the Tibetan nomads who inhabit this region go on a pilgrimage and circumambulate the sacred mountain. As for the five monasteries . . . judging from the conditions of all monasteries in Tibet, it is possible though not probable, that the monasteries in this region are too either destroyed or derelict. This office has no recent photographs of Kailas.
>
> (from a letter to the author from Mr. Samphel of the Information Office, Central Tibetan Secretariat, Dharamsala, India, 28th April 1981)

No information has been forthcoming from official Chinese sources. Lacking more detailed precise information about present conditions at Mount Kailas, it is therefore to the evidences of the past that we must turn in order to find out what this spiritually powerful peak was like and how it was regarded. In consequence, what can be stated hereafter must often be put in the past tense, though it is to be hoped that in many cases the present tense is also in fact applicable.

The landscape of the corner of the great plateau of Tibet in which Kailas is situated is one of desolate beauty. In the high altitudes prevailing there – 13,000 feet and more – virtually no trees and little other vegetation clothe the rugged terrain. Due to the transparency of the rarefied air, however, colours reach the eye with unfiltered intensity: rich reds, browns, yellows, purples – and in fine weather both sky and mirroring water are a deep, noble blue. Climate, on the other hand, is unpredictable, at times violent, and always prone to extremes of heat and cold. It is said that while a man's arm, exposed to the heat of the sun, may be being scorched, his feet, lying in shadow, may at the same time be suffering the ravages of frostbite. Not surprisingly, therefore, this has always been a scantily populated area.

The sacred mount Kailas stands out of this elemental landscape, a compelling and uncannily symmetrical peak. Sheer walls of horizontally stratified conglomerate rock form a monumental plinth thousands of feet high that is finally capped by a cone of pure ice. Such is the regularity of the mountain that it looks as though it might have been carved by human – or more accurately, *superhuman* – hands, those of the gods in fact. Kailas has been frequently compared to a great temple, a cathedral, or a *stūpa* – one of those characteristically Buddhist monuments known in Tibet as *chortens* (see *Fig. 1*). The analogy almost invariably has religious connotations, for in some mysterious way Kailas seems to have the power to touch the spiritual heart of man; in the past this has been as true for hard-headed explorers as it has been for the more impressionable pilgrims.

THE RELIGIOUS ASSOCIATIONS OF KAILAS

Kailas is regarded as a *sacred* mountain by followers of no less than four of the great religions of Asia: by Hindus, Jains, Buddhists and followers of the pre-Buddhist Shamanistic religion of Tibet, the Bon religion.

Hindu Associations
Pious Hindus look upon Kailas as the Heaven or throne of

3. Mount Kailas compared in side elevation with the Kailasantha Temple, Ellora (after E. B. Havell)

Mahadeva himself: the great god Shiva. Here he sits in perpetual meditation with his consort Pārvatī, the daughter of Himalaya. The situation is depicted in a carving in the great Kailasantha temple at Ellora in Central India, with the demon Ravana shaking the mountain in his vain attempt to unseat Lord Shiva and his mate. As the name suggests, Kailas was the prototype for the Kailasantha temple, and indeed for other temples in India of the same type (see *Fig. 3*). The appearance of the mountain is also strongly phallic, for which reason devotees of Shiva identify it with the *lingam*: the phallic symbol characteristic of Shaivism. In the *Mahānirvāna Tantra*, the 'Tantra of the Great Liberation,' a dialogue in which Lord Shiva expounds the principles of *tantra* to his *shakti* or consort, Kailas is described in the following fulsome terms:

> The enchanting summit of the Lord of Mountains, resplendent with all its various jewels, clad with many a tree and many a creeper, melodious with the song of many a bird, scented with the fragrance of all the season's flowers, most beautiful, fanned by soft, cool, and perfumed breezes, shadowed by the still shade of stately trees; where cool groves resound with the sweet-voiced songs of troops of Apsara [heavenly nymphs] and in the forest depths flocks of kokila [cockatoos] maddened with passion sing; where [Spring] Lord of the Seasons with his followers ever abide. . . ; peopled by [troops of] Siddha [holy men of semi-divine status] Chñrana [celestial singers, dancers, bards or panegyrists of the gods] Gandharva [celestial musicians] and Gānapatya [devotees of the god Ganesha].
>
> (trans. Arthur Avalon (Sir John Woodroffe) *The Tantra of the Great Liberation*.)

Another Hindu belief can be found in the *Purānas*, a canon of popular traditional texts, which maintains that Kubera, the god of wealth, ruled from a fabulous city called Alakā, which was situated on or near Kailas, and that eight lesser peaks nearby were his treasure houses. In Kālidāsa's classic Sanskrit epic poem, *Meghadūta* (Cloud Messenger) a love-lorn *yaksha* (a powerful spirit) banished from Alakā recruits a passing cloud to carry a message to his estranged wife, who still resides in Kubera's city. The poet speaks of Kailas being used as a mirror by *Apsarases* (heavenly nymphs), the saddles of its ridges rent apart by Ravana's arms: 'With soaring peaks snow white as lotus blooms/ Cleaving the sky, as stalwart as if they grew/ Through heaping up day by day/ The Three-eyed-One's [Lord Shiva's] o'erflowing laughter.'*

---

* In G. H. Rooke's translation apropos the last line, the commentary states that 'the whiteness of laughter has been adopted as a poetical convention.' (Rooke, p. 40n)

Alakā itself is described as an exotic pleasure-city – a kind of celestial oriental Las Vegas – 'full of lovely girls and pictures;/Deep-toned tabors throb to dance and song,/Floors gem-inwrought, cloud-kissing roofs . . .'.

Finally, the great Hindu epics, the *Rāmāyana* and the *Mahābhārata*, have frequent recourse to Kailas as an analogy for anything of commanding height. It is said to be six leagues high, to be an assembly place for all gods and demons, and to be the site of a great jujube tree. In short, Kailas is the glory of the Himalayas:

> There is no mountain like Himachal, for in it are Kailas and Manasarovar. As the dew is dried up by the morning sun, so are the sins of the world dried up at the sight of Himachal.
>
> (*Rāmāyana* – quoted C. A. Sherring, *Western Tibet and the British Borderland*)

Jain Associations

Kailas is also recognized as a spiritually significant peak by the followers of the Jain religion, a compassionate creed that arose in India at about the same time as Buddhism (around the sixth century B.C.) with which it has many affinities, including emphasis on the attainment of liberation from the painful round of worldly existence. In Jain writings Kailas is called *Astapada*, and is reputed to have been the place where Rishabha, the first *Tirthankara*, attained *Moksha* or liberation. Although the actual and historical founder of Jainism was Mahavira ('Great Man'), the 24th *Tirthankara*, Jains in fact regard their creed as embodying timeless wisdom propounded in the world in all ages. The *Tirthankaras* were the avatars of the present fallen age which has followed the golden age.

Buddhist Associations

Buddhists, meanwhile, associate Kailas with a tantric meditational deity (*yidam*) called Demchog (Skt.: *Samvara* – 'Eternal Bliss') and his consort (*yum*) Dorje Phangmo (Skt.: *Vajravarahi*). This is not really the proper place to delve deeply into the great mystery of *yidams* but basically they figure as tutelary deities in certain practices of Tibetan Buddhism.

While superficially they may be regarded as gods, and as such are represented in great and graphic detail in sacred paintings, initiates regard them more precisely as personifications of purified aspects of human nature, particularly of wrathful or passionate aspects which might ordinarily cause great suffering but which if properly transformed through spiritual training may produce true wisdom. 'The passions are the Buddha nature,' is a well-known saying in Buddhism. Demchog is an awe-inspiring figure, full of fierce energy. Depictions represent him as having four faces, each of a different colour (red, blue, green, white), each with three eyes. He wears a grizzly crown of human skulls and has a tiger skin draped around his waist. His body is blue and the twelve hands of his twelve arms each hold a symbolic object: a *vajra* (thunderbolt), elephant skin, cup, bell, dagger and so forth. Beneath his feet he tramples two prostrate figures. Dorje Phangmo, meanwhile, with whom he unites in a glory of flames, carries a curved knife and a skull cup. Her naked body is red. She is associated with Tijung, a small pyramidal peak adjacent to Kailas, according to Swami Pranavananda, who also maintains that Demchog is associated with two other Tibetan mountains besides Kailas: Lapchi, near Nepal, and Chari, 200 miles east of Lhasa.

Swami Pranavananda also asserts that the Buddha was thought to inhabit the sacred mountain with a retinue of five hundred *bodhisattvas* (realized beings who have deferred their own Nirvana so that they may work for the salvation of all other beings), but this may not have been a generally held view, at least latterly, for in modern times the most important Buddhist association seems to have been with the great *guru*-poet Milarepa, who lived in the late eleventh and early twelfth centuries of the Christian era. He belonged to the Kargyu school of Tibetan Buddhism, and was the pupil of Marpa, the Translator, whom he succeeded as head of the order. He is often shown in Tibetan paintings with his right hand cupped to his ear (like certain modern folk-singers when trying to get a note), his body a strange greyish or greenish colour as a result of his having lived exclusively on nettles at some time in his life. Legend holds that Milarepa was involved in a vital struggle for possession of Mount Kailas with Naro Bhun Chon, a priest of the Bon faith.

Bon-po Associations

The Kailas-Manasarovar region was in fact probably one of the chief centres of the Bon faith long before Buddhism appeared in Tibet around the seventh century A.D. It belonged to a class of mountain that the followers of Bon, the Bon-po, held in especial awe, associating them with certain ancestral gods and hence bestowing upon them the status of 'soul' of a region. Kailas was the soul mountain of Zhang Zhung. It towered above the heavenly sphere like a parasol with eight ribs, and above the earth like an eight-petalled lotus or a spread carpet. It was the navel of the world, the seat of a sky goddess and the dwelling-place of 360 *Gi-kod*, a class of deity exclusive to Kailas and clearly associated with the year's turning. It was also down the 'heavenly cord' of Kailas that the emanation body of Shenrab, the founder of the formalized Bon religion, descended to earth. It was also imagined as a great *chorten* (or *stūpa*) of rock crystal, and as a palace where several families of gods resided. It had four gates, one guarding each of the four cardinal points: Chinese tiger, tortoise, red bird and turquoise dragon.

Clearly, if Buddhism was to prevail in Western Tibet, it had to gain control of this highly auspicious mountain from the Bon-po, and establish itself strongly there. Many legends record the epic struggle that took place but the best known is that of Milarepa's contest of magic with Naro Bhun Chon, which was recorded by the great guru's disciple, Ras-chung-pa, in *The Hundred Thousand Songs of Milarepa*.

THE GREAT CONTEST OF MAGIC

Apparently, when Milarepa went to *Tise*, which is what Tibetans call Kailas (*Kang Rinpoche*★ is another name), he was met and welcomed by the local deities. He was not so

★ Literally, 'Jewel of the Snows'.

cordially treated by Naro Bhun Chon, however, whom he first encountered on the shores of Lake Manasarovar. He showed little respect for Milarepa, who already had a considerable reputation for mystical attainment, and told him that as the Bon-po were in possession of the sacred mountain he would have to change his faith if he wanted to stay and meditate there. Naturally, Milarepa did not accept this. He told Naro Bhun Chon that the Buddha himself had prophesied that Kailas would one day fall under the sway of the followers of the Dharma and that moreover, as his own teacher, Marpa, had spoken of the mountain, it had become especially significant for him personally. He therefore invited the Bon priest to renounce his faith and become a Buddhist. Naro Bhun Chon declined in his turn and suggested that they resolve their differences by holding a contest of magic. The loser should cede the sacred mountain to the winner.

Naro Bhun Chon started the contest by straddling the lake and singing an inflamatory song which vaunted his own mystical prowess while deprecating that of his opponent. Milarepa replied by covering the lake with his own body *without at all enlarging his body*, and singing a counter refrain. Finally, for good measure, he put the whole of Lake Manasarovar on his finger-tip without harming any of the living beings in it.

The Bon priest was impressed and conceded initial defeat but insisted they hold another contest. He then betook himself to Kailas and began circumambulating the mountain in the anticlockwise manner that was later to become characteristic of the members of his faith. Milarepa and his disciples meanwhile began to do likewise in the contrary, clockwise direction that similarly later became established practice for Buddhists. They eventually met up on a large rock in the north-eastern valley of Kailas and began tugging each other to and fro. Milarepa, being the stronger, finally managed to drag the Bon priest off in the direction he wanted to go.

When they reached the northern valley of Kailas, Naro Bhun Chon suggested a trial of strength. He promptly lifted a rock the size of a yak. Not at all disconcerted, his Buddhist opponent lifted both rock and lifter, then, as the latter still would not give in, he sat himself in the Lotus Cave on the west side of Castle Valley and stretched one leg clear across to the mouth of a cave on the east side where the Bon priest was now himself sitting. Naro Bhun Chon attempted a similar feat but failed miserably, at which the 'Non-men spectators' watching from the sky began to hoot with laughter.

Despite intense shame and embarrassment, Naro Bhun Chon declared his resolve to fight on. He began circumambulating the mountain again in his own mode. When he next encountered Milarepa, on the south side of the mountain, it had begun to rain.

'We need a shelter to protect us,' the Buddhist said. 'Let's build a house. Would you prefer to lay the foundations and floor, or put on the roof?'

'I'd prefer to put on the roof,' the Bon priest replied.

They set about the work but in no time it had turned into a competition as to who could split the biggest rocks. Naturally, Milarepa came out well ahead. He then rather unsportingly used his occult powers to make the roof stone too heavy for Naro Bhun Chon to raise. In so doing he also cunningly prepared an opportunity for himself to demonstrate his own virtuosity yet again. He proceeded to dexterously manhandle the huge rock in various ways, leaving various prints of his hands, feet and head upon it. The cave thus made became famous and was called the Cave of the Miracle-Working. Trounced yet again, Naro Bhun Chon was obliged to admit defeat.

But still not final defeat. More contests took place between the two opponents until a final and deciding one was agreed. Possession of Kailas would fall to he who could reach the summit of the mountain on the fifteenth day of the month.

Naro Bhun Chon immediately got into training, applying himself assiduously to his Bon practices. Very early on the appointed morning, Milarepa's disciples caught sight of him flying through the sky on a drum. He was wearing a green cloak and playing a musical instrument. As their own master had not yet got up, the disciples were understandably very upset. Their anxiety was intensified when, on being told what was happening, Milarepa showed little concern and made no move.

The disciples need not have worried, of course. At the very last moment Milarepa was able to halt his opponent's upward progress with a simple gesture. Then, as day broke, he snapped his fingers, donned his own cloak and soared towards the summit. He appeared upon it just as the first rays of sunlight touched it. Seeing him thus, the very apotheosis of victory, what could Naro Bhun Chon do but fall ignominiously down the side of the mountain, his drum clattering after him?

Later, his spiritual arrogance finally subdued, Naro Bhun Chon humbly asked Milarepa that his followers might be allowed to continue to circumambulate the sacred mountain in their own fashion; also that they might be given a place from where they might be able to see Kailas. Milarepa granted the first request and in response to the second picked up a handful of snow and flung it onto the summit of a nearby mountain, thereby bequeathing it to the Bon-po.

SACRED PLACES AND SPIRITUAL PRACTICES

The principal purpose that any latterday pilgrim, be he Hindu, Buddhist or Bon-po, had in view when he undertook the rigours of a pilgrimage to Mount Kailas was to make the great *parikrama* or circumambulation of the sacred mountain.

The usual route was, according to Swami Pranavananda's calculation, some 32 miles long and could be completed 'very comfortably in three days and two days a bit hurriedly'. Some especially keen Tibetans strove to complete the course in a single day, a feat known as *Chhokar*. This does not, however, seem to have been blessed with universal admiration for its practitioner was dubbed *Khi-kor*: 'he who runs round like a dog'. At the other extreme there were those even greater enthusiasts who performed *parikrama* by means of prostration, measuring the full length of their bodies over the ground over the whole distance. Of course, they had to gird themselves up well for this to prevent their bodies being cut to pieces by the rocky terrain. This long-drawn-out and painful method could take anything from 15 to 25 days. Finally, for irredeemably indolent pilgrims reluctant to contemplate even the most benign of these options, it was always possible to hire proxies who, for a fee, would do the whole thing in their stead.

The *parikrama* route started at Tarchen (*alt.* Tarchan

Darchan, etc.) on the southern side of Kailas. This was an important centre of the wool trade, albeit little more than a collection of tents with only one or two permanent buildings. In one of the latter lived a Bhutanese monk-officer, for the place fell under the jurisdiction of the kingdom of Bhutan and had done, according to Swami Pranavananda's account, since a Bhutanese lama named Ngava-Namgyal had been given it by the Tibetan authorities about 300 years before the time the Swami was writing (c. 1950). Two of the five monasteries or *gompa* (*Tib.*, lit. 'solitary place') spaced at intervals around the sacred mountain also fell within the purview of the Bhutanese. These were Nyandi (or Chokku) in the west, and Zunthulphuk (*alt.* Zuprul, etc.) on the eastern side. The latter had strong associations with Milarepa. On the northern side of the mountain, enjoying a commanding view of the spectacular northern face, was Diraphuk (*alt.*, Diripu, Dindiphu, etc.) *gompa*, while there were two *gompa* to the south: Gengta (*alt.* Gyangtrag, etc.) and Silung.

Every inch of the *parikrama* route was replete with powerful symbolism and auspicious association. There were footprints of the Buddha and other religious luminaries, caves where great yogis had lived and pursued their austerities, and tortuous rocks where virtue could be put to the test. There were special places where the pilgrim should pause and prostrate himself before the mountain, and there were innumerable cairns to which he should add a stone of his own in passing. There was a lake, the Gauri Kund lake (*Tib.* Thuji Zimbo, altitude 18,200 feet), where he was expected to perform ablutions, though as it was almost perpetually frozen this seems to have been neither a popular nor exactly feasible proposition; in practice it seems to have been generally regarded as sufficient merely to break the surface ice and sprinkle a few drops of the sacred (and stinging!) water on one's body. Just above the Gauri Kund lay the pass of Dolma La, which at 18,600 feet was the highest point of the circuit. It was considered beneficial for the pilgrim to leave some personal memento on a great butter-daubed rock situated here; literally a *personal* memento – a lock of hair, perhaps, or a tooth. High on the southern side of the mountain, meanwhile, there were two other remote lakes: Tso Kapala (or Rukta), which was thought to contain the key of Kailas, and Tso Kavali (or Durchi). The water of the one was said to be black, of the other, white. Only those who had made at least thirteen circumambulation rounds were considered properly qualified to visit them and, if they so wished, to take away the soft alluvial soil of Rukta as *prasad* (holy gifts).

Interesting features of Kailas included a large rock known as Tyu-punjung, said to resemble the Hindu monkey god Hanuman, and, nearby, a small mountain called Neten-yelak-jung, said to resemble Nandi, the bull mount of Lord Shiva. These lay on the southern side of the mountain while complementing them on the northern side were two small mountains reputed to be symbolic of the Buddhist *bodhisattvas* Chenresig and Chagnadorje (*Skt.* Avalokiteshvara and Vajra-pani). At Serchung, on the way to Nyando *gompa*, there was a great flag-pole called Tarbochhe, where fairs were held on Buddhist festivals. To the inspired eyes of some pilgrims, meanwhile, the markings on the southern face of the sacred mountain were suggestive of a great swan. Cut into the base of that same face there was a row of nineteen *chortens* – Serdung-chuksum – which were monuments to the abbots of Dekung monastery, 100 miles north-west of Lhasa. They were cared for by the monks of Gengta *gompa*, who periodically repaired and painted them yellow. This spot was notorious for avalanches and rockfalls and, if Swami Pranavananda's description is accurate, that air here was frequently wild with the whizzing of falling debris.

Aesthetically, the sacred mountain treated the circumambulator to a visual feast – in Swami Pranavananda's words, every side having 'a peculiar face, charm and beauty of its own . . . each hour presenting a fresh scene and each turn revealing new glimpses and beauties of mountain-grandeur' (*Exploration in Tibet*, 2nd Edition).

In Buddhist eyes, mountain and *parikrama* route were a terrestrial projection of the cosmic *mandala*, each circuit a single turn of the Wheel of Life (see back cover), a progress through life to death and thence to rebirth. One circuit would atone for the sins of one life; ten circuits for those of an aeon; 108 circuits would secure *Nirvana* in this life. Orthodox

Tibetans would ideally make either three or thirteen circuits, travelling either singly or in companionable groups. As they went they might twirl prayer-wheels, mutter a *mantra* or be preoccupied with other practices, though the ritual need not be a solemn or self-mortifying affair and for those so inclined would have afforded opportunity for conviviality.

For Hindu pilgrims, on the other hand, making the orthodox Kailas pilgrimage as laid down in holy writ, there was a plethora of incidental observances – shrines to visit, places to bathe – that were required of them as they toiled up from the plains and on through the mountains. Once across the high passes into Tibet, they visited the monastery at Kojarnath, south-east of the sacred lakes. Then, returning to Manasarovar, they performed *parikrama* there, and perhaps at Rakshas Tal too, before going on to Kailas. There was moreover a school of thought that maintained that no Kailas pilgrimage was complete without a side-trip to Tirthapuri in the west, where there was a satellite *gompa* of Hemis *gompa* in Ladakh; the Sutlej flowed nearby.

According to Charles Sherring, one-time Deputy Commissioner for Almora and himself a traveller in the region, many Hindu pilgrims liked to make an extended tour of the Himalayan and Transhimalayan holy places during the hot season to escape the sweltering heat of the plains. They would assemble at Hardwar, where the Ganges disembogues from the Himalaya, and trek on from there up to the shrines at Badrinath and Kedarnath before going on to Kailas-Manasarovar by way of the Niti pass. If they subsequently returned to India by the more direct Lipu Lekh pass they thus made the whole tour into a kind of grand *parikrama*.

MOUNT MERU, AXIS MUNDI

In discussing the religious and spiritual connotations of Mount Kailas, it is interesting to speculate about the possible connexion between the mountain and the mythical Mount Meru (alternatively, Sumeru, Sineru), the cosmic mountain or *axis mundi* of Hindu cosmology and its Buddhist and Jain variants.

Early Hindu cosmological notions systematized in the

Puranas has Mount Meru standing at the centre of a complex multidimensional system embracing both the material and spiritual dimensions. On the one hand, the various heavens and underworlds are disposed in due order of hierarchy along a vertical axis running through the centre of Meru. On the other hand, the earth, the material dimension, is disposed along a horizontal plane extending outwards from the body of the mountain, rather below the median level. In some versions, the seven continents are shown radiating outwards in succession, each separated from the next by a sea of some exotic liquid. A curtain wall of mountains forms the outer

4. *The Hindu Puranic view of the world as a Great Lotus*

boundary, beyond which is the Void. In other versions, the earth resembles a great lotus flower, with the continents arranged like petals around the great central pericarp of Meru. (see *Fig. 4*)

Meru's reputed height is mind-boggling. A figure of 84,000 *yojanas* is often cited. It is difficult to give an accurate equivalent to a *yojana*, estimates by scholars and translators vary from as little as a league to as much as 9 miles. Probably the best way to view the 84,000 *yojanas* is as a figurative expression denoting sheer vastness of altitude.

As for its other qualities like shape, colour and composition, accounts also vary. Meru may be gold, or self-luminous, or multi-coloured (red, white, yellow and 'dark'); it may be shaped like an inverted cone, or saucer-shaped, or a parallelepiped; it may be quadrangular, octangular, hundred-angled or even thousand-angled.

What is certain, however, is that the sun, moon and other heavenly bodies take their orbits around Meru, and that day and night are in fact caused by the interposition of the bulk of the mountain between the observer on earth and the luminaries in the heavens. The Pole Star stands directly above its summit.

Meru is quite naturally the home and playground of the highest of the gods – a kind of Hindu Olympus. It is principally associated with Brahma, the greatest of them all, and indeed his palace and throne are situated on the summit. Other important deities have their abodes elsewhere upon the mountain.

Finally, Meru is the source of all the life-giving waters of the world. One Puranic myth describes the river Ganges issuing first of all from the foot of Vishnu, the Preserver, and thence descending onto the summit of Meru, washing the moon in its descent. It encloses the city of Brahma on the summit and afterwards divides into four great streams which flow off in the four cardinal directions to water the four quarters of the world. These rivers are the Sita, supposed to flow from an elephant's head; the Alaknada, supposed to flow from a cow's head; the Chaksu, from a horse's head; and, finally, the Bhadra, from a lion's head. There is another Puranic myth that describes the seminal stream as falling initially into the tresses of Shiva's hair, where it is detained until liberated by King Bhagirath; it then divides into seven subsidiary streams: the Chaksu, Sita, Sindhu, Hladini, Nalini, Pavani and Bhagirathi.

The inevitable question is: can Mount Meru be identified with any actually existing mountain or mountain region?

S. M. Ali, author of a substantial study of Puranic geographical notions, argues that there are five possible contenders for
the mantle of original Meru:

1) The region covered by the Karakoram cluster of
   peaks.
2) The region covered by the Daulagiri cluster of peaks.
3) The region covered by the Everest cluster of peaks.
4) The Tibetan plateau enclosed by the Kun Lun and
   Himalayan arcs.
5) The Pāmīr high plateau enclosed by the snow–clad
   peaks of the Hindu Kush, Karakoram, Tien Shan and
   Trans Altai system.

Having weighed up the respective qualities of each, he comes
to the conclusion that the Meru described in the *Puranas* must
be the Great Pāmīr Knot of Asia. Kailas, it will be noted,
isn't even on the list of possibles. Whatever *earlier* classical
tradition may have maintained, however, numerous writers
are agreed that by modern times Kailas and Meru were
regarded as one. Charles Sherring writes:

> In some accounts Mount Meru clearly indicates the mountains to
> the north and west of Cashmere, and in others those in the
> neighbourhood of Kailas and Lake Manasarovar. But whatever
> may have been the original meaning of the description, there is
> no question that all local traditions fix the spot as lying directly to
> the north of the Almora district; and this is the universal belief
> among all Hindus at the present time.
> (C. A. Sherring, *Western Tibet and the British Borderland*)

Sherring concedes that it could not be argued that the
notion of Meru derived from some crucial formative experience at the time of the Aryan migrations, for the routes by
which they entered India lie much further to the west. Once
established on the plains as 'Hindus', however, it would have
been quite natural for them to have been deeply awestruck by
the majestic sight of the snowcapped Himalayas lying to the
north and have come to regard them as the home of their
gods. Finally, had they later dispatched explorers in search of
the sources of the great rivers – all of which would be regarded

as subsidiary streams of the great seminal river that descended from heaven – they might have been led to the Kailas-Manasarovar region. Sherring quotes the persuasive remarks of E. T. Atkinson, author of the encyclopaedic *Himalayan Gazeteer*:

> After traversing the difficult passes across the snowy range and the inclement table-land of Tibet, they discovered the group of mountains called Kailas, and the lakes from which flowed forth the great rivers to water and give life to the whole earth. The rugged grandeur of the scene, the awful solitude and the trials and dangers of the way itself naturally suggested to an imaginative and simple people that they had at length rediscovered the golden land, the true home of their gods. . . .
>
> (E. T. Atkinson, *Himalayan Gazeteer*)

The four great rivers that Atkinson mentions as rising in the Kailas-Manasarovar region are the Indus, Sutlej, Brahmaputra and Karnali. If indeed, as many maintain, Kailas and Meru came to be generally identified by Hindus in later tradition, then it was probably this important point of coincidence that sealed the matter. That Kailas was the

5. *The Jain world view (after D. C. Sircar)*

source of four great rivers was quite simply too remarkable to be overlooked. Other factors, like the unusually regular shape of the mountain, would merely have lent extra weight to the identification.

The notion of Meru also appears prominently in Jainism. Jains display a singular preoccupation with cosmology, and cosmological diagrams form a prominent feature of their art. In the Jain view, the world resembles a great man (see *Fig. 5*) . . .

6. The Buddhist world view

or three cups, placed one above the other, with the lowest and topmost inverted. The disc of the earth lies in the lowest part of the middle or 'waist' section and is again dominated by the august presence of Meru, which, according to H. Jacobi, has grown to a dizzy 100,000 *yojanas* in height. The concentric oceans and continents radiate around it as in the Hindu view, though only two and a half of the continents are inhabited. Meru is finally also regarded as the centre around which the heavenly bodies – the Jains maintain that there are two sets of each – take their orbits.

Meru also figures in classical Buddhist cosmology (see *Fig. 6*), towering as before at the centre of a multidimensional cosmic system 'like the handle of a mill-stone' (Waddell).★ Again the fantastic height of 84,000 *yojanas* is specified, though in this case the mountain is also reputed to penetrate to a similar depth into the nether regions below the terrestrial plane, thus indicating a grand total of 168,000 *yojanas*. It is said to be mounted on the three-peaked Trikuta rock, 'like a vessel upon a tripod' (Spence Hardy).★ As regards its shape, descriptions vary, but one recurring view is that its summit is rather wider than its base, which accords with the old Hindu view. As regards composition and colouring, some Buddhist cosmologers maintain that the eastern face of Meru is silver or crystal (white), the southern face is sapphire or lapis lazuli (blue), the western face is ruby (red) and the northern face is gold (yellow). Finally, various kinds of sweet-smelling plants grow upon the mountain and spread their pleasant perfumes in all directions.

Seven concentric rings of golden mountains radiate out from the Buddhist Meru, each usually said to be separated from the next by an intervening sea. Between the last mountain range and the outer curtain wall of iron mountains (*Chakravāla*), there is a vast ocean in which bask the four great continents: Videha, Godânîya, Jambudvîpa and Uttarakuru. Each is situated at one of the four cardinal points and is accompanied by a pair of satellite continents. Later Buddhist cosmologers have moved the continents in closer to the *axis mundi*, perhaps so that the abodes of men should not be exiled so far from the vital centre. Beyond the *Chakravāla* there is endless dark space in which float innumerable other world systems just like this one, each similarly founded on a two-layered basis of water and air, each with its constituent spheres arranged around a central Meru. All are subject to the Law of Impermanence (*anicca*), however, and thus are in process of coming into being and ceasing to be. Thus every Mount Meru, the hub of each world system and the symbol of

★ See Bibliography.

all that is most fundamental and substantial, will eventually be destroyed:

> Worlds clash with worlds, Himalaya Mountains with Himalaya Mountains, and Mount Sinerus with Mount Sinerus, until they have ground each other to powder and have perished.
>
> (trans. H. C. Warren, *Buddhism in Translation*)

In caverns beneath Mount Meru, well below sea level, there are four towns called 'Shining', 'Star-tassel', 'Deep' and 'Golden Town', each ruled by its respective king. In these towns dwell *asuras*, or titans: bellicose beings who often sally forth from their grim abyss to join battle with the gods (*devas*), their perpetual enemies, who inhabit the upper levels of Meru, the classic cause of their contention being the Great Wish-fulfilling Tree that grows half-way up the side of the mountain.

There are four upper terraces on Meru, separated from each other by 10,000 league intervals. The first three are inhabited by different kinds of *yakshas* (powerful spirits). The fourth is inhabited by the Four Great Kings, the guardians of the four quarters, who are ranked among the gods. They keep watch on the behaviour of human beings on earth and periodically report their findings to the gods on the level above them, who rejoice or lament accordingly. They also enjoy extensive retinues, which include *gandharvas* (celestial musicians).

Half-way up the side of Meru, Buddhist cosmologers maintain that the chariots of the sun, moon and stars are to be found. Then, on the summit, is situated the Heaven of the Thirty-three (*Trayastrimśa*), so named because the sublime beings who dwell there are ruled by an elite of that number headed by Śakra, 'the Indira of the gods', highest of them all. According to mythology, at some remote period, Śakra expelled the *asuras* who had originally inhabited the summit area. He flung them to the bottom of the mountain after having first, rather unsportingly, made them drunk. Thereafter he had to provide his new domain with extensive fortifications to protect it against an *asura* counter-attack. The splendour of the Heaven of the Thirty-three is a wonderful city called *Sudarsana* ('Lovely View': 'Belle View'). It boasts a thousand lofty gates, each guarded by five hundred blue-clad *yakshas*, all armed to the teeth. Like any other city, it has numerous streets of houses and several markets. It also has many distinguished buildings, the finest of which is *Vaijayanta*, a hundred-towered palace that the Venerable Mogollana, one of the Buddha's foremost devotees, thought to be the most beautiful of abodes. On each of the four sides of *Sudarsana* there is a great park containing a magic lake and a tower (*stūpa*) built over relics of the Buddha. On the north-east side of the city, meanwhile, there grows a great tree whose flowers give off a divine perfume, while on the south side lies a great preaching hall: *Suddharma* – 'Hall of the Excellent Law'. Here Śakra sits on his royal throne, flanked by the thirty-three, and listens to the reports of the Four Great Kings. Finally, *Sudarsana* is surrounded by 'districts, depart-ments and hamlets belonging to the *Devas*' (Spence Hardy), extending outward in every direction as far as the elaborate outer defences.

The gods who inhabit the Heaven of the Thirty-three are a most fortunate breed, endowed with every kind of personal advantage, living in commodious palaces made of precious materials, and enjoying almost unstinted pleasure and luxury. Still subject to the Law of Impermanence, however, their sojourn here, though long, is nevertheless of limited duration; the bitter season will inexorably come when their stock of merit is exhausted and they must die miserably. Gautama the Buddha is reputed to have visited this heaven to preach *Abhidharma* to his mother, who was reborn here as a *Devaputra*. He is said to have covered the enormous distance to the summit of the world mountain in three huge strides, and also to have preached to eight million gods from Śakra's own throne in the great preaching hall.

Meru and Kailas

Tradition maintains that Buddhism spread to Tibet from the seventh century A.D., during the reign of King Songtsen gampo. It came by various routes: roundabout via China and Central Asia, but principally and more directly from India. Buddhist cosmological notions, and the concept of Mount Meru which they enshrined, would have been brought to

Tibet with the rest. We know that Kailas was deeply venerated long before the advent of Buddhism and that, in order to establish themselves in Western Tibet, it was vital for the Buddhists to displace the Bon-po and secure possession of the sacred mountain for themselves. What could have been more natural but that, once Kailas had become a manifestly *Buddhist* sacred mountain, the connotations of Meru should be transferred to it? And if such a development did gradually take place, would it not have been consolidated by the fact that, over the course of the next thousand years or more, the Hindus – who had been making pilgrimages to Manasarovar since time immemorial – began increasingly to venerate the nearby Kailas and endow it with, among other things, the connotations of Meru as laid down in their own traditions? Hinduism and Buddhism are not mutually opposed and contradicting religions but rather part of a single tradition and tend to accept and even adopt each others beliefs and practices with an open-mindedness that is hard for westerners to comprehend.

What we are arguing here is not that Meru and Kailas were regarded as absolutely and definitively one at all times, which is the way the Western mind would like to have it, but rather that, in the more flexible, accommodating Eastern mind, the notion of their identity over the centuries gradually gained a certain relative currency.

Finally, by way of closing the matter, it is interesting to note the Tibetan (one might say, *Tibetan Buddhist*) names for the four rivers rising in the Kailas-Manasarovar region as quoted by Swami Pranavananda in his *Exploration in Tibet*. He cites as his reference a work he calls *Kangri Karchhak*, 'the Tibetan *Kailasa Purana*', versions of which he found at the Diraphuk and Gengta *gompa*. These would probably be the works which Professor Giuseppe Tucci found at the same places in 1935 and which he describes as pilgrims' guides to the sacred region outlining its historical, mythological and religious associations. Tucci maintains that the versions he found were independent of each other. Pranavananda's names for the great rivers are as follows:

In the West: the *Langchen Khambab* or Elephant-mouthed river – the Sutlej

In the North: the *Singhi Khambab* or Lion-mouthed river – the Indus

In the East: the *Tamchok Khambab* or Horse-mouthed river – the Brahmaputra

In the South: the *Mapcha Khambab* or Peacock-mouthed river – the Karnali

They are almost identical with the old Puranic names for the four waters that flowed from Mount Meru (see p. 28).

Other Manifestations of Meru
No consideration of the matter of Mount Meru would be complete without a word about the many ancilliary manifestations of the *axis mundi* in the various traditions. These

7. *The Hindu Tantric view of the human body*

exist by virtue of the fact that the ancient Oriental cosmologers were able to discern marvellous correspondences (or 'homologies') between the order of the universe or of its constituent world systems (macrocosm) and the structure of lesser entities, notably man (microcosm).

In the traditional Hindu Tantric view of the human body, for instance, the median nerve which runs through the centre of the spinal column, and which is the chief channel for the psychic forces in man, corresponds to Meru. The practitioner of yoga seeks to divert the energy from the secondary nerves into the median nerve, where as *kundalini* it rises by degrees

8. *A* mandala

from the perineum to the crown of the head, passing en route through the five *chakras* or vital centres. When *kundalini* as *shakti* (Divine Power) reaches the Thousand-petalled Lotus of the brain *chakra*, it unites with *Jnana* (Divine Wisdom) and the yogi experiences realization. The brain *chakra* in this case corresponds to the summit of the world mountain (see *Fig. 7*). Comparable notions are found in Buddhist Tantrism, though scholars would disagree about the degrees of sameness and difference between the two traditions, and about which ways influences travelled.

There is also a Meru of the *mandala* (see *Fig. 8*). *Mandala* are those cosmic diagrams used in connexion with certain

37

meditation practices. Carl Jung called them 'magic circles'. That venerable authority on Tibetan Buddhism, L. A. Waddell, describes a *mandalic* ritual employing rice, where a portion of rice is set down in the centre to represent the world mountain, and the officiating lama chants: 'In the centre of the iron wall is *Hum* and *Ri-rab* (Meru), the king of mountains.' Another writer on Tibetan Buddhist practice, R. B. Ekvall, describes a simple substitute *mandala* that can be created by interlacing the fingers of both hands with the palms turned upwards and the two third fingers, back to back, 'pointing upward to represent Meru'. According to Professor Tucci,★ the symbol of Meru in a *mandala* is the *brahmasūtra*, the 'Thread of Brahma', which effects the fundamental north-south, east-west divisions of the inner surface of the *mandala*. In *mandala* initiations, the neophyte is conducted on a careful progress to the centre; as he approaches it he must encounter the terrible guardians who protect the inner sanctum. The very centre of the *mandala* corresponds to the summit of Meru:

> Transformation from the plane of *samsāra* to that of *Nirvāna* occurs in successive phases, by degrees; just as on the cosmic mountain and round the *axis mundi* are disposed, rank after rank, the Gods ever purer. Little by little one rises towards the peak and beyond the peak right up to the summit of all that becomes and has form (*bhūtakoṭi*), where takes place the passage to the other plane.
>
> (G. Tucci, *Theory and Practice of the Mandala*)

Mountains in general provided the prototype for the classical

---

★ Professor Tucci is disposed to see and indeed emphasize the common ground in the matter of the Hindu and Buddhist traditions of the *mandala*. As he writes in his Preface to *The Theory and Practice of the Mandala*: 'Dealing with the *mandala*, I have considered both the Buddhist as well as the Hindu *mandala*; there may be differences in expression and designs, there may be a different accent laid on the psychological and theoretical situations, but, as a whole, the spiritual background is the same: the same in the yearning to find a way out of time to eternity, to help the primaeval consciousness, which is fundamentally one, to recover its integrity.' Other scholars would perhaps prefer to stress the differences between the two traditions.

Hindu temple, Meru provided that for the most splendid type. Ideally, this should have six sides, up to sixteen storeys, be sixty-four cubits (*hastas*) high and thirty-two or fifty cubits in width; it may only be built with a member of the warrior (*kshattriya*) caste as patron and have as architect either a member of the priestly (*brahmin*) or merchant (*vaisya*) castes. Titus Burckhardt furthermore points out that every classic Hindu temple is built on *mandalic* or cosmic plan and so is symbolically pierced by the *axis mundi*, which emanates from well above the building, enters it through the cupola, proceeds downwards through the successively enlarging pyramidal superstructure to finally penetrate the womblike cavern at the heart:

> The axis of the world corresponds to the transcendent reality of *Purusha*, the Essence that passes through all planes of existence, linking their respective centres with unconditioned Being, situated symbolically at the highest point of the axis, clear of the pyramid of existence, the likeness of which is the temple with its many storeys.
>
> (T. Burckhardt, *Sacred Art in East and West*)

Similar symbolism is to be found in certain Buddhist buildings and monuments. The great Tibetan temple complex at *Samyé* was built on the cosmic plan by the Indian masters Padmasambhava and Sântarakshita in the eighth century A.D., and it too has a token Meru at its heart. The notion of the world mountain is also implicit in that most characteristic of Buddhist monuments, the *stūpa*, by virtue of the fact that this too – as Lama Govinda puts it – has 'psycho-cosmic symbolism'. Of especial interest is the great eighth-century *stūpa*-temple at Borobodur in Java which, so the great historian of religion, Mircea Eliade, maintains, is nothing less than an artificial seven-storeyed world mountain: a man-made Meru (see *Fig. 9*). As the devotee approaches it, he believes that 'he is coming close to the centre of the world and on its highest terrace he breaks through into another sphere, transcending profane, heterogenous space and entering "a pure earth"'. (M. Eliade, *Patterns in Comparative Religion*).

9. Borobodur

Borobodur irresistibly calls to mind the seven-storeyed *ziggurats* of ancient Babylon – and indeed the many other world mountains, both man-made and mythological. For the notion of a great mountain, or alternatively a great tree, a navel or some such appropriate symbol, standing at the centre of the world is by no means exclusive to Oriental tradition. It occurs, so Eliade maintains, in a multitude of cultures from Finland to Japan, and traces can be found among primitives and in the symbolism of prehistoric monuments. It has archetypal power.

If, as we have argued, Meru became identified in later Hindu and Buddhist tradition with Mount Kailas, then all those pilgrims who directed their feet towards the sacred mountain in Western Tibet believed that in so doing they were venturing to the centre of the world, there to perform pious *parikrama* around the *axis mundi*, the essence that unites heaven, earth and hell, the vital Centre where spiritual transformation is possible.

THE SACRED LAKES

Of the two lakes lying to the south of Kailas, the eastern Lake Manasarovar (*Tib*. Tso Mapham – 'The Undefeated' in honour of Milarepa's success in the encounter with Naro Bhun Chon) is the better regarded, the more frequented and the more liberally endowed with both religious and mythological associations. Its beauties have been lavishly praised, in particular the rich colouring of its waters, which grade from a limpid blue near the shores to a deep emerald green as they approach the centre. It is an impressive foreground to the silver dome of Kailas shining away in the north.

At an altitude of 14,950 feet above sea level, Manasarovar is about 50 feet higher than its western neighbour, Rakshal Tal, from which it is separated by a narrow isthmus of land. It is also regarded as the highest body of fresh water in the world. In former times, eight *gompa* (Buddhist monasteries) surrounded its margins: Chiu, Cherkip, Langpona, Punri, Seralung, Yerngo, Thugolho (alternatively Thokar), and Gossul. If the entire lake was seen as representing the Buddhist Wheel of Life (see back cover), with the hub lying at its centre, then the eight *gompa* were situated at those points where the eight spokes intersected with the rim. As in the case of the Kailas *parikrama*, a complete circumambulation of the lake, passing by way of the eight *gompa*, was a single symbolic turn of the Wheel, with all the benefits that that implied. Swami Pranavananda (see pp. 172–84), who made no less than nine Manasarovar *parikramas*, said that they variously took him between two and four days to accomplish. A practitioner of trance running (*Lung-gom-pa*) could do it in a day. The length of the usual *parikrama* route was about 64 miles, while a circuit of the lake by way of its shores was about ten miles shorter, though this could only be performed in winter when the streams that otherwise made it impossible were frozen. All pilgrims had to be on the lookout for *dacoits* (bandits), who infested the area.

Some Buddhists, including Ekai Kawaguchi and Lama Anagarika Govinda (see p. 145, and p. 198), believed that Manasarovar was identical with the legendary Anotatta Lake. Prior to the birth of the Buddha, his mother, Queen Maya, dreamt herself transported there by the gods and bathed in the waters. When her body had been thus purified and she was ready to receive him into her womb, the Buddha appeared from the direction of Kailas (which was one of the five peaks surrounding Anotatta), riding a white elephant. A different legend describes the Buddha and many *bodhisattvas* sitting on lotus flowers floating on the surface of the lake. Yet another maintains that herbs capable of curing all the ills of mind and body abound in the earthly paradise that lies around Anotatta. The environs of Manasarovar have a similar therapeutic reputation, being endowed both with many kinds of curative herb and also with radioactive springs believed to possess healing powers. Thus the association with Anotatta is given added substance.

Nor is Manasarovar unvenerated by the Hindus. Their belief is that the lake was created by a mental effort on the part of the god, Brahma, the Creator. *Manas* means 'mind'. According to legend, Brahma's sons, who were *rishis*, or holy men, repaired to Kailas, where they saw Shiva and Parvati, and they remained there for twelve years performing austerities. Lacking a convenient place to perform their ablutions, however, they appealed to their father for help. Brahma obliged. While rejoicing at the creation of the lake, the Rishis saw and worshipped a great *lingam* (phallus) that arose from its midst.

According to another Hindu legend, the Naga king – the *nagas* were a species of divine cobra – and his subjects live in the lake and feed on the fruit of a giant jambu tree that grows in the middle. Some of the fruit of the tree falls into the water and sinks, uneaten, to the bottom, where it is transformed into gold. Coincidentally – or perhaps not so coincidentally –gold has in fact been found near the north-west corner of Manasarovar, just south of Chiu *gompa*. Swami Pranavananda says that it was mined for some time but that operations were eventually discontinued when small-pox broke out among the miners: a blight attributed to the wrath of the presiding deity of the mines. During the last mining operations a nugget of gold that was either the size or shape of a dog was found and a *chorten*★ built to mark the spot at a place afterwards called *Serka-Kiro* – 'Gold Dog'. Another source suggests that the nugget was sent to Lhasa as a gift for the Dalai Lama but that the prelate regarded its extraction as sacrilegious and ordered it returned to the earth from whence it was taken.

Besides the great *lingam* that the Rishis saw emerging from the lake, Manasarovar has another connexion with Shiva: the god's swans are reputed to swim on its surface. Here again, reality helps substantiate legend, for in fact numerous species of aquatic bird do frequent the lake.

Finally – and demonstrating the continued veneration of Manasarovar by Indians up until comparatively recent times – some of the ashes of Mahatma Gandhi were taken and scattered on the lake on 8th August, 1948, by a party of associates headed by Shree Surendra.†

In comparison, the western lake, Rakshas Tal (*Tib*. Langak Tso) has been far less generously treated. As its name implies –the *rakshas* were a class of demon – it was regarded as a haunt of demons and a place where one of the most notorious of them, Ravana, the abductor of Sita in the *Ramayana* legend, did penance to propitiate Shiva. Some visitors have claimed to have been able to detect a sinister quality in the atmosphere around the lake; although others have found it as beautiful as its eastern neighbour. Nevertheless, it can only boast a single *gompa* and no *parikrama* route. Why should this be so? The most plausible explanation is that, lacking the warm springs with which Manasarovar is endowed, Rakshas Tal and its environs are altogether colder and less hospitable in winter and in consequence are abandoned in favour of the more agreeable climes of Manasarovar.

Of the two lakes, Rakshas Tal is the smaller: around 140

★ *Stupa* – Buddhist monument.
† This is Swami Pranavananda's account, but the 1967 edition of the *Encyclopaedia Britannica* gives the date as 1949.

square miles in area as opposed to about 200. It is also more irregular and indented; it is only in the matter of islands that it seems to have an advantage over its neighbour: it has two, Manasarovar none. One of the two islands, Lachato, is a haunt of wild birds and hence a place visited by egg collectors when the ice of winter makes it accessible; the other island, Topserma, was at one time the refuge of a lama from Kham, who pursued his spiritual discipline there, alone, for about seven years some time at the beginning of this century.

Some writers have been disposed to see deep symbolical significance in the antithetical connotations of the two lakes. To them, Manasarovar represents the light, positive, masculine disposition; Rakshas Tal, the dark, negative, feminine. Like the *yin* and the *yang* of the Chinese philosophy of Change, however, they are not mutually exclusive but flow into one another by way of a channel that pierces the intervening isthmus. This is the Ganga Chhu and was created, so legend would have it, as the result of a fight that took place between two golden fishes that once inhabited Manasarovar. In fleeing from his opponent, one of the fishes carved the channel to the adjacent lake. In doing so, it allowed the waters of Manasarovar to flow into those of Rakshas Tal, which were thereby sanctified and made fit to drink.

Visitors to the sacred lakes during the past two centuries have found water flowing in the Ganga Chhu only occasionally. The flow when it does take place has sexual connotations for the Tibetans, who see it as 'intercourse' between the 'bridegroom' Manasarovar and the 'bride' Rakshas Tal. This is a highly auspicious event, just as, on the other hand, prolonged absence of water in the channel bodes ill for the world.

ROUTES TO THE KAILAS REGION

Mount Kailas cannot be regarded as a mountain of the first rank in terms of altitude. Its summit is a modest 22,028 feet above sea level. Nor is it a peak of the Himalayas but rather belongs to a separate range that is variously called the Gangri or the Kailas Range, or the Southern Transhimalaya, which may be regarded as a branch of the Karakoram.

Lying beyond the mighty wall of the Great Himalaya, Kailas is highly inaccessible for any wishing to reach it from the plains of India in the south. Up until the mid-twentieth century there was a choice of three general avenues of approach. The first, from the east, meant crossing the Himalaya somewhere to the east of Nepal, via the kingdoms of Sikkim or Bhutan. The traveller would then proceed to Kailas along the valley of the Brahmaputra. The western approach, on the other hand, would be by way of Kashmir and Ladakh. The third and most direct route was straight up from the south, travelling somewhere to the west of the Nepalese border. This would involve trekking for upwards of two hundred miles* across the Himalayas and then crossing into Tibet by one of the high passes like the Niti, Lampkiya Dhura, Kungri Bingri or, the most popular and direct, the Lipu Lekh (16,700 ft.).

CONDITIONS IN THE KAILAS REGION IN FORMER TIMES

In the old pre-1959 lamaist days, once across the border the traveller found himself in Ngari or Western Tibet, a province ruled by the Dalai Lama's Viceroys or *Garpons* in Gartok. Local power was invested in district governors or *dzongpons*, who were stationed in some of the more prominent communities. There was a *dzongpon* at Taklakot, a community situated some eleven miles beyond the Lipu Lekh. This *dzongpon* bought his office. Lhasa, the Tibetan capital, was about 800 miles from Kailas and orders from the government there were relayed to local administrators along the high-roads. The Lhasa-Gartok high road passed through a place called Barkha (alternative spelling, Parkha), which was located on the marshy plain separating the sacred mountain from the twin lakes. An official called a *tarjum* presided over a staging post here, where the riders carrying the official mail could change their mounts.

---

* The hill station of Almora, a very popular place from which to start a Kailas pilgrimage, is, by Swami Pranavananda's reckoning, 237 miles from Kailas.

Despite the prevalence of the noble teachings of the Buddha, old Tibet was a backward, even a barbarous place. That very exclusiveness that had kept the outside world at bay for so long and had protected the land from the worst aspects of modern development also effectively stood in the way of any advances that might have alleviated the poverty and generally advanced the lot of the ordinary lay people of what was in any case a very poor country. Certainly valuable religious traditions were thereby preserved and it was possible too for a large proportion of the population to devote themselves to the religious life, a great many of them as monks* and nuns. But critics of the old régime always maintain that such benefits were dearly bought at the expense of the underprivileged. Moreover, while great religious institutions and centres of learning flourished around the principal centres and there were also some fine exponents and teachers of Buddhism in the land, religious life in the more remote parts may not have been of a very high order. Dr. Sálim Ali, a self-confessed 'down-to-earth materialist' and hence a not very sympathetic witness, was in the Kailas region in 1945 and writes as follows:

> . . . on the whole, I was repelled, and sometimes nauseated, by what passed for Buddhism in Tibet at the time of my visit and amazed at the profound reverence given to its philosophy in the outside world. There must doubtless be, and certainly are, some devout and deeply learned scholars of the prevailing brand of Buddhism in Tibet, but I could discern no spark of spirituality or enlightenment among the swarms of initiates and young lamas who hung around every gompa† and dzong.‡ They seemed to me just a pack of dirty, lazy, ignorant louts leading a life of idle parasitism, who could have been more useful to themselves and to society as normal human beings. . . .
>
> (letter to the author from Dr. Sálim Ali, dated 19th March 1981)

---

* The term 'lama' is often used to describe any Tibetan Buddhist monk. In fact it is a term of respect used to refer to a teacher. Not all monks can be called 'lamas' by any means, and not all lamas are monks. A monk is more accurately called a *Ge-long*.

† Monastery.

‡ Fort.

The defenders of the old régime, on the other hand, would no doubt contend that poverty, hard work and privation do not necessarily conduce to misery, and that, in fact, the ordinary lay people of old Tibet were happy with their spiritually-rich environment. Certainly many who have encountered Tibetans both before and after 1959 have been impressed with their general happiness and good nature.

Traditionally, the greater proportion of the secular population of Western Tibet have been nomadic herders, scraping a subsistence living from flocks of sheep and goats. Yaks and horses are their beasts of burden, the wool trade their main economic activity. In former times, many found it difficult to make a living by fair means and consequently resorted to some form of *dacoitry* or banditry. About a day's march beyond Taklakot, the traveller entered an area infested with *dacoits*, many of them armed with old muzzle-loading guns, who would have had few scruples about fleecing anyone they met, be he trader, traveller or pilgrim. Apparently, due to its extreme scarcity in the region, they were chiefly interested in stealing food. Local administration was rudimentary, to say the least, and policing virtually non-existent. The *dacoits* therefore had little fear of arrest. Those who were arrested, however, received the extremely draconian punishments usually dispensed in Tibet during this period: they might suffer some kind of painful mutilation or dismemberment, might even be put to death by being flung from a high place, or left out in the scorching heat of summer to slowly roast.

Zorawar Singh's Invasion (1841)

Probably the most significant event in the nineteenth-century history of Western Tibet – and one said by some to exemplify the native cruelty of the Tibetans – was an invasion by a Sikh adventurer named Zorawar Singh, who was in the service of one of Ranjit Singh's former lieutenants, Gulab Singh, the master of Jammu, for whom he had already annexed Ladakh.

Zorawar forged into Western Tibet in May and June 1841, pillaging villages and *gompas** and destroying every *dzong*†

---

* Monastery.
† Fort.

that lay in his path. At Barkha his comparatively modest force – some number it at 1,500 men – routed a far larger Tibetan force of 8,000 or 10,000 men (accounts vary). He then proceeded to Taklakot, where he established himself and behaved in a generally high-handed manner. Eventually, probably because he had heard that reinforcements were being sent against him and was anxious for his wife's safety, he left his main force under the command of his lieutenant, Bastiram, so as to conduct her out of the area. Returning from Gartok, however, he found himself cut off by a sizeable Tibetan force augmented with Chinese at a place called Toyo, some three miles from Taklakot. He was fatally wounded in the knee (the Tibetan equivalent of the Achilles heel?) by a gold bullet, the only weapon against which the superstitious Tibetans believed this otherwise superhuman warrior was not proof.

Although he had invaded their territory, the Tibetans were inspired with deep respect for Zorawar, upon whom Swami Pranavananda maintains they bestowed the heroic title of 'Singhi-Raja' – 'Lion Raja.' Another writer, Charles Sherring, says that Zorawar's body was immediately dismembered and that the locals hung pieces of his flesh up in their houses for good luck. 'Rumour also says that the pieces sweated fat for many a long day, a sign which the most sceptical regarded as connected with the dead chief's bravery' (Sherring). An imposing *chorten** was also erected at Toyo over his other remains; this was regularly painted with red ochre. Swami Pranavananda reports moreover that one of Zorawar's testicles – which he does not specify – was preserved under lock and key in the Simbiling *gompa* at Taklakot but was brought out once every four years in the second month of the Tibetan calendar (March-April) 'on the occasion of some special *Tantrik* rite called *Chakhar* (iron fort). One hand (wanting in two fingers) is preserved in the Sakya Monastery situated on the west of the Simbiling Gompa . . .' (Swami Pranavananda *Exploration in Tibet*, 2nd Edition).

As for the remainder of Zorawar's force of Dogra soldiers, these had already succumbed badly to the exigencies of the Tibetan winter and it is said they were obliged to burn the

* Buddhist monument.

stocks of their rifles for what small warmth this afforded them. Sherring reports that they were cut down with great brutality by the combined Tibetan-Chinese force; Swami Pranavananda disputes this and imputes Sherring's charge to 'propaganda zeal to damn the Tibetans'. Whatever the real truth of the matter, however, it is certain that only a small and battered remnant of what had once been a glorious conquering army escaped across the high passes to the safety of British India.

Kirghiz-Kazaki Depredations (1941)

In 1941, exactly a century after the depredations of Zorawar Singh, three thousand Kirghiz-Kazaki nomads swept through Western Tibet, plundering and destroying as they went. They had left their homelands in Soviet Central Asia around 1938 and spent the intervening three years travelling in Chinese Sinkiang and Chinghai, before crossing the Kunlun mountains and entering the Chang Thang, the barren northern province of Tibet. Crossing the Brahmaputra, an attempt was made to force an entry into Nepal, but this was resisted by Gurkha border guards and instead the Kirghiz-Kazakis proceeded westwards to the sacred region. Swami Pranavananda stayed at Thugolho (alternative spelling Thokar, Trugo) *gompa* on the shores of Lake Manasarovar from July to mid-September that year and to him we are indebted for information about the affair.

When the interlopers camped on the northern side of Manasarovar, their camp extended for some fifteen miles. By this time their herds had grown to large proportions, as had the quantities of silver and gold in their possession – much of it the spoils of plunder. They were also well armed, if estimates of five hundred guns and rifles are accurate. Nevertheless, they were discouraged from approaching Tarchen or tampering with any of the monasteries of Kailas because the Bhutanese officer at Kailas had a fully-armed garrison. Instead, the Kirghiz-Kazakis moved on southwards between the two lakes, intending to push through Purang and into India by way of the Lipu Lekh. Again they were foiled, this time by the sharpshooting occupants of Tsepgye *gompa* on Rakshas Tal, who shot dead two members of the advance guard, one of them the leader, a woman dressed in a red uniform.

The Kirghiz-Kazakis next withdrew north-westwards, still plundering and destroying wherever they did not meet with sufficient opposition. They passed through Tirthapuri, Khyunglung and Missar, and destroyed buildings at Gartok and Gargunsa, the summer and winter capitals of Western Tibet. Around November, they forced their way into Ladakh, where they were finally disarmed by British and Kashmiri troops before being allowed to proceed through Kashmir to the Hazara District of the North West Frontier Province, where they were subsequently settled.

GEOGRAPHY OF THE SACRED REGION

The traveller, standing in the full blast of the wind on the brow of the Lipu Lekh pass, would therefore have good reason to feel apprehensive about the land he was about to enter. It was indeed a very dangerous place. On the other hand, the overwhelming beauty of the landscape that presented itself to his eye if the day was clear might dispel his anxieties. Indeed, if he was of a religious turn of mind, he might well feel spiritually exalted to know that, after the many rigours of the journey across the mountains, the sacred region now lay at his feet.

Below him, in the valley of the Karnali river, lay Taklakot, the chief community of the populous Purang valley. Here there would have been tents and houses, curious cave dwellings, a *gompa*, a *dzong* and a *mandi* (market).

Beyond Taklakot rose the imposing bulk of the snow-clad Gurla Mandhata (altitude: 25,355 feet). The traveller would have to cross one of the high ridges to the west of the mountain. Once up on the high pass, however, he would be treated to yet another visual feast: the two blue sacred lakes lying in the immediate foreground and beyond them, rising majestically out of the vividly-coloured ranges to the north, the snowy peak of the sacred mountain itself. Again, if he was a spiritual man, the sight would probably have him on his knees, making prostrations and offering thanks to the gods.

And so on to the shores of the sacred lakes, taking due care to steer well clear of *dacoits*. Once he had performed his business there, be it worldly or spiritual, the traveller would then continue north to Kailas, traversing on his way a flat marshy plain crossed by many streams flowing down from the sacred mountain. He would probably find many nomads camped here in their black tents, and might well also catch sight of herds of wild asses or *kyang*. Finally, he would arrive at Tarchen where, if this was his purpose, he might begin the Kailas *parikrama*.

★   ★   ★

For more than twenty years since the Chinese communists supplanted with their own the theocratic régime of the Dalai Lamas, no westerner – and probably no one outside of the Chinese world – has seen Mount Kailas. It is therefore to the accounts of past travellers and pilgrims that we must turn if we wish to find out what this unique mountain and its environs were like, and how they affected the human heart. What emerges most forcefully, as will be seen, is that this was a region of overpowering beauty and profound spiritual resonance: truly one of the natural wonders of the world.

CHAPTER THREE

Travellers in the Sacred Region: To 1850

Even before the Chinese takeover of Tibet in the 1950s, access to the Kailas region – and indeed to the whole of the country – had always been difficult for *Firinghis*, as the Tibetans called Europeans. The Lhasa government had for a long time maintained a total ban on their entry, a xenophobic policy that undoubtedly stemmed from a very realistic assessment of the dangers of allowing even ostensibly innocuous travellers like traders and missionaries to cross their borders. They had seen how commerce and Christianity had been a prelude to guns and annexation elsewhere – in nearby India, for instance. Officials in the frontier districts were therefore sternly enjoined to turn back any European whom they found in their territory. Penalties for failure to discharge this duty, even inadvertently, were draconian. We hear of the execution of comparatively important officials who were discovered to have fallen down in this respect.

For a time after 1904 things were slightly different. The guns of the Younghusband Expedition to Lhasa obliged the Tibetans to be rather more accommodating. During the brief ensuing period we find accounts of visits to Kailas and the sacred lakes written by comparatively relaxed travellers. They contrast with most of the earlier accounts, which were written by travellers who moved furtively and at speed across the desolate landscape, many of them disguised as *fakirs* (holy men) and living in fear of their lives.

Of the few westerners who have set eyes upon the sacred mountain, the first were the Jesuit missionaries Ippolito Desideri and Manuel Freyre, who passed Kailas in the company of a charming Tartar princess en route for Lhasa from Kashmir and Ladakh in 1715. This initial encounter does not seem to have been very auspicious – or representative:

> We left Cartoa [Gartok] in the second half of October, and arrived at the highest point reached during the whole journey in the desert called Ngari-Giongar on the 9th of November. This is held in much veneration by all of this people because of a certain URGHIEN [Padmasambhava – one of the early missionaries who brought Buddhism from India to Tibet], founder of the present Tibetan religion, of whom I shall speak later. Close by is a mountain of excessive height and great circumference, always enveloped in cloud, covered with snow and ice, and most horrible, barren, steep and bitterly cold [Mount Kailas]. In a cave hollowed out of the live rock the above-named Urghien is said to have lived for some time in absolute solitude, self mortification and continuous religious meditation. The cave is now a temple consecrated to him, with a rude, miserable monastery attached, where dwells a Lama, with a few monks who serve the temple. Besides visiting the cave, to which they always bring offerings, the Tibetans walk devoutly round the base of the mountain, which takes several days, and they believe this will bring them great indulgences. Owing to the snow on this mountain, my eyes became so inflamed that I well nigh lost my sight. I had no spectacles, and the only remedy, as I learnt from our escort, was to rub the eyes with snow.
>
> (F. de Filippi, ed., *The Travels of Ippolito Desideri of Pistoia, S.J., 1712–21*)

There seems to be a certain confusion here of legends relating to the Indian tantric adept, Padmasambhava (see *Fig. 10*), venerated in Tibet as one of the seminal teachers of Buddhism in that land, with those relating to the *guru*-poet, Milarepa. If this is indeed the case then the cave referred to as a temple is probably the Zunthulphuk monastery.

Disenchanted with the whole expedition, Freyre quickly returned to India, but Desideri remained in Tibet, mainly in

10. Guru *Padmasambhava*

the Lhasa area, for a number of years, manfully trying to convert the Tibetans from what he considered their misguided Buddhist convictions. Much to his disappointment, he was recalled by the Papal authorities and left the country in 1721.

The British encounter with Kailas and its environs stemmed from altogether more hardheaded motives. They wanted to know what was going on in the territories immediately adjacent to their prized Indian possessions; they were very interested too in the possibility of opening up trading connections; and, finally, they were concerned to improve their knowledge of the geography and other aspects of those areas. The twin lakes, Manasarovar and Rakshas Tal, interested them particularly, for it was known that some of the great rivers of the Indian subcontinent rose in or near them. At one time it was even thought that the Ganges had its source in Manasarovar, but this was finally disproved in 1808 when Lieutenant Webb, assisted by Captains Raper and Hearsey, fixed the principal source of the holy river on the southern side of the Great Himalaya.

The first Britisher to clap eyes on Mount Kailas was a veterinarian from Lancashire named William Moorcroft. Moorcroft was a great energizing and enterprising spirit – a man ahead of his time, whose ambitious schemes and projects were insufficiently understood in his own day, and whose reputation subsequently fell into undeserved eclipse.

Moorcroft was one of the pioneers of veterinary surgery in Britain and in his heyday he had a profitable London practice with premises in Oxford Street. Injudicious speculation in a scheme for manufacturing horseshoes with machinery ruined his finances, however, and in 1808, probably because it looked like the best way of recouping his fortune, he accepted the East India Company's invitation to become superintendent of their stud at Pusa near Cawnpore. In this capacity he advocated the notion of improving the quality of the Company's cavalry horses by interbreeding with Turkoman horses from Central Asia.

Moorcroft had not been long in India before he began to take a keen interest in the mysterious and little known lands lying beyond the Himalayas, and in 1812 he undertook an expedition to Lake Manasarovar. On this expedition, his interest in Central Asian horseflesh seems to have been subordinate to a concern with matters of greater commercial potential, principally the possibility of opening up to British interests the trade in *pashm*, the fine goats' wool from which the best quality Cashmere shawls were made. It is also clear from the precise and highly detailed scientific observations reported in his journal that he was very much a serious explorer. Finally, his journey may have had a political angle: among other things, he showed great interest in the activities of Russians in Tibet.

A young Anglo-Indian adventurer was Moorcroft's companion on the expedition. This was Hyder Jung Hearsey – the same Hearsey who had been with Webb and Raper at the source of the Ganges in 1808. Subsequently there had been unfortunate imputations of skulduggery to the man: that he had attempted to appropriate the glory to himself by cribbing Webb's map and passing it off to London as his own. Nothing untoward seems to have happened during the Manasarovar expedition, however; indeed 'Mr. H.' appears to have acquitted himself to Moorcroft's satisfaction.

There was a strong air of irregularity about the whole project, however, which makes the fact that it miscarried during its closing stages not altogether surprising. For one thing, Moorcroft chose not to obtain the permission of the Nepalese authorities, then in possession of the Kumaon region, to cross their territory; for another, he elected to travel disguised as a Hindu *mahant* making a pilgrimage to Kailas – a device which only partially worked and when it failed served only to arouse the worst suspicions against him.

The outward journey across the mountains ran by way of the courses of the Rama and Alaknada rivers to Joshimath near Badrinath, then via Malari to Niti. The going was difficult, in parts so precipitous that Moorcroft had to crawl on his hands and knees for fear of falling to his death in terrible chasms, but these ordeals were to some extent redeemed by the wild and imposing majesty of the surrounding scenery: snowcapped mountains soaring above the cedars and cypresses that clothed the lower slopes, and rivers roaring in the hidden depths of valleys far below.

At Niti the expedition ran into its first setback. The size of the party and their possession of arms, allied to the fact that for pilgrims to Manasarovar they were taking a highly unusual route, gave the general impression that Moorcroft and Hearsey were in fact *Gorkhalis* or *Firinghis*, 'come with designs inimical to the *Undès*' – and measures were taken accordingly. They attempted to persuade the headman of Niti of their bona fides, and a letter and a present were forwarded to Daba, a major community on the other side of the border, addressed to an official whom Moorcroft called 'the Deba' – possibly a *dzongpon*. He promptly replied, formally forbidding them to enter the country. It was also hinted that large numbers of troops had been dispatched to guard the high passes. Moorcroft was disappointed but not deterred. After much wheeling and dealing, during which large quantities of *timáshás* (a *timáshá* was 'the silver coin of Súnagar and Latakh') changed hands, he managed to get the exceedingly reluctant people of Niti to furnish him with the assistance he needed to proceed into *Undès*, as he called that part of Tibet which he proposed to enter, and so finally the expedition was under way again.

On reaching the high passes across the Great Himalaya, Moorcroft was relieved to find only cairns and prayer flags: there was no sign of the troops with which he had been threatened. He was bothered, however, by a touch of altitude sickness, and experienced difficulty of breathing and 'a great oppression about the heart'. It was now that he obtained his first sight of Mount Kailas:

July 1st. – THERMOMETER at sun-rise 41; march at 5.35 A.M. At 3205 paces reach the summit where there is a heap of stones. Here we found two *Uniyas* [Tibetans], one of whom was busied in lighting a fire, into which the other threw some incense, which he had previously bruised on a stone. He then leisurely walked round the pile of stones, in the midst of which was a statue having a piece of cloth tied to it, and whilst walking, uttered a long prayer. To the East was the sacred mountain near the lake of *Manasarovar*, tipped with snow, and called *Cailas* or *Mahadeo ka Ling*. Turning his face towards this mountain, and after raising his hands with the palms joined above his head, then touching his forehead, he suddenly placed them on the ground, and going on his knees pressed his forehead to the ground. This raising the hands, and prostration of the body and head, was repeated seven times; the other *Uniya*, less devout perhaps, contented himself with three salutations and a short prayer.

(Wm. Moorcroft, *A Journey to Lake Manasarovar*,
Asiatick Researches, Vol. 12, 1818)

The expedition then descended to the blasted plains of the

Great Plateau and followed the road to Daba, where they presented themselves to the *Deba*. He was naturally very annoyed that the people of Niti had allowed Moorcroft's party to proceed in direct defiance of his orders. He was obliged to report the matter to the higher authorities in Gartok and await their instructions. Clearly the Tibetans were not convinced that Moorcroft and Hearsey were what they claimed to be. One of them noted that Hearsey's boots were of the European type (Moorcroft had taken the wise precaution of having his boots fashioned with turned-up toes and tags at the heels after the oriental fashion); and there was the unusual redness of Moorcroft's complexion for which plausible explanation needed to be given. Nevertheless, relations seem to have been passably affable. A certain amount of judicious present-giving may have helped in this, but in any case Moorcroft seems to have been a reasonable and diplomatic man (though a very determined one) and did nothing that might cause offence. Quite the contrary, he seems to have created quite a good impression; and moreover, actual warmth seems to have entered into his relationship with the local chief Lama so that, when orders came that he must leave and present himself in Gartok, their parting was tinged with emotion.

Gartok, it transpired, was just a glorified encampment of black tents, with enormous herds of sheep, goats and yak together with some horses grazing on the adjacent plain. The interview with the *Garpon* (Viceroy) was not the ordeal it might have been, and in the event he allowed himself to be persuaded that the visitors were not *Firinghis*, though Moorcroft admits that the weight of his presents may have had a lot to do with this.

Much of Moorcroft's time at Gartok was spent in investigating the wool trade and especially in the possibility of breaking the monopoly then held by Ladakhi merchants. He did in fact manage to obtain useful concessions from the *Garpon* and was allowed to buy quantities of wool on the spot. The authorities would not, however, accede to his request to be allowed to quit the country by a route different from that by which he had entered; he must go as he had come – by the Niti.

Now enjoying official approval and support, the expedition proceeded south-east to Manasarovar by way of Missar and Tirthapuri. On the way Moorcroft was able to buy quantities of sheep, goats and yak, but he also began to suffer from bouts of fever and when he reached Tarchan (he calls it '*Gangri* or *Darchan*') he had to rest up for a whole day: August 4th. At Tarchan he found four permanent houses and a number of tents; several merchants were staying at the place, including two Chinese tea merchants who claimed that their homes lay two months' journey beyond Peking. The sacred mountain does not appear to have engaged his attention as far as one can tell from the edited published version of his journal.★ Perhaps commercial and scientific concerns kept his eyes focussed at a more mundane level.

When he reached the shores of Lake Manasarovar on 6th August, Moorcroft's concern then and during the succeeding days was to determine whether any major rivers issued from the lake. Harballabh, an old *pundit* who was a member of the expedition, claimed that 'near the south-western corner, a river flowed from it, which flowing in a westerly direction went along the Rawanhrad [Rakshas Tal] and escaping from its Western extremity near the foot of the great mountain, formed the first branch of the *Setlej*'. Subsequent exploration, including a 25-mile walk by Moorcroft himself, albeit in adverse weather and poor health, failed to prove the existence of this river and he was forced to conclude that if it had ever existed it had now dried up and its bed been filled in, possibly as the result of an earthquake. His expedition had therefore shown – correctly, as later exploration was to prove – that Manasarovar gives rise to no large river.

The case of Rakshas Tal was rather different, however. Passing the lake at a distance, Moorcroft thought he saw a river issuing from it 'which probably communicates with the many streams which form the *Setlej*'. He was, however, prevented from actually going and confirming the matter by another bout of fever. The weather also changed abruptly for the worse, and a heavy fall of snow impressed him with the urgency of returning to the high passes before they became blocked.

★ The original was lost.

On 11th August, his retreat already underway across the marshy plain beyond the lakes where his yaks frequently sank up to their bellies in mud, Moorcroft was obliged by a hailstorm in mid-afternoon to halt beside a small river. He notes in his journal:

> *Cailas* mountain is supposed to be the favourite residence of MAHADEVA [Shiva], and is situated opposite to the great lake of *Rawanhrad*, and a little distant from that of *Manasarovar*. As its summit is always clothed with snow, it is but a cool seat: however this cold is said to be necessary on account of the poison which has heated his frame ever since he swallowed it at the period of the *Sankh Avatar*.
>
> (*Ibid.*)

Moorcroft passed through Tirthapuri and Khyunglung on his way back to Daba, and thence up to the Niti again. Once across the pass, however, difficulties began to pile upon the expedition until it was little short of a nightmare. In the first place it was exceedingly difficult to conduct the many animals they now had with them across terrain that was not only highly precipitous but also bedevilled by landslides, broken bridges and swollen rivers; and then soon afterwards the Nepalese authorities began to harrass them. Their failure to get permission for their trip, the size of their entourage of servants and bearers, the fact that Moorcroft and Hearsey travelled in disguise – all these factors had compounded their original suspicion until rampant paranoia broke loose. Rumours gained currency that an army of between 400 and 500 men had proceeded up to the Tibetan border to build forts and encourage the local people into insurrection against their Nepalese masters.

The Nepalese were indecisive at first, merely trying to persuade Moorcroft to delay his journey while its motives were properly investigated. Moorcroft for his part doggedly refused to be delayed and concluded that the best course of action was to show a firm determination to proceed. Intransigence on both sides led to an inevitable confrontation and ensuing violence, which, due to their superior numbers, went in favour of the Nepalis. Moorcroft and his men were seized and detained under duress for some time. Eventually, however, all came out well: they were released on the orders of the Raja of Nepal and given safe conduct out of his territory.

This harrowing experience did not deter the enterprising Moorcroft from further adventures. In fact he was to go on to even more sensational ones. He eventually met his death in 1825 – some say he died of fever, others that he was poisoned – during the course of an audacious and equally pioneering expedition to Bokhara by way of Ladakh, Kashmir, the Punjab and Afghanistan. He was accompanied on that occasion by a German geologist named George Trebeck, who himself died shortly after his mentor. By the time of his death, Moorcroft's star had already sunk low. The East India Company had lost faith and interest in his great schemes for opening up connections with Central Asia and had withdrawn its support and discontinued his pay.

There is a bizarre and implausible footnote to the story of William Moorcroft. In an account of his own travels in Tibet and other parts of Asia published in 1853, Abbé Huc recounts a more fanciful version of Moorcroft's death that he picked up in Lhasa. Far from meeting his end in the wastes of Turkistan, Moorcroft, it was claimed, had turned up in Lhasa in 1826 and lived there for more than a dozen years before finally dying in the Kailas-Manasarovar region while travelling back to Ladakh.

Nearly thirty-five years were to elapse before the next Englishman set eyes on the sacred mountain. In September and October, 1846, Lieutenant Henry Strachey of the 66th Regiment, Bengal Native Infantry, made a journey to Lake Rakshas Tal, which he believed to be of more immediate geographical interest than its neighbour, Manasarovar, because it had been less visited and studied.

As Strachey was a military man, and his narrative suggests quite a typical one, it is not surprising that his journey was altogether different in character from that of his great precursor, Moorcroft, who was after all a Company man. Strachey in fact portrays his own journey as having all the pace and urgency of a lightning strike into enemy territory. His tight, economical party moved with speed and secrecy across the alien landscape, studiously avoiding all contact with the local people and giving all habitations a wide berth or else passing them under cover of darkness. It was, in short, a concentrated military-style operation. In the matter of disguise, however, there was a major point of similarity with Moorcroft. Before crossing into Western Tibet, or *Hundes* as he called it, Strachey donned native costume – 'just enough to pass muster' – though he refused to go to the length of darkening his skin.

During his outward journey across the Kumaon region, Strachey followed the course of the Kali river upstream to its confluence with the Kunti Yakti. He paused at the village of Kunti to exchange his plains servants for mountain people – Bhotias and other Kumaonis – then continued on his way to Hundes with stern warnings resounding in his ears of the perils he might meet at the hands of the Khampa brigands infesting that land. The Khampas are, literally, the inhabitants of the province of Kham in eastern Tibet. They are the most martial of the Tibetans and, apparently, in the old days were much given to banditry, notably in the Kailas-Manasarovar region where the many pilgrims were easy prey for them.

Strachey, his servants and baggage animals – yaks, dzos and ponies – crossed into Tibet by the Lampkiya Dhura pass. It was a difficult transit for both men and animals, through deep snow. Strachey chose the pass because he thought it would give him the most direct line of approach on Rakshas Tal but in fact it brought him over the border much too far to the west and it took him four days, rather longer than he had calculated, to reach his objective, having travelled a considerable way round through Lama Chorten.

Strachey, it would seem, was far more sensitive to the beauties of the Tibetan landscape than Moorcroft and there is a touch of poetry in his descriptions that is entirely lacking in the earlier explorer's record. Strachey felt that what he saw on the northern side of the Himalayas exceeded in aesthetic appeal anything he had seen on the southern side. Rakshas Tal was a sheet of water of the clearest, brightest blue reflecting with double intensity the colour of the sky, except at its northern extremity where it took on the deeper purple hue of the wall of mountain that overshadowed it. Across the low hills in the middle of the opposite bank, he could just make out

Manasarovar – 'a streak of bright blue'. The lakes themselves were bounded by low hills which in places plunged deeply into the water. These hills were bare of vegetation and 'tinted with many shades of red, brown or yellow'. Above them in the south-east rose 'the snowy mass of Momonangli' (Gurla Mandhata); to the north on the other hand, was 'a green grassy plain from the back of which the Gangri Mountains rose in dark steep slopes'. Here 'the main peak of Kailas, now fully developed to its very base, was seen on the extreme left of the range'.

Shortly afterwards, having rounded the northern horn of Rakshas Tal, he was to get a closer and more impressive prospect of the sacred mountain:

The most remarkable object here was Kailas, now revealed in full proportion to its very base, rising opposite [northward] straight out of the plain only two or three miles distant. The south-west front of Kailas is in line with the adjacent range, but separated on either side by a deep ravine; the base of the mass thus isolated is two or three miles in length perhaps; the general height of it, I estimate to be 4250 feet above the plain, but from the west the peak rises some 1500 feet higher, in a cone or dome rather, of paraboloidal shape; the general figure is not unlike that of Nanda Devi, as seen from Almora. The peak and the upper part of the eastern ridge were all covered with snow, which contrasted beautifully with the deep colour of the mass of the mountain below; the stratification of the rock is strongly marked in successive ledges that catch the snow falling from above, forming irregular bands of alternate white and purple; one of these bands more marked than the rest encircles the base of the peak, and this, according to the Hindu tradition, is the mark of the cable with which the Rakshas attempted to drag the throne of Siva from its place. . . . The openings on both sides of Kailas disclose only more mountains in the rear; the Western ravine appears to be two or three miles deep; the back of the eastern recess is occupied by a fine pyramidal mass rising in steps of rock and snow, with a curious slant caused by the dip of the stratification (to the east ward).

(Lieut Henry Strachey, *Narrative of a Journey to Cho Lagan, etc.* Journal of the Asiatic Society of Bengal, July, August and September 1848)

His final judgement is that 'in picturesque beauty Kailas far surpasses the big Gurla, or any other of the Indian Himalaya that I have seen; it is full of majesty, a King of mountains'.

Proceeding in due course to geographical matters, Strachey was unable to locate a visible channel connecting Rakshas Tal with the Sutlej and apart from the possibility of the lake periodically overflowing, 'the only effluence is by

SKETCH OF OUTLET FROM MANASAROWAR, SEEN FROM THE SOUTH.

PLAN OF OUTLET FROM MANASAROWAR.

SECTION OF RAISED BEACH.

11. *Sketches after Richard Strachey of the Dry Channel connecting the Two Lakes*

filtration through the porous soil of the intermediate ground'. He was, however, successful in locating a channel connecting the two lakes with each other, and a broad stream was flowing through it. This was two or three miles west of Chiu *gompa*, near the old gold workings.

The morale of Strachey's Kumaoni servants was low throughout their time in Tibet. They lived in continual fear either of falling into the hands of Khampa bandits and being brutalized by them, or of being caught by the Tibetan authorities – in which case they fully expected to be hung. Unexpected meetings with indeterminate Tibetans invariably put them in a state of funk which on one occasion a disgusted Strachey was to describe as 'little short of rank cowardice'. Discontent and distrust fomented by these not altogether unreasonable fears were bound to grow worse the longer the expedition was delayed on Tibetan soil. They came to a head when, proceeding southwards along the shores of Manasarovar, Strachey mooted the idea of doing a complete circuit of the lake. His men not only reacted with the anticipated lack of enthusiasm but, ominously, baggage ponies and later even some of the men themselves began to mysteriously stray from the party and not return. His 'discontented and dispirited companions' were clearly intent on putting a spoke in the wheel of his *parikrama*; therefore Strachey decided that it would be wiser to forget the notion—it promised to yield little useful knowledge anyway, he consoled himself—and return with all possible dispatch to the other side of the border.

His exit route took him along the north-west slopes of Gurla Mandhata to Taklakot, which he passed at night, and so up to the Lipu Lekh pass, the crossing of which was an altogether easier proposition than the earlier crossing of the Lampkiya Dhura.

Two years later, in 1848, Strachey's brother Richard visited the Kailas region with a certain Mr. J. E. Winterbottom. Richard Strachey was a military engineer with keen scientific interests who was to have a distinguished career in the Indian Army, finally retiring from it in 1875 as a Lieutenant-General. He and his companion crossed the Great Himalaya even further to the west than his brother had done. Starting from Milam, they went over by the Untadhura pass (17,590 feet) and descended to the Plain of Guge. They then took the unusual course of proceeding northwards to touch the Sutlej before turning to approach the *southern* shores of the lakes from the north-west. They skirted the southern shore of Rakshas Tal and then proceeded in the opposite direction to Henry Strachey up the isthmus separating the two lakes. They wanted to prove the existence of the channel joining the two lakes which Henry had observed in 1846. This they were fully able to do. Afterwards they made their way back over the Himalayas at their original crossing point, though they employed a somewhat more southerly route to get there. Their expedition was significant for the valuable geological and botanical information that Richard Strachey collected, in addition to information on glaciers and snowfall.

CHAPTER FOUR

Travellers in the Sacred Region: 1850–1900

During the second half of the nineteenth century the trickle of travellers to the sacred region continued, though their object changed somewhat. Instead of serious-minded explorers and surveyors, we find a motley brigade of sportsmen and adventurers who no doubt found heightened excitement in flouting the strictures of the Tibetan authorities to enter the 'Forbidden Land'. Unfortunately for some – and also for hapless Tibetan scapegoats – this excitement was not without cost.

In 1855 or 1860 – the date given varies – a certain 'Mr. Drummond' committed the terrible sacrilege of sailing an indiarubber boat on Lake Manasarovar. Subsequent rumour had it that the local *dzongpon* was decapitated for allowing this enormity to take place in his territory.

The German Schlaginweit brothers, Adolph and Robert,

both protégées of the great Alexander Humboldt and highly professional in their explorational techniques, planned to visit Manasarovar in 1855 but were intercepted by the Tibetans just short of Daba and diverted north-westwards to Gartok. Along their route, however, they were able to see and sketch part of the Kailas range.

Then in June, 1864, a party of British sportsmen set off from Almora for the 'Land of the Huns'. It included Thomas W. Webber, Late Forest Surveyor for the North-West Provinces and Deputy Conservator of Forests in the Central Provinces and Gorakhpur; Lieutenant Smyth, Inspector of Schools, North-West Provinces; Henry Hodgson; and the Honourable Robert Drummond, B.C.S., brother of the then Lieutenant-Governor of the North-West Provinces. This last-named might well have been the self-same 'Mr. Drummond' whom a later writer, Charles Sherring, identifies as the one-time Commissioner of Bareilly and the person whose sailing interlude on Manasarovar had such dire consequences for the local *dzongpon*.

The party crossed into Tibet by the Nepalese Tinkar pass, fully expecting to be stopped by the Tibetans, but determined to browbeat and bluster their way through to their Tibetan hunting grounds by sheer force of numbers – they had sixty Bhotia servants and many yaks with them – and their formidable array of firepower. They appear to have been, and indeed to have considered themselves, nothing short of a modest private army.

The anticipated confrontation took place just outside Takla-kot. About sixty Tibetan horsemen bore down upon them and began 'wheeling in picturesque confusion right in front of our line of march'. This display was no doubt meant to strike fear into their hearts, but the Tibetans had seriously underestimated the fibre of these British intruders, who merely stood their ground and roared with laughter. So infectious was this laughter, in fact, that the Tibetans were obliged to abandon their attempt at looking ferocious and joined in themselves. Finally they began sticking out their tongues, which Webber understood to be a recognized form of friendly salute among them; also that the correct response was to do likewise and touch tongues – 'a part of the ceremony we felt inclined to omit'.

At Taklakot the party was met by about 200 footsoldiers, some of whom grovelled on the ground begging the Britishers not to proceed while the others drew their hands rapidly across their throats. It was unclear whether the latter was 'a threat or a freemason's sign'. When the British party made a push towards the bridge across the Karnali, however, the Tibetans broke up its timbers before they could reach it. This led to stern remonstrations:

> We held forth by our interpreters that we were friendly travellers. . . ; at the same time that, if any violence was attempted, we were well armed and prepared to defend ourselves and our property. That in pulling down the bridge and preventing us from reaching our camping ground they had committed an unfriendly act, to atone for which they would be required to bring us fuel and supplies, for which we would pay.
>
> (Thos. W. Webber, *In the Forests of Upper India*)

The next day, the British sportsmen were honoured with a visit from the *dzongpon* and the chief lama of Taklakot, accompanied by some soldiers. Drummond received them seated on a chair within a tent – 'the symbol of the Indian Shikar'* – with his companions ranged around him. The Tibetans were obliged to sit on the ground in order to explain their fears to the interlopers, who plied them with *Jameson's* whiskey to weaken their opposition. Nothing was decided that day, but next day word came from the *dzongpon* that they could make a month's trip to the north-east as long as they would give a firm undertaking not to go near the sacred lake. They also had to pretend to have had a great fight so that if his Lhasa masters called him to question the *dzongpon* could claim that he had been overwhelmed by sheer force of numbers.

So the party proceeded north-eastwards, crossing the high ridges east of Gurla Mandhata via a snowbound pass and thence descending to the valleys and plains beyond, where they split up to pursue their various sporting interests. Drummond went to the east and Smyth to the north after antelope and *ovis ammon* (one of the largest species of wild

---

* Hunter.

69

sheep); Webber and Hodgson restricted themselves to seeking wild yak – especially 'big bulls'. These ferocious beasts turned out to have more wit and cunning than their awkward, shaggy appearance suggested, but eventually a fine pair were tracked down. Webber describes a kill:

> The first shot awoke the echoes from the rocks above, and the bullet thud was clearly heard. The great hairy bulls, with bloodshot eyes and heads in the air, faced around and made some startled runs, grunting savagely, but stopped short to reconnoitre for their concealed enemy. Five more barrels were emptied, and still they came on, almost up to the rocks where we were crouched, frantically loading up and cramming in bullets and ramming them down, for the rifles were old-fashioned muzzle-loaders, 14 and 16 bore, loaded with conical bullets and four drachms of powder. The biggest bull had been hit four times, but seemed none the worse, while his companions, also getting a bullet in the chest, thought it wise to retreat up the valley. But the first, discovering his enemy, staggered on, foaming with rage, and fell to the last two barrels, which struck him in the head within a few yards of the moraine. He was game to the last, and was only stopped by weight of lead – a grand beast, seventeen hands to the shoulder and weighing as much as any prize short horn.
>
> (*Ibid.*)

During their sporting travels Webber and Hodgson were also able to get an imposing view of Mount Kailas away to the west:

> On one occasion we crossed another lofty divide, and found ourselves suddenly out on the northern slopes of another watershed, none other than that of the mighty Indus. Far beneath us, some miles away, lay the most brilliantly beautiful blue sea, the celebrated Manasarovar lake, as it proved, which we had promised not to approach. The foreground was flat, rolling hills and ridges sloping gradually towards the lake, all bare and tinted in the most crude colours – reds and pinks and orange – while hundreds of miles to the north and west in the violet distance there stretched range after range of low, jagged hills, all alike, and succeeding one another in endless succession. Conspicuous, and towering above them all, was the snowcapped summit of the

sacred Kailas. We sat down for a while and munched our biscuits and enjoyed the wonderful and expansive panorama, and sketched it in watercolours as a record of our tramp.

(Ibid.)

Having enjoyed good sport, the party were reunited and returned together to Taklakot. After exchanging presents and farewells with their friend, the *dzongpon*, they proceeded back towards the high passes leading to India. No doubt the *dzongpon* was highly relieved to see them go. His relief would, however, have been premature. Smyth and Webber dodged back across the border further west for a spot of shooting on the plains of Gyanima.

A year later another pair of sportsmen made a similar trip: Captain H. U. Smith and Mr. A. S. Harrison. They left Naini Tal in June 1865 and by 31st July had reached 'Shib and Chillum: two camping grounds well known to traders and the turning point for all sportsmen'. It would therefore seem that by this date the border was fairly crawling with British sportsmen eager to slip across into Tibet and to start blazing away at the game roaming the great plateau. The Tibetan authorities kept a keen eye out for them and could usually pick out any planning a long foray across the border by the number of their yaks and the quantity of their provisions. To dupe them, therefore, Smith and Harrison forwarded their main provisions in the care of a trustworthy trader with orders to meet them in due course at 'Kylas'. Meanwhile they themselves proceeded towards the border with only minimal supplies.

They were intercepted at 'Shib' by a party of 'Tartar' guards who tried to turn them back but who eventually conceded that they might proceed to 'Idyum', though they wisely insisted that they accompany them. Smith and Harrison were, however, by dint of guile and devilish cunning, able to give these unwanted chaperones the slip and then proceeded poste haste, marching day and night, to their rendezvous point. At 'Kylas', or more exactly 'the village of Darchin', they were able not only to reclaim their extra gear but they received a warm welcome from the 'high priest'. They had already met this dignitory at 'Shib', where he had gone to trade, and he had assured Smith and Harrison that he would help them if they for their part could successfully spirit themselves to his small domain. This was 'a little territory held by the priests, who were quite independent of the Chinese authorities'. The 'high priest' was as good as his word for the two sportsmen found that preparations had been made for their stay. They gave their benefactor gifts of brandy and an air gun as a token of their appreciation. He returned the gesture by furnishing them with two guides who knew the best shooting grounds thereabouts.

Smith claims to have fished in the holy Manasarovar – surely another terrible sacrilege for which someone's head might roll. Afterwards he and his companion, Harrison, applied themselves to slaughtering the game in the areas to the east and north of the lake. Smith claims to have bagged a black wolf – 'the first ever shot in that part of the world'.

Later they returned to Tarchen to take their leave of the benevolent priest and then travelled east by easy stages towards Gartok, their principal object now being to trace the source of the Sutlej. Their subsequent venture into the field of hydrography was somewhat disasterous for their later reputation. They were foolish enough to cast doubt on the Strachey brothers' findings by denying both the existence of the wet channel joining the two lakes and of the old watercourse connecting Rakshas Tal with the Sutlej. When Smith propounded these notions at a meeting of the Royal Geographical Society, a Dr. Thomson leapt up and staunchly defended the Stracheys' reputation. Perhaps it would have been better if Smith and Harrison had confined themselves to *shikar* (hunting) and not ventured into areas where they were not so well qualified.

If trespassers were going to continue to make such incursions into Tibetan territory in defiance of the authorities, it was more or less certain that eventually one of them would come unpleasantly unstuck. The unlucky head upon which the brunt of Tibetan annoyance was to fall was that of Arnold Henry Savage Landor, the grandson of the distinguished writer and himself the author of such gems of travel literature as *Corea, or the Land of the Morning Calm* and *Alone with the Hairy Ainu*.

It is, however, hard to feel sympathy for this victim, for he seems to have brought his ordeals upon himself by his arrogant, foolhardy and often downright outrageous behaviour. From the pages of the account of his Tibetan travels, *In the Forbidden Land*, Landor comes across as a caricature of a Victorian imperialist: a braggart, a bigot and a bully.

His contempt for the Tibetans was absolute from the start. In his view, not only were they superstitious, insanitary and degenerate in their customs but, worse still, they were spineless cowards to a man; with blood duly boiling, Landor was forever having to teach them salutory lessons. For instance, while still in Bhotia territory, he describes encountering an impudent Tibetan who had a few disparaging things to say about the English:

> This remark was too much for me, and it might anyhow have been unwise to allow it to pass unchallenged. Throwing myself on him, I grabbed him by his pigtail and landed in his face a number of blows straight from the shoulder. When I let him go, he threw himself down, crying, and implored my pardon. Once and for all to disillusion the Tibetan on one or two points, I made him lick my shoes clean with his tongue, in the presence of the assembled Shokas (Bhotias). Thus done, he tried to scamper away, but I caught him once more by his pigtail, and kicked him down the front steps which he had dared to come up unasked.
>
> (A. H. Savage Landor, *In the Forbidden Land*)

Ludicrous as it may seem, this is not at all unrepresentative of the attitudes expressed in *In the Forbidden Land*. The book is little more than an inflated example of the boys' adventure stories of the era, heavily laced with all the characteristic prejudices and posturings. In his own eyes, Landor is always indubitably *right*: he is the noble English hero and the Tibetans are just villainous savages.

Also slightly ludicrous is Landor's stance of being a proper scientific observer. He travelled with mandatory surveying equipment, and was forever making highly precise calculations and dutifully noting them down. Such was his dedication to enlarging the province of scientific knowledge, in fact, that when a prisoner of the Tibetans and denied access to writing materials, he noted his findings in his own blood – and in cypher too. He even claims to have been the first Englishman to visit the northern source of the Brahmaputra and, trusting that he will not be thought immodest, promptly named it after himself.

Sven Hedin, the great Swedish explorer who was in the same region a few years later, makes short shrift of these pretensions:

> The extraordinary Munchausen romance which an English newspaper writer named Landor narrated and which quite set aside all the conscientious reliable descriptions of Moorcroft, Strachey and the pundits, had no effect whatsoever. Among the uncritical, sensation-loving public Landor had a certain temporary success; but among geographers, especially in London, he was received with justifiable suspicion.
>
> (Sven Hedin, *Transhimalaya*)

Tom Longstaff also furnishes further reason to doubt Landor's credibility. He once retraced Landor's ascent of a mountain in Nepal, accompanied by Landor's own guides. He found the cairn beyond which Landor had definitely not proceeded. It lay at an altitude of about 16,500 feet – definitely not at 23,000 feet as Landor had claimed. 'Landor had taken artistic licence', Longstaff concludes – surely an understatement.

Landor undertook his expedition to Tibet in the spring, summer and autumn of 1897. During the early stages of his journey he followed a route similar to that of Henry Strachey. He penetrated into Tibet by the Lampkiya Pass and from there proceeded to Lama Chorten, where he got his first view of Kailas:

> To the north the clouds had dispersed, and the snow-capped sacred Kelas [*sic*] Mount stood majestic before us. In appearance not unlike the graceful roof of a temple, Kelas towers over the long white-capped range, contrasting in beautiful blending of tints with the warm sienna colour of the lower elevations. Kelas is some two thousand feet higher than the other peaks of the Gangir [*sic*] chain, with strongly defined ledges and terraces marking its stratifications, and covered with horizontal layers of

snow standing out in brilliant colour against the dark iceworn rock. . . .

My men, with heads uncovered, their faces turned towards the sacred peak, were muttering prayers. With joined hands which they slowly raised as high as the forehead, they prayed fervently, and then went down on their knees, with heads bent low on the ground. My brigand follower, who was standing close by me, hurriedly whispered that I should join in this act of prayer. . . .

'You must keep friends with the gods,' he said; 'misfortune will attend you if you do not salaam to Kelas; that is the home of a good god!' And he pointed to the peak with the most devout air of conviction.

To please him I saluted the mountain with utmost deference, and, taking my cue from the others, placed a white stone on one of the hundreds of *Chokdens* or *Obos* (stone pillars) erected by devotees at this spot. . . .

(Ibid.)

The Tibetans were hot on his trail by now – as indeed they were to be throughout his time in their land. They were to try the full gamut of approaches to get him to leave: gentle ones initially, like trying to reason with him, begging him, even offering him bribes; only when these failed did they resort to threats and, ultimately, probably in sheer desperation, to direct physical violence. All except the last were of no avail. Landor simply would not be deflected from his intention of pushing right through to Lhasa. Such blind tenacity, if not merely a pose for the benefit of the readership, is hard to credit. Landor himself suggests that the thought of failure was always too galling to bear contemplation. There was moreover always the lure of doing the forbidden. Though he does not mention it himself, there was probably an element of realistic calculation there too: he was banking on the fact that the Tibetans would not dare to do him any harm for fear of provoking a punitive expedition. The British, after all, were extremely powerful and situated just over a couple of hundred miles away on the plains of India – much nearer than Lhasa.

The first confrontation came at Gyanima. The Parkha *tarjum* came in person to ask the Englishman to turn back. Finding Landor obdurate, however, he first recanted and granted him unofficial permission to proceed with a small party to Lake Manasarovar, then retracted and insisted that the whole expedition return directly to India by the way it had come. As there were large numbers of armed soldiers blocking the way, it would have been unrealistic to proceed, so Landor decided to resort to skilful means. Outwardly obeying the *tarjum*'s injunction, he seemed to be making his way back towards the Lampkiya Pass but once out of sight he stopped and divided his party into two groups. The larger group would return to India with Dr. Harkua Wilson of the American Episcopal Mission, who had accompanied the expedition so far. The other, a tight, picked team led by Landor himself and carrying only minimal supplies and equipment, would attempt a commando-like dash across 'unfrequented wilds' to the lakes and afterwards on to the Tibetan capital itself.

After 'adventures and escapes far too numerous to relate here' Landor's group arrived on the southern shores of the sacred lakes, where they obtained another fine prospect of Kailas:

To the N. of the lakes stood the magnificent Tize, the sacred Kelas mountain, overtopping by some two thousand feet all other snowy peaks of the Gagri chain, which extended roughly from N.W. to S.E. From this spot we could see more distinctly than from Lama Chokten the band round the base of the mountain, which, according to legend, was formed by the rope of a Rakas (devil) trying to tear down this throne of the gods.

Tize, the great sacred peak, is of fascinating interest, owing to its peculiar shape. It resembles, as I have said, the giant roof of a temple, but to my mind it lacks the gracefulness of sweeping curves such are found in Fujiama of Japan, the most artistically beautiful mountain I have ever seen. Tize is angular, uncomfortably angular, if I may be allowed the expression, and although its height, the vivid colour of its base, and the masses of snow that cover its slopes, give it a peculiar attraction, it nevertheless struck me as being intensely picturesque, at least from the point of view from which I saw it, and from which the whole of it was visible. When clouds were round it, toning down and modifying its shape, Tize appeared at its best from the painter's point of view. Under these conditions, I have thought it very beautiful,

especially at sunrise, with one side tinted red and yellow, and its
rocky base standing majestic against a background of shiny gold.
With my telescope, I could plainly distinguish, especially on the
E. side, the defile along which the worshippers make the circuit
of the base of the mountain, though I was told that some pilgrims
actually march round it on the snowy ledge directly over its base,
and just above the darker band of rock described before. On the
S.W. side can be seen, on the top of a lower peak, a gigantic Obo.
(*Ibid.*)

Landor was having trouble with his servants by now – not
surprisingly, for they had been discovered by the Tibetans
and, openly hunted and miserably equipped, they had every
prospect of suffering a great deal when their pursuers finally
caught up with them. Their brave leader was incensed at all
attempts at defection and, in true Victorian schoolmasterly
style, liberally administered punitive thrashings to those who
showed such intolerable 'disloyalty' – or merely threatened to
shoot out of hand any man who tried to desert. Nevertheless,
by the time he had reached Thokar *gompa* on the southern
shore of Manasarovar, he admits to being down to nine men.
Five more left him at the lake. Three marches further on all
but two had deserted. No Victorian schoolboy romance is
complete without its complement of faithful native servants
ready to follow their great white leader to the death. Landor's
devoted duo consisted of an ex-policeman named Chanden
Singh whom he had hired back in Almora, and a leper named
Mansing.

Together they forged eastwards, over the 16,900 foot
Maium Pass and down into the valley of the Brahmaputra.
They were now under constant surveillance and desperately
badly equipped and provisioned. The journey became
increasingly difficult. Finally, during a river crossing, one of
their yaks went under the water and, although the animal was
saved, a great deal of the food, money and equipment that it
was carrying were unrecoverably lost. This was a disaster;
from now on they had to live off the land.

On 19th August 1897 they reached a place which Landor
calls 'Toxem'. The villagers received them well and promised
to supply them with food and horses. The next morning,
however, as they were inspecting the horses offered for sale,

they were seized from behind in the most treacherously underhand fashion. Naturally, men of Landor's calibre do not give in without putting up a fight, and his two trusty retainers gave (almost) as good as their master, but eventually all were overpowered by sheer force of numbers:

> All was over now, and, bound like a dangerous criminal, I looked round to see what had become of my men. When I realised that it took the Tibetans five hundred men all counted to arrest a starved Englishman and his two half-dying servants, and that, even then, they dared not do it openly, but had to resort to abject treachery; when I found that these soldiers were picked troops from Lhassa [*sic*] and Sigatz [*sic*], despatched on purpose to arrest our progress and capture us, I could not restrain a smile of contempt for those into whose hands we had fallen.
>
> (*Ibid.*)

And now came the hideous oriental tortures – or so Landor luridly depicts them. Having been tightly bound and subjected to preliminary humiliations, he was made to ride a horse sitting on a spiked saddle, which savagely gouged his back. The Tibetans also took pot shots at him into the bargain. Then he was introduced to a group of 'the most villainous brutes I had ever set eyes upon. One, a powerful repulsive individual, held in his hand a great knobbed mallet used for fracturing bones; another carried a bow and arrows; a third held a big two-handed sword; while others made a display of various ghastly instruments of torture'. Next he was bound to the sharp edge of a prism-shaped log and told by his principal tormentor, the fiendish *Pombo* – Landor defines him as a 'Grand Lama . . . or governor of a province, with powers equivalent to those of a feudal king' – who had worked himself into a frenzy and was foaming at the mouth, that his eyes were going to be put out. In the actual event, although a red-hot iron was flourished in his face, Landor suffered nothing worse than a scorched nose and temporary disturbance of vision. But this was not the end. Afterwards, the butt of a matchlock was placed against his forehead and the weapon discharged. Landor received an unpleasant blow but he merely laughed in order to tantalize his tormentors and demonstrate the absurdity of their every attempt to break his spirit. Not surprisingly, this spurred the Pombo on to greater excesses. He now produced a vicious two-handed sword. After carefully measuring its keen edge against his victim's exposed neck, he raised it aloft. The first swing swept short of its mark. And the second. Landor still had his somewhat inflated head on his shoulders when he was at last led off to meet his next ordeal: being stretched on a rack-like device.

In the end, for all their cowardice and cruelty, Landor assures his reader that the Tibetans could not help being impressed by the native English fortitude with which he bore all. Even the evil Pombo was obliged to concede respect and after a while even became passably affable. Clearly the Tibetans had no real intention of killing him but were just mounting an elaborate display to thoroughly put the wind up him and get him out of their country.

Eventually Landor and his two servants – who had probably been brutalized as much if not more than their master – were led back to Taklakot where they were conveniently allowed to escape and reach the search party led by Dr. Harkua Wilson, which had been sent out when news of Landor's misfortunes had reached the authorities on the other side of the border. More substantial help was also on its way. The Government of India had dispatched a Mr. J. Larkin. Landor ran into Larkin's party after he himself had got back across the frontier. Although severely depleted by his ordeals, he insisted on accompanying the magistrate back to the Lipu Lekh Pass, where they waited for the Taklakot *dzongpon* to obey their summons and present himself to answer for what had taken place. The *dzongpon* did not appear though he did return a good part of Landor's property, which had been confiscated.

And so, filthy, ragged, vermin-ridden, though apparently very little the wiser, Arnold Henry Savage Landor returned to the plains of India. At Bombay he took ship for Italy, where his family home was situated. In due course, without stint of space or hyperbole, he was to tell the world the story of his remarkable adventures in *In the Forbidden Land* – adventures in which he had acquitted himself in a manner befitting an English explorer and gentleman.

Much of the serious surveying work that was done in Tibet during this period was performed by members of the Corps of

Pundits, a group of undercover native surveyors recruited to work in the territories beyond the British frontiers by Major T. G. Montgomerie of the Survey of India. They were given a thorough technical grounding in their work, and when in the field – where they travelled often in disguise – they might use the accoutrements of the peripatetic holy man (prayer-wheel, rosary and so forth), suitably modified, to help them in their surveying. Two who were active in the Kailas-Manasarovar were Nain Singh, the doyen of them all, and Kalian Singh.

The man who initially selected the young Pundits and sent them for training at the Engineering College at Roorkee was none other than the selfsame Edmund Smyth who had been with Drummond,* Webber and Hodgson in Western Tibet in 1864. A later traveller in the sacred region, Tom Longstaff, writes warmly of 'my old friend Edmund Smyth', whom he felt could fairly claim to be the first European at the source of the Brahmaputra – 'which was conveniently ignored by Sven Hedin when claiming its first discovery' (see pp. 97 ff.). Longstaff goes on: 'He was a grand old man with an enduring affection for the beauties of landscape. A notable *shikari*, he was the first European to explore many of the remote byways of Kumaon Garhwal and . . .' – this is particularly interesting – '. . . in 1851 and 1853 he had visited the adjacent parts of Tibet.' Unfortunately, Smyth left no written record of these secret forays, which is hardly surprising since in making them he had been cocking a snook not only at the Tibetans but at his own masters as well, the Government of India, who had banned unauthorized entry into the Forbidden Land by their own servants.

* Charles Allen has identified Drummond as the younger son of the 8th Viscount Strathallan.

CHAPTER FIVE

Travellers in the Sacred Region: The Early Twentieth Century

Around the turn of the present century, British suspicion of increasing Russian influence in Tibet developed into virtual paranoia.* This, allied to impatience with the continuing refusal of the Tibetan authorities to regularize their diplomatic and trading relations with their Indian neighbour, finally tipped the Viceroy, Lord Curzon, into a limited form of direct action. Thus, in 1904, the guns of the British Younghusband Expedition to Lhasa temporarily cowed the Tibetan government into modifying its rigidly exclusive attitude towards the outside world. One of the concessions conceded and duly enshrined in Article Five of the Treaty signed between the two principal parties allowed for the establishment of three trade

* For a detailed account of these events as seen by an observer in Lhasa, the Tibetan capital, see pp. 151 ff.

marts in Tibet. One was to be situated in Gartok in Western Tibet, and a British expedition was promptly assembled and dispatched from Central Tibet to inspect the place. As a survey of the country through which it was to pass was also to be carried out, the expedition included two surveyors among its four officers: Captains C. H. D. Ryder and H. Wood of the Royal Engineers. Ryder had already done sterling survey work in Western China, Burma and along the Indian frontier, as well as distinguishing himself as a first-rate field engineer at Gyangtse during the recent Anglo-Tibetan hostilities. Lieutenant F. Bailey of the 32nd Pioneers also went along as Interpreter and Assistant to Captain C. G. Rawling, of the Somersetshire Light Infantry, who was placed in general control. Surbordinate members of the Expedition included Sub-Surveyor Ram Singh R.S.; Hospital Assistant Hira Singh; three military surveyors; five Gurkha sepoys; five survey Khalassies; seven pony-drivers; two Hindustani and two Tibetan servants; and finally a Ladakhi named Mohammed Isa, later to meet his end in the service of Sven Hedin, who acted as Caravan Leader. Transport consisted of twenty-six baggage-ponies, seventeen riding-ponies and some one hundred yaks; these were to carry the Expedition's considerable supplies and equipment.

When it set off from Gyangtse on October 10th, 1904, the expedition was accompanied by an official of the Lhasa government and carried a 'very strongly worded permit signed with the seal of the Lhasa government and of the three great Lhasa monasteries, and directing all officials along the route to render every assistance' (Ryder). These were unique and highly privileged conditions of travel – ones which would surely have made those earlier travellers who had ventured into the hostile wastes of Tibet highly envious. The expedition leader, Captain Rawling, was indeed fully aware of the great significance of the undertaking: this was the first time that 'British officers, with only a nominal escort, were going to traverse Tibet with the cognizance and assistance of the Tibetan authorities'. Nevertheless, being no stranger to Tibet himself – he had done fine explorational work in remote parts of Western Tibet in 1903 – he was also aware of the many uncertainties that hung over the whole venture, and that it was bound to meet considerable difficulties. Two main problems confronted the expedition: the impossibility of knowing how in fact the provincial Tibetans would treat it and whether they would render the required and necessary assistance; and the fact that the Tibetan winter – an adversary more formidable than the most hostile Tibetans – was advancing fast. Not only could the members of the party expect to bear at least some of its rigours during the course of their thousand-mile journey, but there was the distinct possibility that the high passes back to India would be blocked by the time they reached them, in which case they would have to resign themselves to the prospect of seeing the winter out somewhere in the desolation of Western Tibet.

Rawling need not have vexed himself on the first score. In complete contrast to the experience of his precursors, he and his colleagues were to encounter cordiality, gifts and warm hospitality wherever they broke march. Regarding the winter, however, his apprehensions proved well-founded, though not to the point of realizing the worst possibilities. As the expedition progressed westwards it met with progressively more severe weather conditions. Apart from the occasional sunny days, when it was pleasant enough out of the shade, biting cold was the norm, frequently exacerbated by fierce winds, often reaching hurricane force, which made surveying both difficult and painful. By the time the travellers reached the high country towards Kailas the breath froze in their beards and their faces were covered with ice.

The first leg of the eight-hundred mile stage to Gartok ran through the valley of the Nyang Chu – 'one of the richest and most prosperous valleys in Tibet' – to Shigatse, where the expedition paused for several days. An army of tailors were employed in making warm clothing for everyone: sewing lambskins into their coats, for instance, and fitting them out with fur hats and gloves. There was also time to visit the great Lamaist theopolis at nearby Tashilumpo, seat of the august Tashi lama, second only in the theocratic hierarchy to the Dalai Lama himself. The monastery complex housed some four thousand monks; it was not so large as some of the great Lhasa monasteries but was rather more richly endowed. The monks entertained their British visitors cordially with tea (usually undrinkable), cakes and dried fruit; they also showed them around:

> The bulk of the buildings, the residences of the monks, were of the usual type – narrow paved roads with high houses on each side, dirty, and not picturesque; but we also enjoyed the sight of the tombs of the five previous Tashi lamas, each a separate building with its golden roof and highly ornamented interior, filled with a wealth of turquoises, gold bowls, and rare old jade and cloisonné, the effect being somewhat marred by a fore-ground of small vessels holding lighted tapers fed by very evil-smelling butter.
>
> (Capt. C. H. D. Ryder, 'Exploration and Survey with the Tibet Frontier Commission', etc., *Geographical Journal*, Vol XXV, October 1905)

There was also an audience with the Tashi Lama himself, then a young man of only twenty-three or thereabouts but nevertheless endowed with a quiet dignity that made a lasting impression upon his visitors. Indeed, his personality and the low lighting of the room in which the encounter took place together combined to make the whole proceeding seem like a religious ceremony. It concluded with the traditional presentation of silk scarves and a blessing.

After Shigatse, the expedition's route broadly followed the course of the Brahmaputra (Tsangpo) upstream to its headwaters just east of the Kailas-Manasarovar region. On occasions, members of the survey team split off from the main party to pursue their trigonometrical work in the surrounding hills and valleys. During the initial stages, the country through which they passed was comparatively populous and benign – scattered with pleasant villages surrounded by outlying patches of cultivation, and here and there an imposing fort or *gompa* perched on a rocky pinnacle like a stork's nest. Later on, however, it became increasingly arid, harsh and thinly populated. There were no trees then, not even the occasional oasis of cultivation, and such settled communities as existed were isolated, mean and dirty. This was the domain of nomadic herders and even they were not numerous.

1a. The Snowy Mountains from Mussoorie, North India

1b. The Everest Trek; return from Base Camp, near Dingboche, northern Nepal. Photo: Chris Piper

2. Tibetan painting of Mount Kailas and the Sacred Lakes by Lama Nav-Kushok. Photo: Swami Pranavananda, kindly lent by Shri Uma Prasad Mookerjee of Calcutta

3. Tibetan Thangka painting of the Buddhist tutelary deity, Demchog, and his consort, Dorje Phangmo. Photo: Library of Tibetan Works and Archives, Dharamsala

4. The *guru*-poet, Milarepa. In the background, incidents from the great Contest of Magic with the Bon priest, Naro Bhun Chon, including their legendary race to the summit of Mount Kailas, are depicted. Picture from *The Cotton Clad Mila . . .* by Toni Schmid

5a. A Tibetan lama salutes Mount Kailas. Diraphuk monastery, north side of Kailas. When Herbert Tichy photographed this or a similar scene at sunset, his disguise was nearly blown by the *Garpon* of Western Tibet (see pp. 126 ff.). Photo: Chatter Bhuj Kapur, 1936

5b. Lord Shiva and Pārvatī on Mount Kailas. A carving at Ellora, central India. Photo: Government of India Tourist Office

6a. The route to Mount Kailas: setting off from Almora to cross the Himalaya. Photo: Chatter Bhuj Kapur, 1936

6b. The route to Mount Kailas. View north from above Kalapani; Lipu Lekh Pass into Tibet on the left. Photo: Hugh Ruttledge, 1926

7a. Taklakot from the north. Photo: Hugh Ruttledge, 1926

7b. The Sikh invader Zorawar Singh's Tomb, at Toyo, three miles from Taklakot. Photo: Hugh Ruttledge, 1926

8a. Gurla Mandhata (25,400 feet) from Rakshas Tal.
Photo: Hugh Ruttledge, 1926

8b. Amateur *dacoit* or
freebooter near
Zorawar Singh's
Tomb. Photo: Hugh
Ruttledge, 1926

9a. Lake Manasarovar and Giu *Gompa* from the north. Photo: Hugh Ruttledge, 1926

9b. First View of the Sacred Mountain: Mount Kailas (22,028 feet) and Lake Rakshas Tal from near the Mansyang Pass. Photo: Hugh Ruttledge, 1926

10a. Ganga Chu: the Wet Channel connecting Lake Manasarovar and Lake Rakshas Tal. Looking west from Giu. Photo: Hugh Ruttledge, 1926

10b. *God is here within us . . . and not there on the mountain; the mountain is no more than a heap of stones . . .* Bhumananda, the Indian ascetic with whom Professor Giuseppe Tucci travelled to Mount Kailas in 1935. Photo: G. Tucci, 1935

11a. Mount Kailas from the fertile plain of Barkha to the north of the sacred lakes, *kyang* (wild asses) grazing in the foreground. Photo: Dr. Sálim Ali, Bombay, 1945

11b. Dogpa encampment near Barkha. Photo: Hugh Ruttledge, 1926

12. The Senior *Garpon*, the Dalai Lama's Viceroy, the most powerful official in Western Tibet. Photo: Hugh Ruttledge, 1926

13. The south-west face of Kailas from Tarchan. Photo: Hugh Ruttledge, 1926

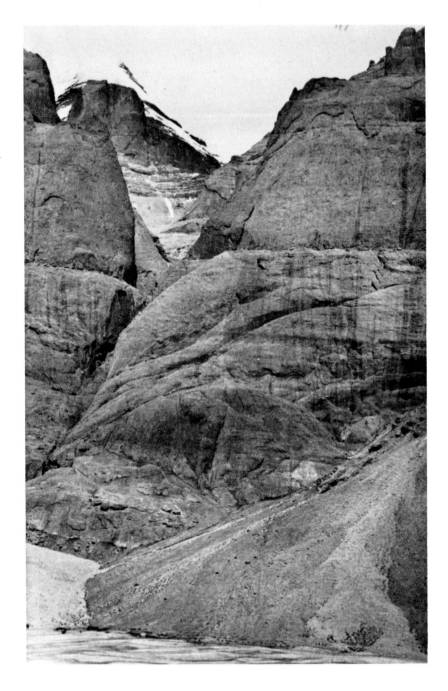

14. West face of Kailas from above the west bank of the Sarsu River.
Photo: Hugh Ruttledge, 1926

15a. North-west face of Kailas from near the Diraphuk (or Dindipu) monastery. Photo: Hugh Ruttledge, 1926

15b. Nun and monks of the Nyandi (Ruttledge's annotation gives it as 'Nindipu') monastery. Photo: Hugh Ruttledge, 1926

16a. The Great North Face of Kailas – a sheer rock wall 5,000 feet high, 'utterly unclimbable' (H. Ruttledge). Photo: Dr. Sálim Ali, Bombay, 1945

16b. Buddhist pilgrims circumambulating Mount Kailas. Photo: G. Tucci, 1935

There were compensations for the harshness of weather and terrain, though. Game became more plentiful as the expedition progressed westwards and its members were then able to indulge in the occasional spot of *shikar*.★ Wild sheep and antelope were among the more plentiful quarry, but Rawling was proud to be able to bag a large and obviously predatory wolf. Wood, on the other hand, was fortunate enough to catch a glimpse of that rarest of carnivores: the snow leopard; and other visual treats included a series of views of the northern side of Mount Everest – the members of the expedition were the first westerners to see the world's highest peak from this aspect:

> We had a magnificent view from a hill a few hundred feet above the pass of the main Himalayan range. Mount Everest stood up towering above the rest of the range in its neighbourhood in one isolated peak, a continuous drop of some 8000 feet separating it from the rest of the range east and west of it.
>
> (*Ibid.*)

The expedition eventually reached the watershed range from the valleys of which issue the many streams that give rise to the Brahmaputra. After a few days of bright sunshine, the weather took a turn for the worse here and the pass of Maium La (16,900 feet) was under a foot or two of snow when the party crossed it. Beyond, after crossing several more, rather lower passes and traversing expanses of undulating ground, they came in sight of the sacred lakes.

Naturally, the members of the expedition applied themselves to the perennial and fascinating hydrological problems of the area. They managed to confirm the existence of the channel connecting the twin lakes, though found it dry. No water was running between the western shore of Rakshas Tal and the course of the Sutlej either, and it was doubted whether it would ever flow again.

And so to the sacred mountain. One might have expected military men to be unimpressed but, as in the case of Henry

★ Hunting.

Strachey half a century before, this was not so. Rawling showed himself highly sensitive to the beauties of Kailas:

> Kailas Parbat is by far the largest and highest of the many pinnacles that tower up in the sky from the range of mountains which lies to the north of the Manasarowar Lake; its summit rises over 22,000 feet above sea-level, or some 7,000 feet above the surrounding plain. Figures, as a rule, convey but a vague idea to the general mind, and it is indeed difficult to place before the mental vision a true picture of this most beautiful mountain.
>
> In shape it resembles a vast cathedral, the roof of which, rising to a ridge in the centre, is otherwise regular in outline and covered with eternal snow. Below this so-called roof, the sides of the mountain are perpendicular and fall sheer for hundreds of feet, the strata horizontal, the layers of stone varying slightly in colour, and the dividing lines showing up clear and distinct. The layers are again divided or split by perpendicular cracks, which give to the entire mountain the appearance of having been built by giant hands, of huge blocks of reddish stone.
>
> At the foot of these Titanic walls a number of caves are said to exist, and dark and gloomy ravines lie on either side, while from the neighbouring and lesser hills rise numberless pinnacles and slender spires of rock.
>
> Wonderful is the appearance of this mountain in the early morning, when its roof of spotless snow is touched by the rising sun and changed in hue to a soft but vivid pink, whilst the ravines below still hold the blackness of the night. As the light increases so do the mighty walls brighten in colour, and form a happy contrast to the blue waters of Manasarowar rippling in the morning breeze, changing gradually, as one gazes, from purple to brightest blue.
>
> No wonder then that this spot is believed by Hindus and Mahomedans [not so] alike to be the home of all the gods, that of the waters of its holy lake they drink, and that it is *the* Holy Mountain, and the most sacred spot on earth a pilgrimage to which ensures both sanctity and renown.
>
> (Capt. C. G. Rawling, *The Great Plateau*)

Rawling and his party visited the staging post* on the main Lhasa-Gartok highway which crossed the lush plain at the southern foot of Kailas, where they were entertained by the

---

* Here the riders bearing the official mail could change their mounts.

tarjum or presiding officer. The building they entered consisted of about nine rooms arranged around a courtyard. Despite having been cleaned in their honour, it was still very dirty – all travellers in Tibet stress the ubiquitous dirt – though the general atmosphere was made cheerful by the Manchester and Indian cotton prints that covered the smoke-begrimed walls. Large quantities of Chinese brick tea were stored here, for which, apparently, the Tibetans had an inordinate thirst. By preference they took it mixed with butter – a rank and souplike concoction that would make even the most gross and long-standing brew of British cafeterias and buffets seem delicate. This tea was exported to Tibet pressed into blocks of about five pounds weight each and finally sewn inside skins for protection in transit. It cost a fair amount on the Western Tibetan market although it was pretty rough stuff; Rawling aptly calls it 'the leavings and sweepings of the Chinese crop'. Superior quality Indian tea could certainly be had at more modest cost but the Tibetans were firmly set against it. Wily Chinese tea merchants had put about the rumour that it induced unpleasant headaches.

After Barkha, the expedition crossed the Indus-Sutlej watershed by way of a 16,200 foot pass called the Jerko La and reached Gartok on December 9th. This was the official summer residence of the Garpons or Viceroys, but they travelled up from their winter residence at Gargunsa some thirty miles away in order to treat with the British. The members of the expedition were exceedingly unimpressed with Gartok; Ryder dismisses it as 'one of the most dreary inhabited places that we had struck in our journey', and continues:

> A long broad plain, absolutely bare, with a dozen wretched hovels in the middle, constitutes at this time of year what is in summer the chief trading centre of Western Tibet. The wind howled round the hut we were in continuously, and, the weather looking threatening, we were not anxious to stay a minute longer than was necessary for Captain Rawling to settle up trade questions with the Garpons.
>
> (Ryder, *Ibid.*)

Rawling was able to discharge his duties in a single day, and then the sprint for India was on. The expedition had first to

cross a number of high passes, however, where they encountered blizzards and scathing winds; then they entered the
bizarre canyon lands of the upper Sutlej valley:

> We were now in the most cut-up country I have ever seen; it must
> resemble to loess formation of China. The bottom of every
> nullah was some hundreds of feet below the general level of the
> valley, with their edges so cut and worn into fantastic shapes that
> it was difficult to believe that one was not looking on the ruins of
> old castles. There are also innumerable caves in which the
> inhabitants live.
>
> (Ryder *Ibid.*)

Rawling and Bailey took off to visit the ruins of the ancient
city of Tholing. These were situated on the summit of an
isolated plateau of sandstone, and the sole means of reaching
them was by means of funnel-like holes carved in the solid
rock. Although largely deserted by modern times, Tholing
continued to enjoy its traditional status as the spiritual capital
of Western Tibet and was the seat of the *khanpo* or regional
patriarch. Nearby was another remarkable relic: an ancient
iron chain cantilever bridge reputed to date back to the time of
Alexander the Great.

Rawling's party crossed the Great Himalaya by the Shipki
La, a 15,400 foot pass. It was Christmas by now and three feet
of snow bedevilled their progress. Their privations were soon
to be over, however. After only eighteen more marches they
were once again enjoying the pleasures of civilization in that
doyen of hill stations: Simla.

Within months another member of this new generation of
privileged travellers was making his way towards Western
Tibet; not a military man this time but a representative of that
other face of the official British presence in India – a civil
servant.

In 1905, Charles Atmore Sherring,★ I.C.S., Deputy Commissioner of Almora, was sent on a tour of the Bhot Mahals
which was subsequently extended to include an official
mission to Gartok to check the functioning of the new trade
arrangements. His line of approach was the most direct and

★ (1868–1940); arrived in India (U.P.), 1899; retired, 1914.

convenient one: up the course of the Kali river, close along the Nepalese border, passing through centres like Ascot and Garbyang, and so on up to the benign Lipu Lekh pass by way of the totally unbenign Nerpani trail. He travelled in appropriate style, lacking nothing in the way of equipment, and accompanied by a sizeable retinue of staff. As he progressed unhurriedly across the landscape, he scrutinized it with a pragmatic eye: noting prevailing conditions of trade, bandying figures of volume and value, devising schemes to expedite traffic. He discerned where new roads or railway connections might be developed and finely calculated what the repercussions would be in terms of intangible political realities like *influence* and *interest*. He had a keen nose for the machinations of rival powers, and could even detect a suspicious Russian aroma on the rarefied air of Western Tibet – and had not his great precursor, Moorcroft, sensed much the same thing as far back as 1812? he reminds his possibly innocent reader.

Yet this was not all there was to the man. Behind the professional persona seems to have lain something of the scholar,★ who took a keen and compassionate interest in the culture and traditions of the indigenous people. Notable among these were the Bhotias, a mountain people of Mongolian stock, though lately espousing Hinduism, who lived in the area adjacent to the Tibetan border. Sherring extended this same humane curiosity to the Tibetans once across the high passes. Indeed, he seems an example of the better type of British servant of India: a responsible man aware that power and privilege entailed a corresponding debt of duty and concern for the people of the land – the very antithesis of Landor. There was in fact a tradition of service to India in his family; his father, Rev. Matthew Sherring – also a writer of books – had lived and died as a missionary out there, although originally trained as a doctor.

But what makes Sherring even more significant in terms of the central theme of the present book is that he was the first of our Kailas travellers to be really awake to the extensive religious connotations of this rare quarter of the world:

★ Sherring had been a Queen's Scholar at Westminster before going on to Trinity College, Cambridge, where he graduated with an M.A. in Classics.

This part of Western Tibet and the British Borderland is a country most sacred to the Hindus and Buddhists, and appealing as it does with its awful solemnity and weird grandeur of landscape to all that is romantic in the human soul, it is clothed the while to the eye of faith with a garment of mystery that makes it the fit abode of the great gods of Hinduism and Buddhism.
(C. A. Sherring, *Western Tibet and the British Borderland*)

On a broader level he takes full cognizance of the spiritual power of the Himalaya in general – there being 'no place in all this fair earth of ours which can compare with the marvellous beauty of these everlasting snows'. Above all, however, Kailas★ rears up pre-eminent, the crowning apex of this whole upward spiritual urge and the seal of the sanctity of the entire region –

There is no mountain like Himachal, for in it are Kailas and Manasarovar. As the dew of the morning sun, so are the sins of mankind dried up at the sight of Himachal.
(*Ramayana* quoted in C. A. Sherring, *Western Tibet and the British Borderland*)

Sherring is depicted in photographs taken during his venture into Western Tibet as dapperly clad in Norfolk jacket and plus-fours, and wearing a compact topi on his head. He regails us in his account of his journey with some vivid descriptions in splendidly augustan prose of the beauties of the passing scene. Beyond the major Bhotia community of Garbyang, his way led along the dizzy Nerpani trail – *nerpani* meaning literally 'no water'. Here the traveller had to gird up his courage and march boldly along narrow stone ledges flashed into the sides of sheer precipices. The final ascent to the Lipu Lekh pass (16,780 feet) was broad and gradual: it could happily accommodate a cart road. Finally, at the top of the pass, there was a revelation:

★ We have already noted in the first chapter that Sherring also discussed the latterday identification of Mounts Kailas and Meru in some depth (see pp. 34–6).

The first view of Tibet from the Lipu Lekh pass is magnificent as, admidst all the other beauties of the landscape, the centre of the picture is occupied by four peaks, all over 22,000 ft., which are quite close together, the highest being Gurla Mandhata, 25,350 ft. This solid mass lends a grandeur to the whole which is quite awe-inspiring, and on all sides the most beautiful coloured rocks heighten the effect, so that the impression on the beholder is that the scene before him is truly one of nature's grandest handi-works. There are no trees or verdure to relieve the severity of what he sees, and the almost total absence of animal life adds to the feeling of intense desolation prevailing everywhere.

These divers colours among the rocks are quite a feature of the country all the way to Taklakot, and of the landscape round that fortress. There are sepia, burnt sienna, raw sienna, violet, all shades of yellow and many lovely shades of red. The brilliancy of the sunshine and the intense sharpness of all lines, added to the clearness of the air, which makes the most distant objects appear close, while all around is a penetrating glare, make one liken the landscape to nothing so much as that part of Arabia which one sees near Suez.

(*Ibid.*)

And so to Taklakot, just a few miles over the other side of the border, where there were the inevitable meetings with the leading local citizenry: the acting *dzongpon*, and his coquettish wife, who insisted on being photographed – alone; and the head lama of the Shivling *gompa*. Sherring tried to impress his hosts with his knowledge of Tibetan Buddhism by showing them his copies of L. A. Waddell's illustrated books on the subject. The stand-in *dzongpon* was rather more impressed, however, with the European magazines that were also shown him, especially with the advertisements for hair-restorers and beauty preparations. All in all the social side of the visit was a great success and their parting was on the very best of terms. Indeed Sherring seems to have generally liked and in many ways admired the Tibetans – in all but one particular, where for a moment his usual open-mindedness fails and he cannot forebear lapsing into classic Victorian prudishness. Having discussed the prevailing institution of *polyandry*, he writes:

REFERENCES :-

A *Bivouac of July 18.19.*
   about 19.000 ft.
B *Camp of July 20.21.*
C *Bivouac of July 22.*
D *Sleeping place in rocks*
   July 23. after Avalanche
E *Sleeping place on*
   Glacier July 24.

12 Rough sketch map illustrating Longstaff's attempt on Gurla Mandhata

The result of domestic life as described above is that a most unsatisfactory state of things exists in the society of this part of Tibet, which leads to very general impropriety between the sexes, and which forms a curse to a nation boasting so many qualities of endurance and manliness which cannot but otherwise call forth our admiration.

(Ibid.)

For part of his journey Sherring was accompanied by the distinguished mountaineer, Dr. Tom Longstaff, who was planning an assault on the hitherto unscaled peak of Gurla Mandhata, and who had therefore brought along with him two professional Alpine guides, the Brocherels. Although they reached heights of 23,000 feet or more, the climbers were denied the summit due to their inadequate knowledge of the topography of the mountain, which made it impossible for them to find a viable route. They also narrowly escaped death twice: firstly, on the mountain itself, when an avalanche swept them down for about three thousand feet; and secondly, having left the mountain, after failing to meet up with Sherring's main party at the appointed place, they found themselves alone in inhospitable, *dacoit*-infested wastes without food, shelter, money or arms to defend themselves.

Sherring had meanwhile passed down from Taklakot, past Toyo where the tomb of Zorawar Singh lay, and so on up to the Gurla pass (16,200 feet), where another stunning panorama greeted him:

The view as one surveys this holy place, venerated alike by Buddhists and Hindus, is one of the most beautiful throughout the whole of this part of the country. The Mansarowar Lake, forty-five miles in circumference, on the right, and Rakas Tal, of equal size and more varied contour, on the left, make with their lovely dark blue a magnificent foreground to the range of the Kailas mountains at the back, while the holy Kailas peak, Tise of the Tibetans, the Heaven of the Hindus and Buddhists, fills the centre of the picture, full of majesty, a king of mountains, dominating the entire chain by 2000 feet. The colouring of the rocks are the hue of the water, softened by the green of thousands and thousands of acres of verdant pasture-land, form a setting to the landscape which is indescribably charming, and although one misses the foliage of the forests, the colours are so exquisite in their brilliancy that they clothe the austerity of the mountains with a mantel that veils all their harshness. As one reaches the heaps of stones (each traveller should cast a stone on the crest according to universal custom) and sees the monuments (Chortens) erected by pious hands which mark the top of the pass, and the view bursts upon the sight, prayers and ejaculations break forth on all sides from the weary travellers, giving place later to a feeling of absolute contentment that they have been blessed to see 'what kings and mighty men have desired to see and not seen'.

(*Ibid.*)

Tom Longstaff and friends, much the worse for their ordeals, rejoined Sherring on the shores of Lake Manasarovar, having been lucky enough to meet up with Thakur Jai Chand, a Kunawari then acting as trade agent for the British in Gartok, who happened to be travelling the same route and gave them assistance.

Passing along the isthmus between the two lakes, Sherring was able to photograph the controversial channel connecting them. No water was flowing through it at the time, however, because the mouth was blocked by a bank of sand. The last occasion when it had flowed had been during the exceptional rains that fell eleven years before; it was clearly remembered because it had been the year of the Khumb Fair at Kailas.

Sherring found his next destination, Barkha, not at all easy to locate. He describes it as lying 'on an enormous plain, viz., the plateau of 15,000 ft., which extends for many miles, and until one actually reaches it it is very difficult to see, being concealed on the east by a bank. The approach is over hummocks of sand and juniper bushes, and it is impossible to travel fast.' The presiding official was absent from the staging-post at the time of Sherring's visit: he had been called to Gartok to stand trial for the murder of a servant of the Shivling *gompa* in Taklakot. His stand-in was also absent, so Sherring had to be content to be entertained by a minor functionary called a *goba*. Afterwards, he journeyed on to Tarchan, the starting-point for the Kailas *parikrama*. The journey was across a 'wilderness of bog, morass and sand hummocks'.

Despite being deeply fascinated by all the lore and mythology surrounding the sacred mountain, Sherring does not seem to have been tempted to circumambulate it himself. He was particularly amused by the fact that proxies were allowed

94

to go round on behalf of indolent or indisposed devotees, thinking this good evidence that 'the element of humour is rarely wanting in Tibet'.

After Tarchan, Sherring proceeded to Gartok to discharge his official duties, which having been duly accomplished he was free to return to India via a more westerly route than that by which he had entered Tibet. He crossed the high Balchh, Kungri Bingri and Untadhura passes to Milam and thence returned to base. Once more upon home ground, with its forests and hamlets and fertile valleys, he writes:

> . . . we could not but help comparing this homely sight with what we had just left behind on the other side of the great barrier of the Himalayas, where desolation is boldly written across a treeless landscape, where, with few exceptions, cultivation is unknown, and a nomad population living in tents is so scattered over the barren wilderness that the traveller can travel for days and see no human being, while the absence of houses makes desolation more desolate; and we felt that, however pleasant our trip, the return home was good.
>
> (*Ibid.*)

Sherring eventually in 1914 returned to roost in England. In later life he was a magistrate for Surrey and a director of the newspaper wholesaling house of Wm. Dawson and Son. He died of a heart attack in East Sheen, in 1940, at the onset of German bombing. His work in India was carried on by his successors at Almora, of course, and indeed their records show that the British took their new political and trading connections with Western Tibet most seriously. Showers of bureaucratic communiqués transmigrated across the Great Himalaya detailing any and every event of significance, and twice in succeeding years important British officials again ventured over the high passes to make personal contact with the Tibetan authorities. In July 1907, W. S. Cassels, Assistant Commissioner, Almora, went to Gyanema by way of Taklakot and the Southern shore of Rakshas Tal; and in July 1911, N. C. Stiffe went to Gyanema via Barkha, accompanied by Captain A. D. Stewart.

British political interest in Western Tibet had now advanced so far that Cassels in the official report of his visit of

1907 openly discussed the problems that would attend on administering the area, and came to the conclusion that these threatened to be so large that the British might account themselves lucky not to have to bear this particular white man's burden. He was also disconcerted to see indications of increasing Chinese interest in the affairs of Western Tibet, and duly noted that the Tibetans seemed favourably disposed to the influence of China. 'Perhaps the effects of the Russo-Japanese War', he concluded.

Trade-wise, on the other hand, the persistent rub was the interference of the *dzongpon* of Taklakot in the Bhotia wool trade – the Bhotias were sponsored by Cawnpore Woollen Mills and large sums were involved – by imposing levies of his own. Neither Cassels nor Stiffe looked forward to much change in the situation while the *dzongpon* purchased his office and would naturally expect a good return on his investment: 'men would hardly exchange the luxury of Lhasa for the bleak exile of Western Tibet for nothing'. This aside, the British were also very eager to promote other forms of trade – and in both directions. Cassels was very taken up with the possibility of introducing Indian Berenag tea and Indian cigarettes into the Western Tibetan market. He saw the matter of roads as vital in trade and argued that investment should be made in their improvement with a view to thereby stimulating economic activity. Sherring's old belief that pilgrims would be the pioneers in matters of trade prompts him to the following fascinating comments, however:

> Kunwar Kharag Singh tells me that at the present time about 150 faquirs visit Kailas in an ordinary year. When the Khumb mela takes place every 12th year, the number of pilgrims from India rises to 400. At present the pilgrim traffic is very small. I myself met three faquirs in Tibet. One of them accompanied my camp from first to last. He bathed in Manasarovar and contemplated Kailas from a distance of 15 miles, has uttered the word 'Kailas' in an extatic way ever since, and will no doubt always claim to have visited Kailas. When I was in Gyanema I met a faquir from Delhi. Kailas is visible from Gyanema, and this faquir told me that the sight of it was good enough for him; he was not going there because it was too cold and the discomfort too great. I met a third faquir. He spoke excellent English and was a tahbildar in Jaipur

state before he resolved to forsake the things of the world and become a sadhu. He went from Gangutri as far as Gyanema. He fell ill in Gyanema and returned thence to India without visiting Kailas or Manasarovar. He told me that the *pujari* in Kailas were ignorant; that there were no religious devotees in Kailas learned in Indian philosophy and religion, and that nothing was to be gained by a visit to the place. I conclude, therefore, that many of the faquirs who claim to have visited Kailas have gone no further than Taklakot or Gyanema. On paper the journey to Kailas appears easy. In practice it is difficult and attended by great discomfort. The pilgrim must take his own food with him; the climate is bleak; the wind is a blizzard; there is the fear of dacoits; the road is very bad, and the country eerie and almost uninhabited.

It will be many years before the pilgrim trade from India becomes considerable. . . .

(*Report by W. S. Cassels, Assistant Commissioner,*
Almora, on a visit to Western Tibet in July 1907,
India Office Library, L/P&S/7/207/No 1873)

Cassels might also claim fame in the annals of Western Tibet as the man who brought the strains of Harry Lauder's *Stop Your Tickling, Jock!* and Dan Leno's *Red Poppies* to the desolate wastes of the great plateau . . . on gramophone records! He held little gramophone concerts and much delighted the Tibetans with them. He also showed the wife of the Taklakot *dzongpon* her own picture in Sherring's book – naturally much to her delight.

If anyone can be said to have played the part of a Richard Burton or a John Hanning Speke in the search for the sources of the great rivers of the Indian subcontinent, it must be Sven Hedin, the distinguished Swedish explorer. During the course of a long and highly successful career of Central Asian exploration, Hedin chalked up a number of claims to geographical 'firsts', including claims to have discovered the sources of both the Indus and Brahmaputra rivers. He was also the first westerner to make the *parikrama* or circumambulation of Mount Kailas.

In 1901–2, Hedin had penetrated deep into the heart of Tibet, only to have been turned back by the authorities. A man of remorseless determination and will, he returned to

India in 1905 with his heart set on exploring those areas of the Forbidden Land which appeared on the maps of the day as a great amorphous white patch bearing the summary legend 'Unexplored'. In Simla he was lionized by the luminaries of British India: Viceroy Minto, Kitchener, Younghusband —they were all behind his new Tibetan project to a man. The India Office in London was not so acquiescent, however, and refused to lend its sanction. In consequence, it looked for a while as though the whole enterprise was in jeopardy.

Hedin had managed to obtain a Chinese passport, however, and eventually the British authorities allowed him to proceed to Kashmir and Ladakh on the understanding that he would visit Turkistan. In Ladakh, he assembled a considerable caravan of some thirty porters and servants, one hundred and thirty animals, and bought provisions sufficient for a very long march. He had brought special equipment with him from Europe: the usual surveying and photographic gear, a collapsible boat made of oiled canvas, and a fabulous cornucopia of medical resources contained in a splendid case of burnished aluminium, supplied courtesy of Messrs Burroughs and Wellcome. When all was complete, the caravan moved off towards the high passes.

Of course, Hedin had no intention whatsoever of going to Chinese Turkistan. The directives of the bureaucrats meant little to him. He was a man whose thinking was cast in the old heroic mould; his obsession was to win fame and glory through explorational achievement; anything that did not work toward this end was trivial, not worthy of consideration. Once he was into the high country where the borders of Ladakh, Tibet and Turkistan blur into each other, therefore, he quite cynically pointed his caravan in the direction of his only real objective: Tibet.

Hedin's route took him across the awesomely barren Chang Tang plateau; Capt. C. G. Rawling (1903) was one of the few westerners who had ventured there before him. For over eighty days, Hedin saw no other human beings besides the men of his own party. Biting winds and withering sub-zero temperatures decimated his pack animals. Both caravan and supplies were seriously depleted by the time they at last encountered the first nomads, from whom they were able to buy replacement animals and a few spare supplies. Money was about the only thing that was not in short supply during the expedition. Hedin carried sacks containing thousands of rupees with him, a high proportion of them supplied by Nobel, the dynamite millionaire.

Outstanding adventures during the first leg of the route included two dramatic lake interludes: one at Lake Lighten, where Hedin sailed his collapsible boat and nearly came to grief in a terrible night storm; the other at Ngantse-Tso, which was frozen and in consequence explored by sledge. There were also perilous encounters with wolves and crazed yaks.

Despite all hardships and crises, Hedin pushed doggedly on. He seems a deeply lonely figure, more emotionally involved with his favourite animals than with the people with whom he travelled. An amusing incident with a favourite puppy or horse will warrant several sentences in his journal, and he is deeply moved when one dies. People do not command the same space or depth of sentiment. Thrust back on his own resources, partly by circumstances, partly by choice, he seems to have fortified himself spiritually by constantly meditating on notions of heroic achievement. The Swedish hero, Marcus Curtius, who ended his life in a glorious horseback leap into an awesome abyss, was frequently in his thoughts. To Hedin, geographical 'firsts' were quite simply the contemporary counterpart of the legendary feats of the heroes of old.

The whole time he travelled, Hedin was bedevilled by uncertainty as to how the Tibetan authorities would treat him when they eventually found out about his presence in their land. Would he be simply turned back as in 1902? As encounters with Tibetans became more frequent, it did look as though this was what might happen. Then, ironically, at Ngangtse-Tso, Hlaje Tsering, the self-same provincial governor who had done the honours in 1902 turned up in person to repeat the old routine. As luck would have it, however, no less a person than the brother of the Tashi Lama turned up at precisely the same time, carrying Hedin's mail from Shigatse. Seeing that the old interloper had friends in high places, Hlaje Tsering allowed Hedin to proceed to Shigatse to have his fate determined there.

To get into the Brahmaputra valley, where lay the principal routes to Shigatse, Hedin had first to cross the great mountain system which he subsequently named the *Transhimalaya*. On those sequestered heights, his spirits soared, for he realized that he was on one of the great watersheds of the world and could in fact lay claim to a highly significant 'first':

> It was delightful this evening to sit at length in the warmth of the camp fire. In silent meditation my eyes swept from the rocky crests, brightly lighted by the moon, down to the dark shadowy depths of the valley, where there were only wolves crouching in their holes. It seemed as though all belonged to me; as though I had marched into this land a conqueror at the head of victorious legions, and had crushed all opposition. Oh, what splendid legions! Five-and-twenty ragged fellows from Ladakh, ten lean jades, and about twenty worn-out yaks. And yet I had succeeded! Marcus could not have been prouder of the triumphs he achieved in the war against Jurgurtha than I was when I had won my victory over the 'Trans-Himalaya' at Sela-la, that Sela-la which, now bathed in moonlight, seemed to us the extreme outpost on the limits of boundless space.
>
> (Sven Hedin, *Transhimalaya*)

Hedin arrived at Shigatse at a timely moment. Thousands of pilgrims had arrived from all parts of Tibet and from adjacent Buddhist countries to witness the New Year celebrations at Tashilumpo, the Tashi Lama's great theopolis. Hedin witnessed the celebrations, and also met the Tashi Lama. The young prelate's palpable spirituality impressed the Swede as strongly as it had impressed the British group led by Rawling. Hedin also took the opportunity of visiting and sketching – he was an accomplished draughtsman and watercolourist – the temples, mausolea and inhabitants of Tashilumpo, and he studied Tibetan Buddhism closely, sometimes with a sympathy that suggests that he may himself have had leanings towards the spiritual life, at other times with rather less sympathy and indeed a certain admixture of Christian prejudice against 'false faiths.'

All the time Hedin was at Shigatse the usual battle of wills was going on. On the one hand, there was the Swedish explorer doggedly set on doing what he had a mind to do. On the other hand, there were the Tibetan authorities, equally determined to uphold their own policies and have the foreigner obey them. The Tibetans wanted to send Hedin back the way he had come – this was their usual course with foreigners who succeeded in illegally entering their country. The whole notion was anathema to Hedin, however, because it would be to retrace old ground and thus give him no opportunity for new geographical discoveries. An alternative possibility was that the Tibetans, in order to achieve a quick riddance, might insist that he leave the country by the most

13. Drawing of Tashilumpo by Sven Hedin

immediate route: that is, the direct southerly one back to India via Gyangtse, Sikkim and Darjeeling. This would also take him through much-travelled and therefore geographically uninteresting territory. What Hedin wanted was a chance to get into some more of those blank spaces on the map, and he was prepared to use any trick, tactic or ploy to swing things his own way. He would stall, bluster, threaten, bargain, lay red herrings. . . . Where discoveries were concerned, he was utterly without morals.

Eventually a compromise was agreed – and it says a great deal for the stature of the man that even in the heart of alien territory he could yet contrive to get a large measure of his own way. He *should* return to Ladakh, but by a route rather to the south of his outward one: a route that would in fact take him up the Brahmaputra valley to Gartok – broadly the same route taken by Rawling's party. At every stage, however, Hedin conspired to dodge the restraints of the officials who were meant to control him and strayed off his ordained route into unfrequented byways where he could make fresh explorations.

In mid-July 1907, Hedin located what he claimed to be the true source of the Brahmaputra river on the main glacier of the Kubi-gangri mountains, at a height of 15,958 feet. A few days later:

> . . . we rode over the Tage-tsanpo, where its valley opens into the flat basin of Manasarovar – a new chapter in the chronicles of our journey. Again, Gurla Mandhata showed itself in all its glory, and in the north-west Kangrinpoche or Kailas, the holy mountain, like a great *chorten* on a lama's grave, rose above the jagged ridge which forms the horizon in that direction. On seeing it, all our men suddenly jumped out of their saddles and threw themselves on the ground. Only Rabsang, a confirmed heathen, remained seated on his horse, and was afterwards well scolded by Tsering.
>
> (*Ibid.*)

Hedin was to top the Drummond sacrilege of 1855/60. Not only did he sail his collapsible boat on Lake Manasarovar, but he also sailed on the neighbouring Rakshas Tal as well, though there were no subsequent reports of decapitations. When he initially proposed his Manasarovar venture to his guides, Hedin was told the whole thing would be quite impossible. As the lake was the home of the gods, they told him, any mortal who ventured upon it must surely perish; moreover there was a practical problem deriving from the fact that the lake was said not to be flat at all but formed like a transparent dome – if anyone succeeded in sailing a boat up one side of it, they would only come to grief when their craft came shooting down the other side.

Nevertheless, the days on the lake were idyllic. Hedin tacked to and fro on the turquoise waters with the great crystal bulk of Kailas looming up to the north, complemented by that of Gurla Mandhata in the south. He did not neglect his scientific duties, of course, but took innumerable soundings and generally made close study of the lake before going to Rakshas Tal to do likewise.

Naturally Hedin also visited the channel connecting the two lakes. He found it dry, though it was reported that water had flowed through it four years earlier. He went on to the old dry bed of the Sutlej discovered by Henry Strachey in 1846, and, though he found no water there either, was convinced that there was subterranean filtration between the western lake and the main stream of the river. If this were the case, the source of the Sutlej could then be traced back to Rakshas Tal and, further still, via the connecting channel back to Manasarovar, and finally to streams flowing into that lake from the highlands to the east. This theory in fact upheld local tradition and also a thesis advanced in Chi Chao Nan's *Hydrography*, an eighteenth century Chinese work, which maintained that the upper headwater of the Sutlej was the Tage-Tsangpo, a stream arising from the Ganglung Glacier, which lay not many miles north-west of the source of the Brahmaputra. Hedin insists that this assertion would be good even though many of the channels were dry for most of the time, and he dismisses as 'prognostication' the notion that the hydrography of the area might have changed permanently and that water would never flow through these old channels again.

During his sojourn at the sacred lakes, Hedin repeatedly observed, admired and sketched Kailas:

> The sun sets and we sit still and wait, confused by the rush of the spirits of the air and water. This time they have played a pretty trick, and we have been caught. To the north rises Kang-rinpoche, lofty and bright as a royal crown. Its summit is like a *chorten* on the grave of a Grand Lama. Snow and ice with vertical and slightly inclined fissures and ledges form a network like the white web of a gigantic spider on the black cliffs.
>
> (*Ibid.*)

It was, however, seen to best advantage from a distance:

The nearer we came to the holy mountain, the less imposing it
appeared; it was finest from Langak-tso [Rakshas Tal]. In form it
resembles a tetrahedron set on a prism. From the middle of its
white top a belt of ice falls precipitously down, and below it
stands a stalagmite of ice, into which a thick stream of water
pours from above. The stream splits into glittering drops of
spray and thin sheets of water – a grand spectacle, which one
could watch with pleasure for hours.

(Ibid.)

Hedin seems to have had no doubt that this was truly a *holy*
mountain – the most famous in the whole world. This being
the case, he was prepared to join with the other pilgrims –
Buddhists, Hindus, Bon-po – who were engaged in making
the *parikrama* of Kailas. On 3rd September, 1907, laden with
only minimal supplies and accompanied by a single servant, a
Buddhist named Rabsang, Hedin gave the slip to the Gova of
Barkha who was keeping him under surveillance, and rode
north from his camp at Khaleb, a few miles due west of
Tarchen, to the mouth of the Dunlung valley. Three other
servants had already gone on ahead – Tsering, Namgyal and
Ishe. Hedin rejoined them at the first moraines and the whole
party proceeded in close column across the undulating,
debris-strewn ground. To the east they could see a party of
pilgrims from Kham resting on the banks of the Dunlung
river, their horses grazing on the fresh grass, their tents
nearby.

Riding on up the valley, they soon found themselves
hemmed in by solid walls of hard green and violet conglomerate rock, at the foot of which lay cones of scree debris. The
main pilgrim road – the *Kora kora* or Gangri circle – lay on the
left bank of the river, where there were also several rows of
manis and *chortens* and a small cubical house. As the party went
on, the cliffs assumed 'ever wilder forms, falling perpendicularly to terraces and pebble screes, forming steps and ledges,
fortifications, battlements and towers, as though built by
human hands'. They were composed of sandstone conglomerate and appeared horizontal to the naked eye, though in fact
there was a 10° dip in them to the south.

They passed another pilgrim group, who were crossing a
small bridge that spanned the river. Hedin's party held to the

right bank, however. On the sheer rock face above them was a ledge where a hermit lived and nearby a terrace where the first *gompa* (monastery) of Kailas was situated: Nyandi *gompa*. The perilousness of the *gompa's* situation had been demonstrated some five years before when a huge boulder had fallen and shattered half the building. Dominating the cliff from the top was a prayer-flag called *Nyandi-kong*.

Hedin was well received at the *gompa* which, like others in the region, fell within the purview of the Raja of Bhutan. He was told that pilgrims flocked to Kailas in especially great numbers every twelve years. That year, 1907, five thousand had already called at the *gompa*, most of them being from Ladakh. Among the treasures of Nyandi were a huge copper vessel, said to have flown from India long ago, and a fine pair of elephant's tusks set up before the altar. Hedin found the view from the roof magnificent.

After three hours, Hedin's party left Nyandi and descended a steep, zig-zagging path running through boulders and scree. 'At every turn I could stand still in astonishment,' he writes, 'for this valley is one of the grandest and most beautiful wildernesses I have ever seen.' The right-hand precipice was divided into two stages, separated by a gaping ravine; the left hand precipice was a single vertical wall of rock carved into forms of rococo intricacy. Melted ice-water cascaded from the heights above, dousing the rock walls as it fell and turning to spray when whipped up by the wind.

Hedin noticed that the members of the next two pilgrim groups he encountered were not socializing with each other at all but grimly murmuring the sacred mantra, *Om mani padme hum*, as they hurried on their way. One pilgrim from Gertse was said to be on his tenth circuit. There were numerous cairns about the place at this point; apparently it was customary to add a stone to them in passing. The icy peak of Kailas, meanwhile, had vanished from view but became visible again a little later through a gap in the ubiquitous rock walls. The sun also broke occasionally through such gaps to dispel with bright, yellow light the shadow trapped in the tight, enclosed places.

At Dunglung-do, three valleys converged: the Chamo-lungchen, the Dunlung and the Hle-lungpa. Hedin's party ascended the last. They now found that granite was the prevailing rock; and the summit of Kailas, turning a sharp edge to the north, appeared more like a tetrahedron than ever.

Diri-pu was the next *gompa*; it stood on a slope to the right of the valley. The sacred mantra was carved on a huge block of granite that stood beside the path that led up to it. There were also long *manis*, streamers and cairns. The *gompa* itself was full to capacity because all the pilgrim parties encountered during the day had stopped there for the night. Accommodation was free and extended even to members of the Bon religion. Hedin

The Kailas from N.

The Kailas from S.W.

The Kailas from N.E.

The Kailas from S.E.

14. Views of Kailas by Sven Hedin

pitched his tent on the roof amid the pilgrims' luggage, and was able to enjoy a fine view of the dramatic north face of the sacred mountain. The temperature was decidedly cool, however, and an uncomfortable wind was blowing.

When he discovered from the monks at Diri-pu that the

source of the Indus – the river that issues from the mouth of the lion – lay just three days' march to the north, he was sorely tempted to abandon his *parikrama* and repair there immediately. After holding a council of war, however, it was decided that it was not an opportune time to make the trip: money was in short supply and, anyway, things were too uncertain back at Khaleb for any more risks to be taken for the moment.

Accordingly next morning, 4th September, Hedin's party took their leave of the monks of Diri-pu, crossed the river again and began the ascent of a rough, boulder-strewn slope. This became progressively more steep as they proceeded eastwards until they reached the brow of the first ridge, after which the ground levelled out for a while. Here they enjoyed a splendid view of a short, truncated glacier that was fed from a sharply-defined, trough-shaped firn basin lying on the north side of Kailas. From the sacred mountain itself, a sharp, jagged ridge ran off to the east. It had a furrowed appearance due to being covered with alternating belts of snow and stones. From all parts of the ice-mantle and snow fields, streams cascaded down to the river that flowed to their right. To their left, northwards, the mountains consisted of vertical, fissured granite sculpted into 'wild pyramidal forms'. The summit of Kailas rose above this 'sea of wild mountains' like a 'mighty crystal of hexagonal form'.

A party of impoverished women and children were toiling wearily up towards the next pass, at the summit of which Hedin met an old pilgrim who had already completed nine of the thirteen circuits he intended to make. With this kind of experience to his credit, he clearly knew his way around the sacred mountain, so Hedin sensibly secured his services as guide. At Tutu-dapso they encountered literally hundreds of votive cairns.

The ascent to the next pass was the most arduous of the whole *parikrama* so far. The path was cluttered with a proliferation of granite boulders which ranged in colour from pink to light-grey and off-white. Between two such boulders a pathetic heap of rags was found. This turned out on closer examination to be the clothing of an emaciated pilgrim who had collapsed. A little later they encountered the *Dipka-karnak*: the test-stone for sinners. If a person could scramble through the narrow passage beneath the rock here then he showed himself innocent of sin. A sinner, on the other hand, be he ever so lean, would surely get stuck. The servant Ishe attempted the test and was promptly exposed as a sinner. His companions left him to kick and struggle for a while by way of penance before releasing him. A little later Ishe was able to redeem himself by triumphantly passing at the next test-stone: a double passage formed by three huge stone blocks, where the candidate had to creep through by the left and return by the right. His master was not very impressed by this achievement, however, as he estimated that the passages were wide enough to accommodate small yaks and thus did not constitute a particularly rigorous test of virtue.

The enthusiasm which the *parikrama* clearly provoked in Hedin caused him to write at this point:

> Our wanderings round Kang-rinpoche, the 'holy ice mountain' or the 'ice jewel' is one of my most memorable recollections in Tibet, and I quite understand how the Tibetans can regard as a divine sanctuary this wonderful mountain which has so striking resemblance to a *chorten*, the monument which is erected in memory of a deceased saint within or without the temples. How often during our roaming have I heard of this mountain of salvation! And now I myself walked in pilgrim garb around the path between the monasteries, which are set, like precious stones in a bangle, in the track of pilgrims round Kang-rinpoche, the finger which points up to the mighty gods throned like stars in unfathomable space.

> From the highlands of Kham in the remotest east, from Naktsang and Amdo, from the unknown Bongba, which we have heard of only in vague reports, from the black tents which stand like the spots of a leopard scattered among the drear valleys of Tibet, from Ladak in the mountains of the far west, from the Himalayan lands in the south, thousands of pilgrims come hither annually, to pace slowly and in deep meditation the 28 miles round the navel of the earth, the mountain of salvation.

> (*Ibid.*)

He goes on to imagine the innumerable winding roads and paths, starting in the remotest regions of Asia, and converging inexorably on Kailas. He compares them to the migratory flight-paths of wild geese: that they exist is known, but not their precise course, or how they would look on a map.

The *parikrama* path now snaked downhill between boulders to the Dung-chapje: a basin of rock with a stone the shape of a yak's cloven hoof lying in it. The established practice here was to strike the hoof-shaped stone against the wall of the basin, and then run it around the inside like a pestle, thus helping deepen it. Beyond, a stream flanked either side of the path that ascended to the next ridge. There were cairns on every rock flat enough to serve as a base for one.

Straight ahead now lay the Dolma La (pass), which gave access to the eastern valley of Kailas. The Dolma-la was the highest point on the *parikrama*, and was generally thought to mark its half-way stage. It was crowned by a huge boulder, the mass of which Hedin estimated to be anything up to ten thousand cubic feet. This was topped by a grim profusion of cairns, bones, horns and prayer flags. The custom was for pilgrims to daub this rock with butter as they passed, and then stick something of themselves – a lock of hair, perhaps, or a tooth – as well as fragments of their clothing to the surface. In consequence, the great rock had something of the appearance of a bedraggled wig. It was permissible to take a relic from the rock as a talisman – Hedin's old guide had many such relics hanging around his neck.

Hedin sketched the scene from the pass, although the summit of Kailas was not completely in view at this point. As he was engaged in this work, a lama appeared who was making the *parikrama* with a sick child slung in a basket around his neck. Later he was also to encounter those especially enthusiastic circumambulators who made their circuits by measuring the length of their bodies on the ground the whole way round. Hedin gave the lama alms to help him with his holy work; the lama then began chanting *mantras* and the last the Swede saw of him he was prostrating himself before the great rock with its matting of rancid butter and human remains.

Hedin next seems to have left the usual *parikrama* route and cut across country in a south-westerly direction to join the route that came directly northwards from a place he calls

'Draxhan',★ up the valley of the Silung-chu to the southern foot of Kailas. He visited the small, circular lake of Tso-kavala, which he was told was permanently frozen. He could not linger there as time was pressing so he and his party went slipping and sliding down into the valley known in its upper portions as Tselung and in its lower ones as Lam-chyker. Through the large valley which entered on the right, called Kando-sangham, he could again see the summit of Kailas – 'which has a sharp edge towards the north-east, and again looks like a crystal'. Here also two *manis* marked the place where the prevailing granite gave way once more to conglomerate; thereafter the way was choked with boulders of conglomerate.

Hedin now cut back to the main *parikrama* route to bivouac for the night on the roof of the Zunthulphuk *gompa*. He had heard *Om mani padme hum* chanted so much that day that the rhythms of the sacred *mantra* went on echoing round and round in his brain as long as he remained awake.

As the Zunthulphuk *gompa* did not contain anything of particular interest, it did not detain Hedin long the next morning. His party was therefore soon riding down the gradually widening valley, past more *chortens* and *manis*, until, at the boulder-choked entrance, they caught their first glimpse of Rakshas Tal and the Gurla group since setting off on their circumambulation. They duly ended their *parikrama* at Tarchan, where they left the pilgrim road to cut back to Khaleb, catching sight on the way of the 'fourth monastery' of Kailas – probably Gengta *gompa* – which was perched high up on a terrace in the valley immediately below the sacred peak.

On his return to Khaleb, Hedin told the Gova of Barkha – 'who had the hopeless and thankless task of watching my proceedings' – that he intended to visit the source of the Indus. The Gova retorted that he could in no way countenance this, but, after a great deal of haggling, a skilful solution to the dilemma was devised. If Hedin would like to divide his caravan into two parts, the main portion could proceed in a proper manner to Gartok along the high road. Hedin, meanwhile, could go off with the remainder for a brief

★ Darchan?

excursion to the north – provided he understood that he was doing so entirely at his own risk.

Needless to say, this suited Hedin perfectly, and on 8th September, accompanied only by five companions, he again set off up the western valley of Kailas for Diri-pu. From there he crossed the Transhimalaya by way of the Tseti-la pass and so on down to the source of the Indus at Singhi-khambab. This was another explorational 'first' which, with the earlier one gained at the source of the Brahmaputra, made a neat pair that gave Hedin no inconsiderable satisfaction.

Hedin subsequently met up with his main party at Gartok, as arranged, and thereafter, for the moment becoming uncharacteristically compliant, proceeded in a more or less straightforward way back to Ladakh.

This was all a cunning pose, however. The lure of those beguiling blank spaces on the map had not yet loosened their grip on Hedin's imagination. On reaching Ladakh, he threw up an elaborate smokescreen of false reports and rumours to mislead *all* parties while at the same time covertly re-equipping himself and establishing a new caravan. He then turned east into Tibet once more to make a second and far more secret transit of the blank area, adopting a route rather to the south of his earlier ones. He himself travelled in disguise, acting the part of a servant whenever Tibetans were encountered. However, it was all putting a terrible strain upon him – for one thing, Hedin had not seen another westerner for two years – and so when the inevitable discovery came it was rather a relief. Nevertheless, even then, the Tibetans were to find Hedin still dogged and slippery, and he made several more crossings of his beloved Transhimalaya before they were eventually able to get rid of him.

Hedin's final exit route took him to the south. A year after his initial visit, he was back in the Kailas-Manasarovar region en route for Simla, via the upper Sutlej valley and the Shipki-la pass. In India, Minto, Kitchener and other of Hedin's auspicious Raj friends turned out to welcome the conquering hero in fitting style. Yet the man who had braved the worst hazards of the Great Plateau not once but twice still suffered the pangs of stagefright as he went before a glittering social gathering to lecture upon his travels. This was no real cause for shame. He had, after all, proved himself thoroughly worthy of his idol, Marcus Curtius.

After days of rest and recuperation whiled away amid the civilized amenities of Simla, first as the guest of the Viceroy and Lady Minto, then of Lord Kitchener, Hedin returned to Europe, fully expecting to receive the acclaim his great achievements merited. Sadly for the old lion of Central Asian exploration, the final act was not to be all laurels and honourable tranquillity. That very high-handedness and remorseless drive for personal achievement that had taken him thrice into Tibet against all the odds had also alienated many, including influential people at the Royal Geographical Society in London. A number were out to dispute his claims to geographical 'firsts', notably that young upstart, Tom Longstaff, who instead was advancing the claims of Edmund Smyth and his sporting comrades to have been the first Europeans at the source of the Brahmaputra and those of the Pundit, Nain Singh, to have discovered the Transhimalaya. Longstaff and others didn't like the name that Hedin had given the range either, and he was moreover in favour of Henry Strachey's location of the main source of the Sutlej at the head of the Dharma Yankti. He would only concede to Hedin that he might claim 'the distinction of being the first traveller to reach the ultimate source of the Indus'. Despite diplomatic attempts to smooth the situation, the public debate★ grew heated and ugly and eventually the Swedish explorer, that massive ego badly mauled, withdrew to the Continent in high dudgeon. A subsequent knighthood conferred through the good offices of Lord Curzon failed to salve his resentments and thereafter he turned to Germany for that appreciation that the perfidious British had denied him. Open support of Kaiser Wilhelm in the First World War and of Adolph Hitler in the Second lost him respect not only in this country but in his own as well, and it was a sad and largely forgotten man rather than a revered conqueror who passed away in Stockholm in 1952.

★ For a full account, see Charles Allen, *A Mountain in Tibet*, London, 1982, final chapter.

CHAPTER SIX

Travellers in the Sacred Region: The 1920s and After

By the 1920s, Mount Kailas was under threat. European travellers had already committed the sacrilege of sailing on the sacred lakes, and, in 1905, Tom Longstaff had made a mountaineering assault on the summit of Gurla Mandhata. Clearly, it would not be long before mountaineers were setting their sights on the summit of the sacred mountain itself and, perhaps, if they were successful, trampling on the very cushions of the throne of the gods with their Alpine boots.

In July 1926, the gods might well have felt especially uneasy. Two distinguished mountaineers had arrived in Tarchan. One was Colonel Commandant R. C. Wilson, D.S.O., M.C., of the Indian Army; the other, Hugh Ruttledge of the I.C.S., lately appointed Deputy Commissioner for Almora. Ruttledge had begun his mountaineering career in the Alps, while on leave in 1921. He would later go on to lead two notable, though unsuccessful, Everest expeditions: that of 1933, when a height of 28,000 feet was reached on the first assault, and that of 1936. Ruttledge, who was accompanied by his wife, was primarily in Tibet on official business on this occasion, however. Reports had been received from Bhotia traders complaining of infringements of their trading rights in Tibet, and it had been considered advisable in official circles that these reports should be investigated.

At Barkha, Ruttledge discovered that the newly-appointed senior *Garpon*★ of Gartok, whom he was hoping to meet, was not expected to pass through the *tarjum* en route for Lhasa for several days more, so he decided to put the spare time to advantage by making the Kailas *parikrama* with his wife. Accordingly, on 21st July, they travelled north to Tarchan with Colonel Wilson. Of Tarchan Ruttledge writes:

> The place was full of interesting types: nomads from the north, one of them a smartly dressed youth armed with an old but well-kept Russian Army rifle, and accompanied by an equally smart wife whose fur toque was the admiration of us all; pilgrims from Kham on the Chinese frontier; big hulking Nekarias; soi-disant traders, but obviously of doubtful respectability; beggars of every description; and three devoted Hindus from the Central and United Provinces, recently robbed, and miserably cold and underfed, requiring assistance. One cheerful party of Tibetans was busily engaged in performing the parikarma [*sic*] a distance of 28 miles, once a day for twelve consecutive days, thereby acquiring sufficient merit to last a lifetime. The altitude of Dorchan [*sic*] is about 15,200 feet.
>
> (Hugh Ruttledge, 'Notes on a Visit to Western Tibet', *Geographical Journal*, Vol. LXXI, May 1928)

At 7 a.m. on 22nd July, the main party set off westwards along the pilgrim route. Colonel Wilson and his Sherpa, Satan [*sic*], meanwhile struck up the nearest valley with the intention of reconnoitring approaches to Mount Kailas.

★ Viceroy.

Wilson's account of his experiences casts an interesting light on the topography of the sacred mountain.

> The mountain is best seen from a distance, and has the appearance of a somewhat lopsided white bowler hat placed on a square plinth of considerable steepness. As one approaches [from the south] the summit is more and more concealed until one can only get an occasional glimpse of it between ridges running down from the snow cap. This cap ends abruptly at the plinth and forms little or no glacier.

> It [Kailas] stands up prominently in a massif of its own, projecting S. from the Kailas Range of the Himalayas, to which it is joined by the Dolma pass ridge.
>
> (Col. R. C. Wilson, 'Kailas Parbat and Two Passes in the Kumaon Himalaya', *Alpine Journal*, Vol. 40, 1928)

The following sketch map accompanies his account:

KAILAS

Scale $\frac{1}{250,000}$

Dotted lines indicate the writer's routes.

Having passed close to Kyangda (Gengta?), Wilson and Satan emerged from the valley by a col to the north, and thence reached the foot of Point B without loss of altitude. They then kept on up the valley, maintaining the ridge HB on their right. This valley was deep and dark, and proved to be a cul-de-sac. When they reached the end, they found the perpendicular plinth towering before them – 'black and forbidding'. On the right, at Point H, where the long ridge marked HF sprang from the plinth, there was a small glacier which reached the valley in the form of fragments of ice and snow. On their left, leading up to the gendarme marked G, there was a shale slope as steep as anything Wilson had hitherto encountered in his mountaineering career. Meanwhile, straight ahead, at the foot of the plinth, there was a fan of snow which had fallen from the gulley which was so prominent a mark on the centre of the summit cap. To the right of this fan, between it and the debris of a tiny glacier, there was a small niche, partly natural, partly man-made, in which a row of clay votive tablets had been placed, probably, Wilson felt, by the lamas of Kyangda *gompa*. From this point, Wilson noted a very marked flattening of the south-east ridge of the snow-cap. There was also a flat continuation of that ridge, which could be gained by a short but steep climb at Point H.

'Sahib, we can climb that!' Satan exclaimed, as he too saw that this represented a feasible route to the summit.

Time, however, was against them. They had to look for a way down, though this was not easily found. The shale slope to their left proved impossibly unstable. Then, to make matters worse, snow began to fall as well. Finally, a brilliant flash of lightning and a shattering crash of thunder heralded the breaking of one of those violent storms for which Kailas is notorious. Clearly, the gods of the sacred mountain were showing their displeasure at this impertinent intrusion upon their sacrosanct domain. There was nothing to be done but to place their ice-axes at a safe distance and sit it out.

An hour and a half later, Wilson and Satan achieved the col between Gendarme G and the plinth. Above them, the mountain towered almost perpendicularly; below them lowered a pitch-black abyss of forbidding depth and steepness – 'quite the most awesome place I have ever looked into'. The sides were composed in part of slatey black shale, in part of snow. Descent by this way was not to be contemplated.

The south-west ridge offered the only viable alternative. They attained this by climbing up a steep shale slope from Point E only to find that the other side was perpendicular. Or almost so. Looking back, however, they could see a slight bend in the ridge about a mile away, which might indicate a more reasonable slope on the west side. A hole was poked in the snow overhang on their side and they forced their way up. Once through, they found that they had been correct in their supposition and now had a comparatively easy (though visually sensational) descent into the western valley ahead of them. That night, they met up with the Ruttledges at Diraphuk.

Wilson drew the following conclusions from his day's reconnaissance:

> Should fate again take me to Torchen [*sic*] with a couple of days to spare, I should make for the ridge HF, moving either round the foot of D or via Kyangda and over ridge FD. I should expect to get on the ridge HF about point F and to have an easy passage to the foot of the final ascent. A reasonably comfortable camp could be made here and the carriers sent down again to the foot of F for the night.

> Next day the carriers could return to H and remove camp to the foot of F, whilst the climbers went on to the top and back. As regards altitudes, Torchen is probably about 15,500 feet, point H about 20,000 and the summit is 22,028.

> The photograph shows the final slope to be reasonable, though the snow might be found powdery and treacherous.

> Should the route suggested above prove impracticable, an alternative line to point H would be to leave C and the ridge HB on one's right and to trust to finding a way up on to H from near the foot of the mountain where the small glacier falls into the valley and the niche with the images has been made.

> In this event one would have to be content with a light camp, as the climb to H might prove too much for laden carriers.

> Finally, there remains a third possible route: to get on up the long N. ridge somewhere near the Dolma Pass.

> (Wilson, *Ibid.*)

117

16. The Ruttledges' route to Kailas

Meanwhile, the Ruttledges had passed up the western valley
of Kailas and called in at Nyandi *gompa* before going on to
Diraphuk, where they arrived in the evening and met up with
Wilson and Satan. At Diraphuk, they admired the imposing
view of the north face of Kailas, which Ruttledge estimated to
be a sheer precipice of 6,000 feet, 'utterly unclimbable'. Near
the summit there was some snow and ice, but the rest of the

face was composed of limestone slabs of brown and chocolate colour that were entirely unbroken and far too steep to hold snow.

Next day they went on to the Dolma La, passed the great boulder with its bunting of human and other relics, and proceeded to the Gauri Kund lake, the surface ice of which had melted a little in the heat of the sun, enabling pilgrims to perform token ceremonial ablutions.

From this point Ruttledge contemplated the north-east ridge and, impressed by its mountaineering possibilities, was tempted to try an ascent, but was unable to do so due to lack of time. The north-east ridge rose steeply for about a thousand feet and then carried on at an easy angle for about two miles until it articulated with the north-east arête leading sharply to the summit.

A steep descent down execrable boulders led the party into the beautiful green eastern valley, which was watered by a river, and stood in sharp contrast to the savage grandeur of its western counterpart. Although the summit of Kailas was then obscured by cloud, Ruttledge was of the opinion that angles on the eastern side were less severe than those elsewhere and might offer other viable lines of approach for future mountaineers. The permanent snow-line seemed to be mainly around the 19,000 foot mark.

Having spent the next night at Zunthulphuk *gompa*, the party left the usual pilgrim route and cut across country, hoping to see more of the sacred mountain from the south. Cloud obscured their view, however. They visited 'Kyangda' *gompa*, where the head lama seemed none too pleased by their visit, though he did consent to show them around. One of the things they saw was a suit of chain armour said to be a relic of Zorawar Singh's army.

On their return to Tarchan, Ruttledge's party found that the *Garpon* had already arrived and himself set off on a *parikrama*, so they had to sit tight and await his return. The interview with him, when eventually it did take place, was both interesting and pleasant, for he was the scion of a good Lhasa family and possessed both quick perceptions and charming manners. Afterwards, Ruttledge and his companions journeyed to the market centre at Gyanima by way of

Lejandak, where the Sutlej properly begins to flow as a continuous stream. Ruttledge was of the opinion that Rakshas Tal must be the true source of the river as there was a long chain of pools stretching between the two. At Gyanima, they met both the British Trade Agent and the Tibetan Government Trader, Jung-Chun, who proved to be a 'most amusing and sagacious person, fully alive to the iniquities of his traffic'. After three days of official business, they set off for the Kungri Bingri, Jayanti and Unta Dhura passes, and thence returned to base at Almora – 'after some 600 miles of enjoyable trekking, performed entirely on foot to the scandal of right-thinking Indians and Tibetans'.

For Mrs. Ruttledge this was an outstanding achievement. She was, so far as research has revealed, the first and only Western woman to visit the sacred mountain and perform the 32-mile *parikrama*.

Ruttledge was followed into Western Tibet by another official, E. B. Wakefield, who ranged extensively there, mainly in the area west of the sacred lakes, for some five months in 1929. He left Simla on 4th June with a Gurkha escort (one havildar and four riflemen) and eighteen baggage mules. He visited Taklakot and was at Gartok twice; also while at Barkha he took the opportunity of strolling over to Darchan to inspect the mart there. At the local *gompa* an old lama lit candles and said prayers for him – and for the Government of India as well!

Then in 1932 came F. Williamson (Officer on Special Duty in Sikkim) and F. Ludlow, who visited both Kailas and Manasarovar as well as making a Kailas *parikrama*. At Gartok they met the *dzongpon* of Tsaparang, who took them into the area then under contention in a border dispute between Tibet and the State of Tehri.

Finally, Swami Pranavananda maintains that a Captain R. K. M. Sekas – was it perhaps Saker? – 'B.T.A. of Gyangtse', came on 'special duty' in Western Tibet from Ladakh. He visited Gartok and performed the Kailas *parikrama* before leaving by the Lipu Lekh. A contact at B.B.C. Television has informed the author that colour film taken during Saker's mission has recently come to light.

In the mid-1930s, Herbert Tichy, then a young geology

student at the University of Vienna, was growing restless in the cloistered academic life. A previous trip to India had afforded him an unforgettable taste of freedom and adventure, and his imagination was brimming with visions of the East. One in particular haunted his hours in the enervating lecture halls. He had come upon it in a book on Tibet by Sven Hedin: 'a bare rocky countryside out of which the summit of a snow-clad mountain rose up like a glittering pyramid of silver'. Reasoning with inexorable Germanic logic that it was senseless to merely sit and dream of distant marvels, Tichy determined to see this wonderful far-off mountain for himself.

Accordingly, he conjured out of the ether a noble undertaking called 'The Austrian Central Asian Expedition', whose imposing letterheads were soon bearing requests for support and sponsorship to numerous newspapers and commercial concerns. In due course, the Expedition – or rather, Tichy himself, for he *was* the Expedition – was receiving quantities of free supplies and equipment, which included a motorcycle from the firm of Puch. Solid financial support arrived in the form of an advance paid by a newspaper editor to his 'Special Correspondent in Asia' – Tichy, of course. Finally, as this was in the Thirties, the young adventurer did not intend to abandon his academic career, so with characteristic initiative he persuaded his professor to allow him to make the Himalayas the subject of his doctoral thesis.

With everything thus neatly arranged, Tichy sailed for Bombay. His expedition was to take him to various parts of India, as well as to Burma and Afghanistan, before he was to make a brief foray into Tibet to realize his ambition of seeing Sven Hedin's sacred mountain with his own eyes. He had three companions with him on the last adventure. There was an Indian friend, a student of law at the University of Lahore, whom he had met on his first visit to India: Chatter Bhuj Kapur. There was a sixteen-year-old Hindu bearer named Ranschid. And finally there was a Sherpa porter from Darjeeling named Kitar, a veteran of many Himalayan mountaineering expeditions, whom Tichy had engaged because he was himself planning an assault of Gurla Mandhata.

Starting from Almora early on the morning of 4th May 1936, Tichy's little expedition followed the Kali river across the Kumaon region. Being on the main pilgrim route, they met many yogis and ascetics: men ready to brave icy winds and snow, in order to realize a spiritual ideal. Perhaps the most unlikely encounter was in a small cave, to which Tichy was attracted by the sound of muttered *mantras*. Inside, he discovered an ancient sage swathed in blankets, who addressed him in fluent German. Apparently, this ascetic had been sent in his youth to study in Europe. On his return to India, however, the spiritual had presented its higher claims to him, and in the classical manner he had renounced all his worldly goods in favour of the solitude and discomfort of a cave in the mountains.

Tichy and his friends reached Garbyang in pouring rain on the evening of 20th May. It was still early in the season, and many of the inhabitants had not yet returned from their winter quarters in the lower valleys. Thus the Austrian found the place largely deserted – but spectacular: surrounded on all sides by imposing snow-clad peaks. He also found the Bhotia girls very attractive – and surprisingly liberated – but he was not able to realize his full romantic potential with them because his friend Kapur had put it about that he was an idiot. This was not an underhand move so that the Indian law student could gain a monopoly of the girls' favours; rather it was an attempt to offer some kind of plausible explanation of why his companion was unable to speak Hindustani when to all intents and purposes he looked a thoroughgoing Hindu.

During the course of their march Tichy had in fact been progressively slipping into disguise, for, as an unofficial European traveller, he could not expect sanction for his journey from the Tibetan authorities. He therefore resorted to the long established device of masquerading as an Indian *fakir*: dying his hair and beard jet-black, and allowing them to grow long and unkempt. He also donned a greasy old turban and other Hindustani articles of clothing, and to perfect the effect restricted himself entirely to eating native fare, its very liberal hot chillie content notwithstanding. Kapur, on the other hand, as an Indian, could readily gain entry to Tibet as a bona fide Hindu pilgrim.

Unable to get baggage animals because the high passes were still snowbound, Tichy engaged a couple of coolies in Garbyang to carry his party's luggage into Tibet. He also obtained the services of a Tibetan-speaking guide named Nan Singh. This company duly set off from Garbyang around 23rd May, and two days later camped at Synchum just below the Lipu Lekh pass. The snow lay thickly all around and, laden with heavy packs, the travellers sank deeply into it at every step. They therefore had to bivouac at Synchum, cowering for shelter from the bitter wind behind a small stone wall until the early hours of the next morning, when the snow had frozen hard enough to bear their weight. Then, having toiled upwards for many hours, they at last saw, in the grey light of dawn, the prayer flags and *chortens* that marked the summit of the pass, and when the sun rose a little later they were presented with a splendid view of the great treeless plains of Tibet:

> We seemed serenely apart from the noisy turmoil of humanity, and, bathed in the healthy morning sunlight, I was able to drink in all the spirit of loveliness around me.
>
> (C. B. Kapur, 'A Pilgrimage to Mount Kailas',
Modern Review, August 1936)

They proceeded directly to Taklakot – with some trepidation, for they knew that they must, like all pilgrims, present themselves to the local *dzongpon*; in addition, a high official from Lhasa was also paying a visit to the place, which might lead to embarrassing complications. Initially, Tichy was tempted to try to slip past without declaring himself but eventually decided that this would be foolish because they had already met several Tibetans and their presence in the country would soon be widely known. Alternative strategems were therefore devised. His party timed their arrival at Taklakot very precisely so as to arrive in the failing light of evening. Then, just outside the place, Tichy began to feign sickness. The locals who witnessed his pantomime sagely diagnosed 'mountain sickness', a commonplace malady even among the Tibetans themselves. He was hurried to the shelter of the local *dharmasala* or guest-house, where he remained in a pitiful condition while his companions dutifully went to see the local officials, who were so completely satisfied that they did not require to see the sick member of the party.

At Taklakot they also had their first experiences of real Tibetans. They were not impressed. Chatter Kapur describes his impressions of them thus:

> They were all awfully dirty and wore greasy clothes. Men and women looked very much alike, for in Tibet men (except the lamas) do not cut their hair and very few have hair on their chins. They all smelled profusely and touched nearly all the things we wore or carried with us, like children. They have never seen the things which we had, modern material civilization not having reached their country yet.
>
> (*Ibid.*)

Finally, pack horses and a driver were engaged at Taklakot to replace the Garbyang coolies, and when all preparations were complete, Tichy and company marched to their next camping place near the village of Rungong. This was to be their base camp for the long-projected assault on Gurla Mandhata.

Tichy had prepared his attempt on the mountain very carefully, studying Tom Longstaff's account of his own attempt. He planned to employ the 'rush' method, whose principal exponents at the time were Eric Shipton and Longstaff himself. Accompanied only by the Sherpa, Kitar, and carrying only minimal supplies and equipment, Tichy grappled with the great mountain for five days and forged to a creditable altitude of 23,500 feet, before sheer exhaustion obliged him to return to base camp. He fully intended making a second attempt, but back at Rungong ominous developments were afoot. The local people had seen the two climbers on the mountain and had leapt to the conclusion that they were looking for gold and silver. They had decided to report the matter to the officials at Taklakot, and were even debating whether to arrest these trespassers-on-sacred-ground themselves. Fortunately, Kapur had been able to make them believe that Tichy and Kitar had really been inspired by more lofty motives: had, in fact, gone to the snowy heights to be nearer the gods. The pious people of Rungong naturally found such motives quite understandable and let the matter drop. Tichy and his friends therefore quickly struck camp and proceeded northwards in respectable pilgrim fashion before the villagers were disabused of their false impressions.

The party were now well and truly into *dacoit* country. Their guide, Nan Singh, was very put out that they had no arms to defend themselves, so before leaving Rungong he had skilfully wrapped their ice-axes in pieces of cloth, leaving only the ends exposed. They carried these imitation guns throughout their time in Tibet, and they served them well. Not long after they had crossed the Gurla pass – where they obtained their first imposing view of the sacred region – they were approached by a gang of fearsome-looking *dacoits*, armed with spears, who wanted to know why they carried their guns in such an unusual fashion. Nan Singh explained that they were exceptional weapons of their own manufacture which could fire fifty rounds without reloading and therefore required special protection. The *dacoits* were appropriately impressed and passed on without causing trouble.

It was not long before the party were on the shores of Lake Manasarovar. Here they performed the ritual ablutions, though Tichy and Kapur, being rather less pious than their companions, did not prolong their stay in the icy waters. They subsequently found accommodation at Thokar (Thugolo) *gompa*, which, like all the *gompa* they visited in Tibet, was exceedingly dark and dirty, though it contained a wealth of ancient books and ritual objects. They frequently heard the lamas chanting the mantra, *Om mani padme hum*: the monotonous rhythm building up towards a crescendo to the accompaniment of drums, cymbals and thigh-bone trumpets, then dissipating into a formless cacophony and finally into silence – the characteristic sound of Tibetan Buddhism. Tichy was very impressed with the *gompa*, which seemed to ride on the waters of the sacred lake like a vessel, commanding a fine view of Kailas in the distance. It was so far removed from the hurly-burly of 'civilized' life, a place of 'rest, peace and adjustment' – yet, of course, he had to admit that in the last analysis all that was really pure supposition: who could really tell what was in these lamas' minds?

After Thokar, they journeyed up the narrow isthmus separating the two lakes; they passed Chiu *gompa* on its eminence, the connecting channel and the old gold fields, then

over the lush pasturelands to the north of the lakes, and so to
Barkha, which they found hard to locate as it lies in a hollow.
Here they were entertained by the *tarjum*, the staging-post
official, and also witnessed the Tibetan method of slaughtering
a goat: the beast's mouth and nose were closed for about two
minutes until it suffocated.

They finally arrived at Tarchan, which they left at 6 a.m. on
the morning of 2nd June, to commence their *parikrama* of
Mount Kailas, despite the fact that it had snowed heavily the
night before. They also knew that no less a person than one of
the *Garpons* of Ngari (Western Tibet) was engaged in making
several *parikramas* at that time, which also occasioned a certain
trepidation. The first leg of the circumambulation passed off
without mischance, however, and it looked as though the
whole thing might pass off safely, but at Diraphuk Tichy
blundered. Up until then he had assiduously maintained his
cover, augmenting his physical disguise by playing the part of a
pious idiot, suffering the abuse and impositions of his
companions with apparently boundless good nature, and
avoiding all conversations by diligently twirling his prayer-
wheel and intoning his *mantra*: *Ram, ram, ram* . . . Then at
Diraphuk he was suddenly overwhelmed by the beautiful
spectacle of a group of lamas coming out and bowing to the
sacred mountain as its great northern face reflected the radiance
of the sunset. He could not resist trying to capture the scene in a
photograph, and had to grovel at full length on the ground in
order to compose both mountain and lamas in the viewfinder.
Nothing was said at the time, but later, when he and his friends
were taking their evening tea in their own quarters in the *gompa*,
a lama entered and announced that the *Garpon*, who was also
lodging there, wished to see them immediately.

The interpreter, Nan Singh, who had hitherto represented
himself as a man of invincible courage and fortitude, blanched
horribly. Still, there was no way out – though before
answering the *Garpon*'s call they took the precaution of hiding
their Leica among some rocks.

The *Garpon* received them in an open, well-illuminated
room. He was a tall man, slightly on the stout side, but clean
and better dressed than any Tibetan they had hitherto seen.
Everything about him, in fact, indicated his being of high rank

and used to obedience. Tichy and his companions duly prostrated themselves.

The *Garpon* motioned them to rise from the floor and fixed them with a penetrating gaze. This particularly upset Nan Singh, who turned a sickly green and seemed on the point of fainting. When called to translate the *Garpon*'s questions he could hardly stammer out the words. The viceroy was not, however, interested in Nan Singh; Tichy was the real object of his curiosity.

'Take off those glasses,' he ordered the Austrian.

Tichy was obliged to obey, though to do so might well be to give himself away by showing the *Garpon* his blue eyes, the unmistakable hallmark of a European. Nevertheless, he tried to maintain a brave façade, and once the glasses were off returned the *Garpon*'s gaze as squarely as he was able.

'Take off the turban,' was the *Garpon*'s next command.

Tichy again obeyed without demur, and the greasy cloth was removed to reveal long tangles of neglected and – most importantly – jet-black hair. He noted with satisfaction the good effect this had on the viceroy; it seemed to offset the bad impression made by his blue eyes. Tichy and Kapur were in fact passing themselves off as Kashmiris, who may indeed have comparatively light skin.

Then the *Garpon* fired the inevitable question: 'What were you doing in front of the *gompa* with a camera?'

So he knew. . . . Tichy felt trapped. There was nothing for it but to desperately try to bluff his way out. Nan Singh translated his phonily innocent retorts:

Camera? What a strange idea! What could have made the lamas think he had such a thing. . . ?' He paused for a moment to reflect. *Ah, yes: he had it. They must have seen him looking through his telescope – the one given him by the English sahib whom he'd served so faithfully. . . .*

A really desperate game – but, played with conviction, somehow it worked. The *Garpon* was swayed. The atmosphere lightened. Even Nan Singh's nerve revived, and soon he was translating away with his usual panache. The telescope was produced and presented to the *Garpon*, who took it and focussed it on the summit of Kailas. He became instantly chastened to see the abode of his gods brought so unbelievably close. *Would it be possible to actually see the gods themselves through this wonderful instrument?* he wondered. Tichy assured him it would; explaining that he and his friends had been graced with such a sight themselves, though it had taken a great deal of patience, and anyway, they were men whose unusual piety had gained them a great deal of spiritual merit.

Naturally, as the *Garpon* was so taken with the telescope, he was made a present of it. The awkward questions did not end there, however. The viceroy next wanted to know what had brought them to Tibet so early in the season. The main pilgrim influx was not expected until August, when the high passes would be completely free of snow.

To this, Kapur supplied an astoundingly inventive reply. 'We have come so early because we are mad with love,' he explained. 'A year ago we saw our neighbour's daughters – girls of such ravishing beauty. . . .' And here he proceeded to go into juicy detail about the girls' charms, amplifying his description with extravagant curving gestures. 'Their parents are so pious, however, that they would not allow us to marry them until we had purified ourselves of the sins of our youth by making a pilgrimage to Mount Kailas,' he continued. 'Naturally, we set off at once. What is a little snow on the passes to we who care only to be in the arms of our beloved beauties. . . . You understand?' And he concluded by smacking his lips lasciviously, a sound that Tichy tried to imitate, but unsuccessfully, as his mouth was dry with fear and excitement.

The *Garpon* understood only too well. He also expressed himself very interested in hearing more about these girls' finer parts, but here the travellers had to invoke the claims of honour and discreetly draw a veil over the already over-exposed bodies of their imaginary sweethearts. Tactfully, the *Garpon* did not press the matter further.

Their friendship now seemed sealed and the atmosphere to have relaxed sufficiently for the ensuing conversation to range comparatively freely over a variety of topics. Emboldened, Tichy asked through his interpreter whether European mountaineers might attempt the sacrilege of climbing Mount Kailas as they had already begun to commit comparable enormities in Kashmir.

The *Garpon* smiled indulgently. 'Only a man entirely free of sin could climb Kailas,' he replied. 'And he wouldn't have to actually scale the sheer walls of ice to do it – he'd just turn himself into a bird and fly to the summit.'

And why were the Tibetans so reluctant to allow Europeans into their country?

'I have seen many Europeans, and many Indians who are ruled by Europeans,' the *Garpon* said. 'They all seemed very unhappy to me. We have our gods and we are content. If the Europeans came, however, they would drive the gods away and bring us nothing in their place. That's why we prefer to be left alone.' He went on to sum up the situation in Tibet. 'In your country, Kashmir, you may be a great lord, a tax-collector or a substantial landowner. Here, you are nothing. Even I, the ruler of this whole province, am nothing. *Only the gods rule here.*'

The sun had now fully set; it was night. The *Garpon* rose and bowed deeply to the sacred mountain. Tichy followed his example, and as he did so he did not feel that he was dissembling. At that moment he felt as completely sincere in his salutation as any pious Hindu or Tibetan pilgrim. He was simply overawed by the overwhelming sanctity of the sacred mountain. Afterwards, he squatted on the floor in an attitude of prayer and stared up at the luminous peak, absorbing its image into his soul.

Next morning, when they awoke, the travellers found that the *Garpon* had already left to go on his *parikrama*. They took their time over their breakfast and then set off themselves, toiling up the steep ascent to the still-snowbound Dolma La. On the way, they passed a group of prostrating pilgrims, and again Tichy was tempted to use his camera – much to the consternation of Nan Singh, who prudently thought it unwise to risk another crisis when they had so narrowly wriggled their way out of the last.

A little beyond the frozen Gauri Kund lake they met up again with the *Garpon* and his party, who were resting on the grass of the agreeable green eastern valley. He motioned Tichy to join him, apparently pleased to see him again, and plied him with butter tea and *tsampa*.★ He was very amused at

★ See footnote p. 4.

Tichy's ineptitude in eating this typical Tibetan fare with his fingers. Then the questions started again. Rather than risk giving himself away by transmitting his answers through Nan Singh in faltering Hindustani, Tichy opted to recite rousing passages of German poetry and leave it to the interpreter to make up his own plausible answers. This device worked excellently, and the *Garpon* later proceeded on his way apparently completely satisfied.

That night, that of 4th June, Tichy and his friends returned to Tarchan, their *parikrama* completed. Now all that remained was to slip out of the country without further trouble. The plan was to go out by a different route from that by which they had entered. This involved making a wide detour to the west, following the course of the Sutlej for the first lap of the way, passing near Tirthapuri and Kyunglung, then veering south for Chitichun and so to the Kungri Bingri pass. They were repeatedly told that this pass would still be snowbound and impassable but, being young and adventurous, they were prepared to chance their luck that way rather than face the monotony of retracing their former route.

It took them six days of enervating, waterless marching to reach Chitichun. For some of the way, they had Tibetan travelling companions – nomads for the most part. They also had another brush with *dacoits* – three of them this time: young men armed with muzzle-loaders. They openly declared their profession and even seemed to think it a perfectly respectable means of livelihood. To discourage them from discharging their professional duties, Nan Singh concocted a fanciful tale about their being agents of the Maharaja of Kashmir sent to survey the land in preparation for a pilgrimage that their master was to make to Mount Kailas in the following year. Should any mischance befall them, the Maharaja would most certainly dispatch an entire army to wreak the most terrible revenge. Duly warned, the *dacoits* took themselves off quite meekly. Had they sought to rob them, however, their main concern would have been to steal food, which was at a premium in that arid, barren region, where markets were only held once a year.

As the party approached the towering white chaos of the Great Himalaya, it became clear that they might not find it at all easy to locate their chosen pass. Nan Singh, who had assured them that he could point them straight to it, turned out to have a far less exact knowledge of the land than he had claimed, and, in any case, he intended to leave them at Chitichun in order to make his own way back to Garbyang, his home, via Taklakot and the Lipu Lekh. The horse-dealer whose animals had carried their baggage since Taklakot was also scheduled to split off from the party at the same place. Tichy was therefore in something of a dilemma, faced with the possibility of being without guides or transport in an inhospitable and bewildering area. He decided to act summarily, threatening to withhold Nan Singh's pay until substitute guides had been found. This Nan Singh managed to do and duly went on his way with the horse-dealer, but the new coolie-guides – a pair of Tibetan nomads – were unreliable and temperamental, and it was only by dint of much cajoling and *baksheesh* (handouts of cash) that they were kept to their original undertaking to guide the party across the high passes.

Tichy and his friends did finally reach the Kungri Bingri pass (18,300 feet), however. It was indeed still snowbound, so they had to cross it at night when the snow was frozen hard. No evocative moonlight illuminated their high transit: cloud obscured the moon, and scything winds sliced up from the glaciers far below.

They pushed on over moraines to the next pass, the Jayanti (18,500 feet), where their guides left them, though by mutual agreement. The view from the head of this pass was tremendous: Nanda Devi, Nanda Kot and other ice giants soared magnificently all around. Tichy also cast one final look at Tibet over his shoulder. Despite the rigours that that inexorable, primordial land had imposed upon him, the Austrian knew that it had worked a potent magic. The sheer scale of the landscape, its rarefied and impossible beauties, would always linger in his memory, calling him back. And if he had any choice in the matter, he would choose to die within sight of Mount Kailas rather than anywhere else.

The way ahead was quite straightforward now: over the final Unta Dhura pass (17,590 feet) and on to the village of Milam, from where the route back to Almora would be no more difficult than that up to Garbyang. One final and potentially insuperable obstacle barred their way. A crucial bridge across a torrent had been dismantled by the people living on the Indian side to prevent marauders coming into their territory from Tibet. Tichy and his friends had two options: to return to Tibet and make their way round to the Lipu Lekh, or somehow to get across the torrent. Tichy eventually decided on the latter course, and so he and Kapur stripped off, armed themselves with a rope and braved the turbulent waters. They made it to the far side, where they roped up the dismantled timbers and hauled them back into place so that Ranschid and Kitar could come across with their gear.

No sooner was this crisis over than someone started shooting at them. It turned out to be Captain John Locke, a British sportsman, who claimed to have mistaken them for quarry. Appropriately apologetic, he invited them back to his camp for a slap-up meal complete with wines and spirits. He also filled them in on the latest news: the Italians had attacked Addis Ababa, and the Japanese had bombed Manchuria. The travellers were back to 'civilization' with a vengeance!

Not long afterwards, Tichy and Kapur took leave of their friends Kitar and Ranschid, on the platform of the railway station at Kathgodam. It was a sad parting. A few moments later, through the window of the departing train, they saw the mountains sliding into the distance. Finally, they disappeared.

At the time of writing, Herbert Tichy is still alive and living in Vienna. His later life continued the pattern set in his youth: he has travelled widely and written many books about his travels. He passed the Second World War in China, where he lived for some eight years in all. True to his resolution, he has returned many times to the Himalayas, and among his many achievements can claim to be the first man to reach the summit of Cho Oyo, which is probably the seventh highest mountain in the world.

As for his friend, Chatter Bhuj Kapur, he is also still alive and lives in London, in a street behind the Exhibition Hall at Olympia. I have met him a number of times and recalled with him his remarkable journey to Mount Kailas. He was surprised that anyone should be taking an interest in it at all. Retired now, he left his native Punjab at the time of Partition and spent several years in Delhi before coming to London, where he worked first as a teacher and later as an educational administrator. He is a sensitive person, unobtrusive in manner. When asked what his motive in going to Kailas was, he answered, 'It was an adventure!' Even though he does not claim to be a religious person, he admits that Kailas had a deep spiritual effect upon him, which has remained alive and fresh during the intervening forty years. He is in no doubt that there is something intrinsically sacred about the mountain. When asked where the particular spiritual potency of Kailas might reside, he simply raised both arms till they were horizontally presented across his chest, then raised a simple pyramid with his flattened hands. It lay in its unique and unusually symmetrical shape, he explained, and in the fact that it stood out as a single snow-clad peak in an otherwise snowless desolation.

The fate of the third member of Tichy's party, Kitar, was not so fortunate. Shortly after returning from Tibet he fell ill and died while serving the Anglo-American Expedition that successfully climbed Nanda Devi in 1937.

Of young Ranschid, all that remains is a blank.

After the mountaineers, the scientist; after the ice-axe, the geologist's hammer strikes the sacred rock of Mount Kailas.

Also in 1936, during an expedition with his colleague, Arnold Heim, the Swiss geologist Augusto Gansser found himself in the village of Kuti, where the local inhabitants were preparing for their festival of the dead. For this to be properly performed, two sheep reared at the foot of the sacred Kailas were required; therefore, on 28th July, two sturdy Bhotias were dispatched to procure them. They travelled with two additional companions: a Sherpa porter named Paldin, and a rather paunchy, bearded lama wearing a heavy red sheepskin caftan and fur cap. The lama's obesity was not due to body fat, however, but because beneath his robes he carried a small armoury of scientific gear: sketchbook, hammer, aneroid, field-glasses, Leica, and even a bottle of hydrochloric acid. It was Gansser himself, who, denied proper credentials, was continuing the tradition first established by William Moorcroft, of disguising himself in order to penetrate the Kailas-Manasarovar region.

The four men crossed into Tibet by the Mangshang pass and then made their way to Tarchan by the western shore of

Rakshas Tal, where Gansser came to several important conclusions concerning the present hydrography of the lakes region:

> The domain of these mighty lakes is undergoing depression, and it has long been known that the Sutlej has ceased to derive any of its waters from them. They have no outlet now, and I can find plain evidence of changes in the direction of the flow – very recent changes in the course of the rivers that rise in the Transhimalaya.
> (A. Gansser and A. Heim: *The Throne of the Gods*)

During the journey the travellers slept rough: either under the stars, or in the tents of nomads, where adults, children and animals all lived together in atmospheres made acrid by the smoke of yak-dung fires.

At Tarchan, Gansser and Paldin embarked upon the Kailas *parikrama*. The Sherpa first performed the ritual prostration, then looked at his employer to see his reaction – 'No, Paldin . . . the mountain is just as sacred to me as it is to you, for I too am a pilgrim,' Gansser reassured his porter. 'Just as those two lamas who passed a moment ago. Like you, like them, I am in search of the beautiful, the sacred in this wonderful mountain.'

But if the pilgrim in Gansser had been awakened, the geologist had not fallen into abeyance. He realized that the remarkable position of Kailas presented fascinating geological problems for solution:

> Strangely enough, it consists of horizontally stratified conglomerate masses with erratic admixture. In the course of geological aeons, these strata have been elevated many thousands of feet without any change in the horizontal lay-out.

> (*Ibid.*)

As the collection of specimens would, however, be regarded as sacrilege by pilgrims and lamas alike, he had to proceed with extreme caution and employ what he calls 'peculiar methods'.

Having marched up the western valley of Kailas between high walls of conglomerate rock, he at last reached the northern side, which was of far greater interest from a geological point of view. Here he examined closely the granite pediment upon which the great conglomerate mass of the mountain itself stood, until one of those sudden electric storms so characteristic of Kailas put an end to his investigations and forced him to seek shelter for the night at the nearby *gompa*, unnamed in his narrative but undoubtedly Diraphuk.

Here the authenticity of his disguise was really put to the test. It was established practice for all visitors to the *gompa* to seek an interview with the head lama. Gansser, posing as a lama of importance from a distant region, could not evade this custom without giving offence. Moreover, in the interests of complete authenticity, he should not only ask for an interview but do so with enthusiasm.

Having been schooled in his part by Paldin, Gansser duly presented himself at the head lama's chamber with bare feet and lowered head. The chamber was dark inside, lit only by the tiny and unstable flames of guttering butter lamps. The head lama was squatting 'tailor-fashion' behind a long altar. 'He had sharply cut features and an intelligent expression,' Gansser writes. Paldin having announced him, the geologist silently presented the lama with two small goblets of marbled vulcanite. The Tibetan reciprocated by hanging a red scarf around Gansser's neck, and also presented him with a bag of pills said to be good against every kind of mischance. By invoking the universal convention that among men of really deep spirituality communication by so gross a means as the spoken word is not necessary, Gansser was able to leave the chamber with his cover intact.

The next morning the weather was glorious, and Gansser took advantage of it to go out and take photographs. As he returned to the *gompa*, he saw the head lama make his daily salutations to the gods and demons of the sacred mountain. Re-entering the *gompa*, Gansser prostrated himself before the gilded images, offered up the customary butter lamp, spun the great prayer wheel, and then left to continue his *parikrama* with his porter. They ascended to the Dolma pass, then descended to 'a small sacred lake', almost undoubtedly Gauri Kund, where masses of rock littered the frozen surface: evidence of many pilgrims' unsuccessful attempts to break through the ice and make their ritual ablutions. 'It seems to be an unfavourable year for pilgrimages,' Gansser writes.

Moving on southwards down the eastern valley, Gansser found himself leaving the savage granite landscape of the north and once again stood immured between imposing walls of conglomerate:

For the moment I am wholly taken up with my geological investigations. The strata of the conglomerate, which had hitherto been horizontal, are somewhat inclined, as if by pressure from the south. As we negotiate a curve in the valley, this impression is confirmed, and suddenly I come across a most interesting geological phenomenon. At a well-marked transitional line, the conglomerate strata have been covered by a number of convoluted strata sharply contrasting with the flat Transhimalayan sedimentary rocks, and the granites. Compared with the Transhimalayan rocks, this superimposed series must have undergone recent and intensive convolution. These observations show that we have to do with the northernmost vestiges of the Himalayan chain proper, which has been superimposed upon the Transhimalaya from the south – backwards, that is to say.

(*Ibid.*)

'Look out, the sadhus [holy men] are coming!'

A warning shout from Paldin jerked Gansser from his scientific speculations, and together they took cover in a small side valley. Later, however, they resumed their work and continued till nightfall, when they sought shelter at Zunthulphuk *gompa*.

The *gompa* was comparatively uninteresting, and its running had become rather disorderly due to the absence of the head lama, who had gone on a trip to Lhasa. The following day, Gansser and Paldin visited some unoccupied hermit caves excavated in the cliffs nearby. Much to the dismay of his porter, the geologist filched a finely-carved *mani* stone to take home as a souvenir. They then proceeded back to Tarchan.

While they were waiting for their pack animals and the sacrificial sheep to be got ready, Gansser and Paldin made another foray into the foothills on the southern flank of Kailas to further trace the superimposition of the rock strata first detected the day before. On their return to Tarchan, they found all ready, so they could return to Kuti with their original Bhotia travelling companions. They reached the Mangshang glacier without crisis, and found Heim waiting for them there, the Swiss flag flying over his tent. They recrossed the Mangshang pass the following day.

Gansser subsequently published a fine, scholarly *Geology of the Himalayas*, in which he describes the geology of the Kailas region in technical detail. According to him, the northern portion of the low-lying belt separating the Himalaya and the Transhimalaya comprises a sandy alluvial plain over twenty kilometres wide, bordering the foothills of the Kailas range. This Gansser calls the *Kailas Flysch* zone:

> The Kailas Flysch represents the last remnant of the Himalayas, thrust steeply northwards over the autochthonous Kailas conglomerate which transgresses over the Kailas granite.
>
> (A. Gansser, *Geology of the Himalayas*)

North of the thrust there is a completely different region: one characterized 'by huge fantastically shaped conglomerate mountains sitting on granites', of which Kailas itself is a beautiful example.

In 1939, the Austrian mountaineer, Heinrich Harrer, found himself in Karachi after having completed a reconnaissance of Nanga Parbat with a German expedition. The outbreak of the Second World War led to the whole expedition being interned as enemy aliens. After spending several years in various camps in India, Harrer was incarcerated in the largest of them at Dehra Dun, right beneath the Himalayas. In 1944, after various abortive attempts at escape, he and a few companions succeeded in crossing the mountains and entering neutral Tibet by the Tsangchola pass (17,200 feet). They made contact with the local authorities and applied for asylum, but received the usual unwelcoming reception and were told to return to India. They were given a choice of routes, however, and elected to take the more westerly one by the Shipki pass, fully intending to slip back into Tibet further along the frontier and put their request for asylum to more senior officials. They were successful and eventually arrived at Gartok, where they were granted an audience with the *Garpon*. He was sympathetic to their suit but could only grant them a passport to travel in his province; they could not enter the central provinces without permission from Lhasa.

On 13th July, Harrer and his companions, Aufsnaiter, Kopp and Treipel, travelled eastwards with the intention of going to Nepal. They soon arrived at Barkha, where they caught a glimpse of Kailas. They would have liked to have made the *parikrama* but the master of the 'Barkha caravanserai' (the *tarjum* perhaps?) blocked them in this and obliged them to proceed straight on their way. Gurla Mandhata, majestically reflected in the turquoise waters of Lake Manasarovar, impressed them rather more deeply than the holy Kailas, however, and also engaged their mountaineering instincts. They would have liked to have attempted to climb it, if it had been at all possible – which it was not. Harrer bathed in the icy waters of the sacred lake, though more in the interests of physical hygiene than of spiritual purification. Altogether, the beauty of the sacred region impressed him deeply. 'This is certainly one of the loveliest spots on earth,' he writes.

From Barkha, the fugitives proceeded to 'Tokchen', where they had a pleasant meeting with the new Governor of Tsaparang; then they continued on to the source of the Brahmaputra, which they subsequently followed eastwards for the next fortnight.

Harrer ultimately reached Lhasa, where he eventually rose to become tutor and confidant of the present exiled Dalai Lama, then in his teens. Harrer spent seven years in Tibet all told, only leaving – and then with great reluctance – when the Chinese began to mount the final phases of their takeover of the country.

In 1931 and again in 1942, an American Christian named Steiner apparently visited Kailas and Manasarovar on 'missionary propaganda work' and performed both *parikramas*. Beyond a brief recitation of these facts by Swami Pranavananda, no other information about this pious (and intrepid) gentleman has been forthcoming.

The very last European at the sacred mountain was a Buddhist monk and so his story rightly belongs with those of the pilgrims in Chapter Eight. His immediate predecessor, the penultimate European visitor and the last *traveller* proper, arrived at Mount Kailas in the summer of 1945. He was another distinguished mountaineer: Major T. S. Blakeney, who had begun to climb in the Alps in the early 1920s. He went to the East about ten years later and worked on tea plantations, first in Ceylon and later in the Madras district. On the outbreak of War in 1939, he joined the Army.

Blakeney's notes on his reconnaissance of Kailas were

published in the *Alpine Journal*; they are brief and may therefore be quoted here in full:

APPROACH TO KAILAS. – Major T. S. Blakeney has sent us the following notes, the result of an expedition undertaken with little opportunity of preparation in August and September, 1945.

I had only a very small scale map, so I cannot give exact heights etc. As a climbing proposition, I think only the E. arete of Kailas is feasible. The W. ridge forks into a N.W. and S.W. arete, subtending an unclimbable W. face of about 4000 feet, and I could not see any way of getting on to either of these aretes. The N. face is terrific (about 5000 ft.), very sheer, and stones fall a good deal. From the Diraphuk Gompa or monastery one can approach the N. face easily enough by a small valley giving on to the moraines beneath the face. The valley lies between two peaks called, I gather, Jambyang and Chenresi, the latter being furthest west. It might be more useful for reconnaissance purposes to climb Jambyang, but as we had nothing but sleet and mist we saw nothing, whatever we did. East of Jambyang is another peak, Changnadorje, and the valley between can also be ascended, and ahead of it I got a glimpse of a pass that looked certainly easy and should, I estimate, give out on to the lower slopes of the E. arete of Kailas. Normally, pilgrims making the circuit of Kailas pass from the Diraphuk Gompa on the N. to the Zunthulphuk Gompa on the E. by the Dolma La, a pass further N. than the one I could see, but Swami Pranavananda, author of a *Pilgrim's Companion to the Holy Kailas* etc., and of *Exploration in Tibet*, tells me that Tibetans are allowed, after they have made ten circuits of Kailas, on future occasions to short-circuit the route by what I think must be the pass I saw. If so, then a simple route to the E. arete may lie here, though I fancy it would be better approached by a climbing party straight from Zunthulphuk Gompa, without spending the time going round to Diraphuk.

The only fine day I had was on the S. side of Kailas; above the Gengta Gompa a mild ridge runs parallel to the S. face, but separated from it by a deep valley. Direct ascent of the S. face seems quite out of the question. This parallel ridge is joined by another at right angles that runs northwards to merge in the snows of the E. arete of Kailas; this looked practicable so far as I could see, and I would have liked to try, but my Tibetan guide would not hear of it, and even had he agreed I doubt if I could have braved your editorial strictures on anyone approaching a substantial Himalayan peak in unnailed boots and armed only with that invaluable asset to monsoon climbing, an umbrella. I do not recommend this route, actually, as I still think direct access is more easily obtained to the E. ridge from the E. flank; but once up on the snows of the lower E. ridge I think a camp could be pitched (we were at approximately 19,000 ft. and, I reckoned, slightly lower than the beginnings of the steep portion of the E. arete) and the summit reached next day. Probably plenty of step-cutting, but Kailas is only 22,028 ft., and there would be barely 3000 ft. to climb.

It is a grand peak; the N. face is usually considered the finest view, but my one fine day on the S. side impressed me greatly. The view from here southwards was magnificent – in the foreground, the bright blue lakes of Manasarovar and Raksas [*sic*] contrasting vividly with the barren hills around them; and the huge mass of Gurla Mandhata (almost a range in itself) and behind, the vast extent of the Zanskar range, from Kamet in the W. to Nalkankar and the unnamed peaks of Nepal in the E., with Nanda Devi, Nanda Kot, Panch Chhuli and others raising their heads in the background.

(*Alpine Journal*, Vol. 55, 1945–6)

Blakeney, the last Englishman to have seen Mount Kailas, died at Chichester in 1976.

CHAPTER SEVEN

Pilgrims to the Sacred Mountain – 1

EKAI KAWAGUCHI

On 25th June 1897, a small group of well-wishers standing on the quay at Kobe in Japan waved goodbye to a Buddhist priest who was sailing that day on the ship *Idzumi-maru*. His name was Ekai Kawaguchi; his destination, Calcutta, and ultimately Tibet; his mission, to obtain rare Mahayana Buddhist texts. At least, that was the overt story. It has been alleged, however, that this pious Buddhist priest was in fact a secret agent of the Japanese government, briefed to gather information on the political situation in the Forbidden Land.

In pictures taken at the time Kawaguchi looks every inch the Buddhist priest. In one, he poses in a Japanese garden with a rosary playing through his fingers. His head is shaven to billiard-ball smoothness, he sports a whispy beard of the

Chinese variety and he wears a most splendid, though heterodox, set of robes – they combine elements of the vestments of both the Nichiren and Obaku Zen sects. Then, as the eye travels downwards, it suddenly notices a discordant element: the highly polished toecaps of a pair of oxfords peeping from beneath the capacious hems. They suggest incipient European inclinations – which were to subsequently manifest themselves in the form of an interest in Theosophy.

As regards his background, Kawaguchi tells us that he was a native of Akashi, that he was Rector of the Monastery of Gohyakurakan in Tokyo until March 1891, when he left to spend three years in Kyoto, living the life of a hermit and occupying himself with studying his extensive collection of Chinese Buddhist texts. It was with a view to augmenting and improving this collection that he embarked upon his epic journey to Tibet. This kept him away from Japan from June 1897 to May 1902. He left Japan again in October 1904 for India and Nepal, hoping to make a second foray into Tibet for manuscripts.

Kawaguchi's route on his first visit to Tibet was a long and roundabout one. Initially landing at Calcutta, he went north to Darjeeling, where he spent the whole of the next year preparing himself for the Forbidden Land. He studied the Tibetan language with Rai Bahadur Sarat Chandra Das, who himself had also combined scholarship with a career as an undercover agent. He had been on secret missions into Tibet on behalf of the British, as a result of one of which a notable lama named Sengchen Dorjechan had been put to death by drowning for having harboured him. Then, as the route into Tibet was known to be closely guarded, Kawaguchi decided to try to make his entry by unfrequented byways. He therefore went to Nepal, which he believed himself to be the first Japanese to visit, and where he also hoped to be able to obtain Buddhist texts. Having visited both Kathmandu and Pokhara, he eventually travelled north to a village near the Tibetan border called Tsarang, where he also lingered for many months.

'The days I spent in Tsarang,' he wrote, 'were, in a sense, the days of my tutelage in the arts of living amidst filth and filthy habits.' Here he pursued his Buddhist studies under the guidance of a lama of the Nyingma (Red Hat) sect, who had been obliged to leave Lhasa and live out his life in this obscure backwater because he had at sometime succumbed to 'feminine temptation', as Kawaguchi quaintly puts it. The Japanese traveller was himself something of a puritan and particularly disapproving of sexual lapses on the part of a religious. He also found the erotic symbolism of Nyingma tantrism highly offensive, and held the founder of the sect, the Indian guru Padmasambhava – Lobon or Padma Chungne★ to the Tibetans – in special odium:

> Lobon was in practice a devil in the disguise of a priest as if he had been born for the very purpose of corrupting and perverting the spread of the holy doctrines of Buddha.
> (Ekai Kawaguchi, *Three Years in Tibet*)

Naturally, such views inevitably led to heated arguments with his Nyingma lama friend, who on one dramatic occasion lost his self-possession entirely and physically attacked Kawaguchi.

While at Tsarang, Kawaguchi got himself into training for his eventual penetration into Tibet by doing a considerable amount of mountain walking, sometimes carrying heavy loads of stones on his back. He actually crossed the border in June 1900, taking a route by the northern slopes of Dhaulagiri, after which he cut straight for the Kailas-Manasarovar region. As usual, he ran the gamut of trials and tribulations – 'hunger and thirst, the perils of dashing stream and freezing blizzard, the pain of writhing under heavy burdens, the anxiety of wandering over trackless wastes, the exhaustion and the lacerations. . . .'

Passing himself off as a Chinese lama, Kawaguchi seems in fact to have fared considerably better than his secular precursors. Moreover, being a Buddhist priest, he was able to command respect and get invaluable help from the people he met along the way by performing small religious services, like reading from the scriptures, preaching or divining. He also had a smattering of simple medical knowledge which he put

★ Also Guru Rimpoche or Urghien (see *Fig. 10*)

to good use as well. No doubt his Buddhist philosophy and the depth of his faith helped him to survive. Whereas so many westerners had gone into Tibet with loud and often violent arrogance, Kawaguchi was a consciously restrained and humble man, and while some of the philosophical beliefs that he held do not seem to have been strictly orthodox – he appears, for instance, to have believed that the Buddha was a kind of god, and that the ultimate ground of being has a personal character – his grasp of the practical, down-to-earth basis of Buddhism seems sound enough; altogether he appears to have been a conscientious Buddhist. He was not without his human faults and failings, though: he had, for instance, to infringe the Buddhist injunction to Right Speech in order to mislead people about his true identity; and he can at times be very unBuddhist in the scathing remarks he sometimes makes about the Tibetans themselves:

> I was struck by the notion that the Tibetans are characterized by four serious defects: filthiness, superstition, unnatural customs (like polyandry), and unnatural art.★ I should be seriously perplexed if I were asked to name their redeeming points; but if I had to do so, I should mention first of all the fine climate in the vicinity of Lhasa and Shigatze [!!] their sonorous and refreshing voices in reading the Text, the animated style of their catechisms, and their ancient art.
>
> (*Ibid.*)

Nor, as he comes to see more of it, does he hold Tibetan Buddhism in much higher regard. He is appalled by the decadent practices and superstitions that have crept into it, at the low level of scholarship and the ignorance of the majority of lamas, and of their general moral turpitude. It is, however, redeemed for him by the occasional rare lama of real quality, who stands out like a precious jewel in a heap of rubbish.

Early in August 1900, when he was travelling with a group of pilgrims from Kham – the province of eastern Tibet notorious for its robbers and murderers, he reminds us – Kawaguchi had just bivouacked for the night when he

★ He is referring here to the erotic imagery to be found in Tantric iconography.

chanced to look towards the north-west and saw 'a great snow-clad mountain'. It was Kailas:

> As far as my knowledge goes, it is the most ideal of the snow peaks of the Himalayas. It inspired me with the profoundest feelings of pure reverence, and I looked up to it as a 'natural mandala,' the mansion of a Buddha and Bodhisattvas. Filled with soul-stirring thoughts and fancies, I addressed myself to this sacred pillar of nature, confessed my sins, and performed to it the obeisance of one hundred and eight vows. I also took out the manuscript of my 'twenty-eight desires', and pledged their accomplishment to the Buddha. I then considered myself the luckiest of men, to have been enabled thus to worship such an emblem of the Buddha's power, and to vow such things in its sacred presence. . . .'
>
> (*Ibid.*)

Kawaguchi's pious devotions aroused the curiosity of his Khampa companions, of which he took immediate advantage, treating them to a brief but calculatedly inspiring sermon. This had an immediate and profound effect upon the hearts of these people who belonged to a stock who 'took mens' lives with the same equanimity with which they cut their vegetables' – and Kawaguchi consequently 'blessed the power of Buddhism more than ever, and could not hold back my tears as my companions shed theirs'.

A day or so later, seeing Kailas rising in the distance across the placid waters of Lake Manasarovar, Kawaguchi though he saw in it 'the image of our mighty Lord Buddha, calmly addressing his five hundred disciples'. He also describes it for a second time as a 'natural mandala', inferring thereby that the sacred mountain and its environs are a model of the order of the universe. This would also imply identification of Kailas with the mythical Meru or its equivalents. Furthermore, he goes on to identify Lake Manasarovar with the legendary Anotatta or Anavatapta of Buddhist mythology, though the Buddhas and bodhisattvas said to sit in lotus flowers floating upon its surface are not visible to mortal eyes. 'The real thing in the region is its wonderfully inspiring character,' he continues; 'and a wonderfully holy elevation is to be found there.' He describes his own elevated feelings in an *uta*, one of the brief (and sometimes not-so-brief) poems he composed during his travels to express his responses to the changing faces of the landscape and his own changing moods and thoughts:

> Among these mountains high here sleeps the lake
>   Serene – 'devoid of seething cares' – so named
> By native bards; its broad expanse appears
>   Like the octagonal mirror of Japan.
> The grand Kailas, majestic, capped with snow,
>   The moon o'erhanging from the skies above,
> Bestow their grateful shadows on the lake.
>   Its watery brilliant sheen illuminates me;
> All pangs of pain and sorrow washed away.
>   With these my mind besoothed now wanders far
> E'en to Akashi in Japan, my home,
>   A seashore known for moonlight splendours fair.

Kawaguchi and his companions skirted the southern shores of the lakes and then made a loop detour to the west of Kailas, visiting Gyanima, Gya Karko and Tirthapuri. This was to be a spiritually perilous phase of his journey for a young Khampa lass declared her love for the good Buddhist priest and began to beset him with all the wiles of female cunning. He was not insensitive to her attractions either, not being, he assures us, 'a block of wood, nor a piece of stone'. He compares himself under such sweet assault to the Buddha on the eve of his Enlightenment when he was tempted by the daughters of Mara, the Deceiver – though he has to concede that little Dawa, bold though she was, was a siren of rather an inferior order. Ultimately, however, Kawaguchi was able to use skillful means to divert and defuse the girl's passion for him by reminding her of her far-away mother and her deep feelings for her. Still, no doubt, he escaped by the skin of his teeth.

Kawaguchi found Tirthapuri to be an important religious centre. He paid a *tanka*★ to see Padmasambhava's imprint in the local *gompa*. It was said to have been etched into the rock by supernatural means. Though he deplored the veneration paid to this Tantric *guru*, he found the scenery around

---

★ A Tibetan coin (see Fig. 17, p. 178).

Tirthapuri altogether delightful – in fact, 'one of nature's best essays in landscape'.

Returning eventually to the foot of Kailas, the pilgrim party broke up, each individual member apparently wishing to make his or her *parikrama* in a special way. Kawaguchi himself chose to make the outermost circuit, not concerned to break any records or subject himself to particularly gruelling austerities. He carried with him enough food to last four or five days.

His first call on his *parikrama* was at the Nyandi *gompa*, which he found to be dedicated to the Buddha, Amitabha, and very popular with pilgrims in consequence. There was an image of Amitabha in the *gompa* made of 'white lustrous stone'; the features 'were of the Tibetan type, and looked mild and affable, awakening in me pious thoughts'. Two thick ivory tusks, five feet high, stood in front of the image, and behind them a quantity of books were arranged on shelves, though more as objects of veneration than of study. 'This use of Buddhist books is peculiar,' Kawaguchi thought, 'though it is preferable to the outrageous treatment to which these books are sometimes subjected by impious priests, who do not scruple to tear out leaves and use them for improper purposes.'

After Nyandi, he travelled up what he calls the 'Golden Valley' –

> The adjective 'golden' should not be taken in a literal sense, for gold is not found near this place. Rhetorically, however, the valley deserves this distinction, the scenery all around being really magnificent. There are séveral fantastic rocks of great size towering far into the sky, while beyond them peeps the snow-clad summit of the peak of Tisé.
>
> (*Ibid.*)

His next stop was at Diraphuk (Diripu or Dindiphu), where the head lama and he struck up such a good relationship that Kawaguchi could only conclude that they must have a spiritual affinity dating back to previous lives.* His host in fact

---

* This implies mutual belief in reincarnation.

gave up his own room to his Japanese guest. This commanded a spectacular view of the great north face of Kailas and its surroundings, the symbolism of which he explained when he brought Kawaguchi his butter tea in the evening (his precepts forbade the taking of an evening meal). The main peak of Kailas represented the Buddha, the lama maintained, while the three smaller peaks in front of it represented the Bodhisatt-vas Manjushri, Avalokitesvara and Vajrapani. That night was one of the most delightful interludes of Kawaguchi's whole three-year sojourn in Tibet:

> . . . it was a pleasure of an elevating kind. My mind was subdued and captivated as I looked, in that still night and in that far-off place, at the soft rays of the moon reflected on the crystal-like current that was flowing with pleasant murmur. Just as, in the holy texts, the soft breeze stirring the branches of trees in paradise is said to produce a pleasant note, that sounds to the ears of the happy denizens of that blissful abode like the voice of one reading the Scriptures, so that sweet murmur of the moon-reflecting stream deluded my enchanted ears into believing that they were listening to the divine music of Buddhism. Staying in that sacred place, and surrounded by such soul-subduing phenomena, my mind soared higher and higher, till it flew up to the eternal region beyond this world of woe and care. The holy Founder tells us that the most sacred region lies in one's own pure mind, but I, sinful mortal that I was, felt elevated and chastened when I found myself in such an environment.
>
> (*Ibid.*)

He liked it so much at Diraphuk – he in fact calls it 'Ri Ri Puri' – that he stayed the following day as well. Its name, he claims, means 'The Place of the Female Yak's Horn', and derives from a legend that Gyrva Gottsang Pa of Bhutan was led on his Kailas *parikrama* by a female yak, which he took to be a manifestation of the Buddhist deity, Vajra. The yak eventually concealed herself in a cavern at Diraphuk and struck her head against the rock there. This cavern was situated beneath the *gompa*, which at the time of Kawaguchi's visit was the most prosperous of all four Kailas *gompa* and had most lamas attached to it.

When he eventually left Diraphuk, his lama friend sent

17a. The Diraphuk or Dindipu monastery on the north side of Mount Kailas. Photo: G. Tucci, 1935

17b. A large rock venerated by pilgrims, who discern in its corrosion the footprint of a great ascetic. Photo: G. Tucci, 1935

18a. The north-east ridge of Mount Kailas. Photo: Hugh Ruttledge, 1926

18b. The Dolma La or pass (18,600 feet), the highest point of the 32-mile *Parikrama* or Circumambulation Route around Mount Kailas. Photo: Hugh Ruttledge, 1926

19a. Pilgrims' teeth extracted and inserted into the great rock on the Dolma La. Photo: G. Tucci, 1935

19b. The Gauri Kund lake or 'Lake of Mercy', north-east corner of Kailas. Photo: Hugh Ruttledge, 1926

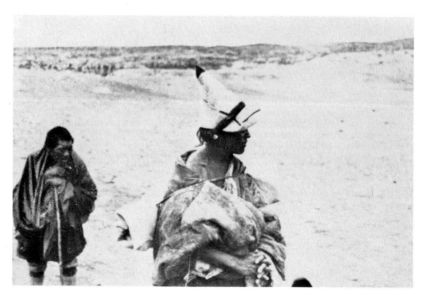

20a. A Bon-po pilgrim. Photo: G. Tucci, 1935

20b. The cave where the great *guru*-poet, Milarepa, lived and meditated. Zunthulphuk, east side of Kailas? Photo: G. Tucci, 1935

21a. Camp at Tarchan. Photo: Hugh Ruttledge, 1926

21b. The Gengta (or Gyangtrag) Monastery, south side of Mount Kailas.
Photo: G. Tucci, 1935

22. William Moorcroft and Hyder Young Hearsey at Lake Manasarovar. Mount Kailas in the background? Hearsey's own watercolour. Picture: India Office Records and Library

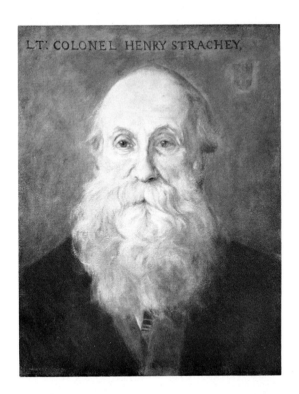

23a. Lieutenant-Colonel
Henry Strachey.
Picture: Royal
Geographical Society

23b. Arnold Savage Landor, before and after his Tibetan ordeal

24a. Colonel C. H. D. Ryder

24b.
Captain C. G. Rawling

25a. Dr. T. G.
Longstaff. Photo
kindly lent by Mrs.
Charmian Longstaff

25b. Charles Atmore
Sherring, I.C.S.
Photo kindly lent by
Mrs. Vera Sherring

26. Sven Hedin with members of his expedition

27a. Mr. and Mrs. Hugh Ruttledge and Colonel R. C. Wilson with members of their party after their 1926 tour of Tibet. Photo kindly lent by Major David Ruttledge

27b. Herbert Tichy and Chatter Bhuj Kapur (1936). Photo kindly lent by C. B. Kapur, Esq.

28a. Herbert Tichy in
disguise en route for
the Sacred Mountain.
Photo: Chatter Bhuj
Kapur, 1936

28b. Heinrich Harrer.
Photo kindly lent by
H. Harrer, Esq.

29. Ekai Kawaguchi

30a. Swami Pranavananda

30b. Bhagwan Shri Hamsa

30c. Edwin Schary

31. Giuseppe Tucci with a Tibetan official (the *Dzongpon* of Taklakot?).
Photo: I.S.M.E.O. (Rome)

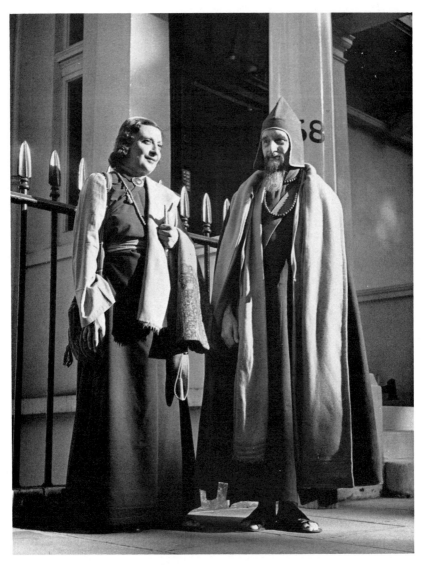

32. Lama Anagarika Govinda and Li Gotami at the Buddhist Society, London. Photo: The Buddhist Society

Kawaguchi on his way with a yak, a guide and a supply of food and delicacies. Thus he plodded on up the 'Hill of Salvation' towards the Dolma pass in comparative comfort. By sharp contrast, many of the other pilgrims he passed were making the *parikrama* by the most arduous and painful prostration method. Kawaguchi did not feel moved to join them. He also passed a burly fellow who was 'frantically confessing to and worshipping Kailas'. This man, his guide informed him, was an especially notorious bandit from Kham: a man whose murders and other crimes were legion. While he now seriously regretted these sins and was earnestly doing penance for them, he evidently did not trust himself not to commit similar offences again, for he was also doing penance for future crimes. 'This fellow,' Kawaguchi wrote, 'was decidedly original in his conception of penance. . . . Yet, I was told that this convenient mode of repentance was universal in the robber district of Kham.'

Approaching the Dolma la, Kawaguchi could see the mountain ranges to the north of Kailas, called in Tibetan, *Gyalpo Norjingi Phoprang*: 'Residence of King Kuvera'.★ Recalling Kāildāsa's great poem *Meghadūta* – 'Cloud Messenger' – Kawaguchi mused: 'Is it not really the mansion of the God of Wealth – that crystal abode shining in the emerald sky?' He also reflected that any 'mammon-worshipper' exploring the region would be sure to mistakenly expect to find a diamond mine there.

On the crest of the Dolma la he found the great stone, which he calls 'the natural stone image of the Mother of the Saviour'. Similarly, other strangely-shaped rocks nearby were, so his guide assured him, other images of the same person. He was now beginning to feel the effects of altitude and had to travel on the yak. On the other side of the Dolma la he encountered the Gauri Kund lake, and recounts the legend that explains how the lake came to be frozen all year round. Apparently, in ancient times it did not freeze in summer, and Kubera and his family used to take advantage of this to go there and wash their hands. One day, however, the child of a female pilgrim happened to accidentally slip into the lake and

★ Or Kubera – Hindu god of wealth.

was drowned, so the guardian spirits decided that thereafter, in the interests of safety, it should remain perpetually frozen.

Kawaguchi was obliged to dismount from his yak to make the difficult descent down the eastern valley of Kailas to the Zunthulphuk *gompa*. Its name, according to him, means 'Cave of Miracles', and he duly notes the association with Milarepa. He stayed one night there before going on to Gengta *gompa*, which he found to be dedicated to Dorje Karmo – 'White Thunderbolt'. He did not spend a night here, however, but travelled the mile or so on to Tarchan, where he found lodging in a house.

His *parikrama* duly accomplished, Kawaguchi met up with his Khampa friends the next day and they set off together on their travels again, moving in a south-easterly direction to the west of Lake Manasarovar. The following day they passed the foot of Ponri (19,590 feet), the peak sacred to the Bon religion. Now that they were properly out of the sacred region, however, his companions returned to their unregenerate worldly ways and began, for one thing, to slaughter animals. This was offensive to Kawaguchi's Buddhist conscience, and so he decided that the time for the parting of the ways had come. He subsequently set off on his own, following the Brahmaputra eastwards to Shigatse and eventually reaching Lhasa itself. Again, he had to run the full gamut of misfortunes and hardships. These included two attacks by robbers. He had long before decided that he would offer no resistance should he encounter any such people: they could freely take whatever they wished of him in the way of goods or money if they would leave him his life – which, after all, was his most valuable possession. Not that he feared death if it came. As a Buddhist, he subscribed to the doctrine that all that is born must die. If he wished to prolong his life it was only that he might work for the benefit of other beings:

> Whate'er my sufferings here and dangers dire
> Whate'er befalls me on my outward march
> All, all, I feel, is for the common good,
> For others treading on Salvation's path.

He also nearly froze to death in a terrible blizzard: a harrowing

experience that did not, however, unduly disturb his philo-
sophic equanimity:

> Upon these plains of snow, my bed is snow,
>   My pillow snow; my food also the same;
> And this my snowy journey, full of pain.

Whatever may be asserted about Kawaguchi's possible undercover activities, there is no doubt that he was a sincere
Buddhist, assiduous in his practices, which included the
virtues of self-control, truthfulness (though occasionally
infringed for reasons of security), compassion, friendliness
and non-violence. These no doubt in the long run helped him
to survive all difficulties and, after six months of hard
travelling, to arrive safely at Lhasa, the Tibetan capital, a little
footsore but essentially in good spirit.

Such was the benighted state of medical knowledge in Tibet
at the time that Kawaguchi was able during his stay in Lhasa to
win fame and fortune by employing his small medical skills.
This gained him access to the highest circles of society. He
met the Dalai Lama, and became a close friend of the
ex-Minister of Finance, at whose home he lodged for a time.
He also stayed at the great monastery of Sera, a notable centre
of Buddhist scholarship, where he sought and obtained
Buddhist texts and studied Buddhism under Ti Rimpoche, a
lama of distinction.

Aside from the religious and medical aspects of his life in
Lhasa, the Japanese priest was a keen observer of all aspects of
the Tibetan scene. His book, *Three Years in Tibet*, contains a
wealth of material on a wide variety of subjects, notably
political ones. Here the sheer volume of information amassed
is cited by some writers as clear evidence that Kawaguchi was
in fact a secret agent. Whole chapters are devoted to such
matters as Foreign Explorers and the Policy of Seclusion; the
Government; Tibet and British India; China, Nepal and
Tibet; and – most ominously – Russia's Tibetan Policy. This
latter was at this period a highly sensitive issue among all
powers with interests in Asia. The chief cause for concern was
the proximity to the Dalai Lama of a certain Buriat lama from
Russian Central Asia called Arguan Dorjiev. Kawaguchi

gives his honorific Tibetan title as *Tsani Kenbo* – 'Instructor in the Lamaist Catechism'. Dorjiev, who seems to have been both a good Russian and a good Buddhist, trotted dutifully back and forth between Lhasa and St. Petersburg. In order to encourage the Tibetan leaders to look towards Russia for support against the other powers active along their borders – notably Britain and China – Dorjiev is reputed to have disseminated the fiction that the Tsar was about to become a Buddhist and would one day found a great worldwide Buddhist empire. Russian arms were also flowing into Tibet at this time: Kawaguchi himself saw a consignment arriving by camel caravan. He also found out about the lavish presents that the Russians were bestowing on the Dalai Lama and other members of the Tibetan hierarchy through Dorjiev.

It may be possible that, if he was a secret agent of some sort, Kawaguchi was also working for the British. We know that he was sending letters from Lhasa to his old teacher of Tibetan, Chandra Das, himself at one time a British agent. If he was in contact with the British, Kawaguchi may well have been one of the channels, possibly even the main channel, whereby information of Russian activities in Lhasa, including those of Dorjiev, came to the ears of the Viceroy, Lord Curzon, who was so disturbed by them that he eventually ordered the Younghusband Expedition to Lhasa (1904), which resolved matters to Britain's immediate satisfaction.

Towards the middle of 1901, the secret of Kawaguchi's real identity began to be leaked in Lhasa. Worse: the possibility of his being both a Japanese and a British spy was also mooted. He himself strenuously denies that his Tibetan journey had any political dimensions. Whatever the true facts of the matter, he could not remain in the capital much longer, though when it came to the matter of flight he paused out of consideration for his many Tibetan friends. Perhaps recalling the fate of Chandra Das's protector, Sengchen Dorjechan, he realized that if he were to suddenly vanish the Tibetan authorities might well suspect the worst and accordingly punish and torture his friends for harbouring him. He sweated on the horns of this dilemma for a long time before deciding to go to the ex-Minister of Finance and make a clean breast of everything. He told his friend who he really was and suggested that he arrest him himself and deliver him to the authorities by way of proving his own innocence in the matter. The ex-Minister would have none of it. It was entirely contrary to his Buddhist principles, he said, to deliver another person over to danger in order to save his own skin – especially a fellow Buddhist who had come to his country for the noble motive of studying Buddhism. The decision to leave was finally clinched when Kawaguchi heard a mysterious voice telling him to do just that while he was strolling in the Dharma Garden at Sera.

With his collection of Buddhist texts and other possessions packed up and dispatched to Darjeeling in charge of a Chinese merchant, Kawaguchi sadly took leave of his Tibetan friends and, accompanied only by a single bearer, stole out of Lhasa. He took the direct southerly road for India, travelling fast for fear of pursuit. Ahead of him lay five serious obstacles: five 'challenge gates' notorious for their bureaucratic complications and for the extreme corruption of their presiding officers. In the best traditions of spy literature, however, Kawaguchi was able to exploit his now nationwide reputation as the 'Physician of Sera' to convince these officials – at whose merest whim he could have been held up for days – that he was in fact engaged on a mission of the utmost urgency and delicacy for no less a person than the Dalai Lama himself. He got through each of the gates without delay and was across the border without crisis.

Safely back in British India, he was still not at rest, however, for conflicting but nonetheless disquieting reports about the fate of his Tibetan friends filtered across the border to him. To settle the matter once and for all, he returned to Nepal for a second time in order to directly entreat the Maharaja to intercede personally with the Dalai Lama on behalf of his Lhasa friends. After initial reluctance and suspicion, the Maharaja was finally convinced of Kawaguchi's sincerity and concern, and agreed to cooperate.

And so, his conscience set at rest, Ekai Kawaguchi was able to return to his native Japan with his new collection of Buddhist texts. His ship, the *Bombay Maru*, came alongside the quay at Kobe on 20th May, 1902. He had arrived home safely, his mission fulfilled:

> My heaped up sorrows and calamities
>   Now all are melted like th' eternal snows
> With that unfailing Beacon-light, my Guide;
>   The Universal Leader, Buddha Great, my Guide
> Has been in all my travels in Tibet.

BHAGWAN SHRI HAMSA

The opening scene takes place at Victoria Terminus, that extravaganza of neo-Gothic railway architecture in Bombay. On the morning of the 4th April 1908, a yogi boarded the Delhi Express. Forty-eight hours later, during which time he had changed trains three times – at Bina (where he boarded the Punjab Mail), Lucknow and Bareilly – he finally arrived at the railhead at Kathgodam. Here, with the aid of the Government coolie contractor, he engaged two bearers at a rate of a rupee and a half a day, and a pony at a rate of six rupees. These were to accompany him to Almora in the foothills of the Himalayas on the first leg of a pilgrimage to Mount Kailas.

The yogi in question was one Bhagwan Shri Hamsa, and the narrative of his pilgrimage, *The Holy Mountain*, is a wonderfully exotic piece of literature, characteristically Indian and highly devotional. The style is quaintly formal, as though the author has thoroughly immersed himself not only in the writings of the Victorian masters of prose but also in the jargon of the Indian compilers of civil service regulations and railway time-tables. Purple passages descriptive of the most sublime spiritual experiences sit alongside the detailing of very precise, but very prosaic, facts – particularly facts relating to costs. The indications are that while Bhagwan was a deeply religious man, this did not preclude his also having a very keen eye for economy.

The English translation of *The Holy Mountain* from the original Marathi was made by Shri Purohit Swami, while the Introduction was penned by no less a luminary of English Literature than W. B. Yeats. Bhagwan Shri Hamsa was Shri Purohit Swami's spiritual teacher, who in turn collaborated with Yeats in the translation of the *Ten Principal Upanishads*. The poet had a great appetite for various kinds of esotericism at certain phases of his life and it is interesting that the tendrils of his curiosity reached as far as the sacred region in Western Tibet. He seems to have had no doubt that Kailas and Meru were identical, and furthermore, in 1935, in the anthology entitled *A Full Moon in March*, he actually published a poem under the title, *Meru*. Amid the usual Celtic sound and fury, this asserts that the world is an illusion, human life merely the product of mind, and man's lot a dreadful, violent struggle down the cycles of the ages to 'come into the desolation of reality'. He continues:

> Hermits upon Mount Meru or Everest,
> Caverned in night under the drifted snow,
> Or where that snow and winter's dreadful blast
> Beat down upon their naked bodies, know
> That day brings round the night, that before dawn
> His glory and his monuments are gone.

It seems, in short, a hymn to the transience of things.

Bhagwan Shri Hamsa's outward journey took him by the familiar route through Almora, Ascot, Garbyang, along the Nerpani Trail and into Tibet by the Nepalese Tinkar pass; then on to Taklakot, the lakes, Barkha, and finally to Tarchan and Kailas. It was hard and difficult going the whole way, beset with many perils: encounters with lust-maddened elephants, venomous cobras, tigers, ghosts and – perhaps most alarming for the chaste ascetic – licentious mountain girls. His intense faith in both himself and his spiritual master, Lord Dattātreya, added to the practice of continence and the determination to fulfil his spiritual ideal, saw him safely through every time. In Tibet he even fell into the clutches of a gang of ferocious *dacoits*; his reaction –

> I cried the sweet name of my Master and bowed down in mind, in reverent adoration before his lotus-feet, and to Shri Kailas and Lake Manas. . . . I closed my eyes in cool and quiet meditation, with my head projected a little forward.
> (Bhagwan Shri Hamsa, *The Holy Mountain*)

When he opened his eyes –

The man who a few moments ago stood with his naked sword

drawn over me, now knelt down before me with his head bent, resting on his thumbs in a suppliant posture.

(Ibid.)

There were other problems in Tibet besides the *dacoits*: the intense heat of the day; the equally intense cold of the night; the inhospitable terrain; and the people themselves, whom Bhagwan found semi-barbaric. Moreover, what passed for justice among them was summary and nauseatingly cruel. A young *dacoit* who had been caught at Taklakot was sewn up in a yak-hide sack and left to roast to death in the searing sun.

Nevertheless, the first sight of Kailas, when it came, was a species of beatific revelation that thoroughly made up for all the adverse experiences of the journey:

I washed my hands and feet in the lake [Rakshas Tal] – and turned to look towards Mount Kailas, whose peak shone in a clear sky. The realization of my cherished object, for which I bore so much physical and mental suffering, seemed near at hand – the haven of my pilgrimage, Mount Kailas stood before my eyes though still at a distance. The idea, the hope, exalted me, and soon I forgot the worry and exhaustion of the journey. I sat down on the beach of Lake Rakastal with my eyes fixed upon Mount Kailas, meditating upon the lotus-feet of my master. Kailas' peak shone clear till my meditation was over.

The peak of Mount Kailas is in the shape of a dome. At that hour the sun shone clearly upon its summit, which resembled a radiant ball of burnished silver. I was reminded of the golden dome of the temple of Shri Chidambaram, in the Madras Presidency, and its inexpressible beauty when shining in the sun's rays. There is one great difference between the two. The golden dome of the temple of Chidambaram is man-made, while the silvery peak of Mount Kailas is the work of nature.

(Ibid.)

Before going on to Kailas, Bhagwan took lodging in one of the *gompa* on the shores of Lake Manasarovar and performed *Anushthana* – religious observance – for twelve days. This involved bathing in the icy waters in the morning and in the evening, going without all nourishment except a cup of tea in the evening, and performing meditation. Sitting crosslegged on his meditational tigerskin, he did, however, allow himself the occasional indulgence of watching the frolics of the local wildlife – hamsa duck and hares mostly – and of generally admiring the stunning beauties of the scenery through his binoculars:

> Lake Manas is the home of sanctity, the abode of peace. It is the very Heart of Nature, full and throbbing. The region seems to be not of this earth, but of Heaven, and the blessed Land of the Soul. Sunrise and sunset, the canopy of the sky during the day and the shining moon and stars at night – all these are scenes of ineffable beauty. . . . At such a beautiful and solitary place, the mind loses itself and there is harmony full and complete.
>
> (*Ibid.*)

Possibly as a result of the austerities practised while performing *Anushthana*, he began to hear mellifluous singing and afterwards discovered footprints along the shore of the lake leading in the direction of Mount Kailas. He became convinced that these belonged to some great sage or Mahatma, and therefore decided that it was indicated that he proceed forthwith to the sacred mountain.

The *Pradakshina*, as Bhagwan calls the *parikrama*, went uneventfully enough until he reached the eastern side of Kailas. Then his Tibetan guide pointed to a cave high up on a perpendicular ridge, bounded by glaciers, where he claimed that a Hindu Mahatma was engaged in contemplation. Hamsa naturally decided that he must visit this Mahatma and although he could see no visible route to the cave, set off to try and reach it with his guide. Half-way up, the guide collapsed and had to be sent back down, so Bhagwan continued alone. About fifty yards from the mouth of the cave, he had to traverse a steep ice slope, and then a glacier. The final seven feet up a perpendicular precipice were climbed by using minute finger- and toe-holds.

At the mouth of the cave, Bhagwan hesitated in indecision; then resolution overcame prudence and he plunged inside – only to fall headlong into a four foot pit lurking just beyond the entrance in the totally dark interior. Bhagwan groped his way on into the darkness until his head butted against something hard which, on examination, he discovered to be 'a human head with hair on it'. It was the Mahatma.

Friendly greetings were exchanged, and as Bhagwan's eyes gradually became habituated to the darkness he saw before him the naked body of a man in his sixties – 'a noble, full and serene figure sitting in Padmasan' – the lotus posture – 'on a tiger skin'. The Mahatma's face seemed to be 'the abode of serenity, joy, peace and light, a veritable fountain of love'. There was absolutely no doubt that he was a fully-realized Master of Yoga: one who knew Brahma. Bhagwan was also certain that this was the person whose mellifluous singing he had heard and whose footsteps he had seen along the shores of Lake Manasarovar.

Bhagwan spent three days with the Mahatma, during which time he slept with his head in the sage's lap and lived on water alone. Their waking hours were spent in conversation spoken in a number of languages, ranging from perfect English to perfect Marathi. The Mahatma answered all Bhagwan's questions on matters relating to the spiritual life. It was, however, 'impossible to describe, even meagrely, the nature of our conversation. . .'. On the fourth day, having told Bhagwan to visit a fellow disciple of his own guru living at Tirthapuri, the Mahatma indicated that it was time for him to leave.

The coolies and the Tibetan guide were greatly relieved when they saw their employer returning safely from his perilous expedition, but more anxieties were shortly in store for them. Bhagwan's next hair-raising project was an expedition to the Gauri Kund Lake. This he undertook alone, taking all his warm clothes with him, a good supply of biscuits and a stout, metal-tipped staff. The last proved invaluable when scaling the snow- and ice-bound slopes that he had to ascend. The cold was excruciating; the breathing difficult. Then an avalanche swept him away. When he came to his senses, he found himself 'pitched in ice up to the waist' and 'at the very brink of death'. After two terrible nights bivouacked in holes in the ice, he managed to get back to his men.

Despite all these ordeals and the earnest entreaties of his coolies, Bhagwan determined on a second attempt to reach the Gauri Kund. This was successful, though the ascent took him nearly fifteen hours. Conditions at the lake, moreover, were arctic – 'My lips became green and blue with severe cold; my nerves seemed ready to burst, and respiration was difficult.' He broke the surface ice in order to get holy water; this stung like a scorpion's bite as he sprinkled it on his body in the prescribed manner. Then, as the sun began to set, he looked at the sky and at Kailas, and cried; 'Victory, Victory to the Lord, my Master. . . !' and sat down upon his tiger skin in the *Siddhasana* posture, facing north. Finally he closed his eyes and passed into profound meditation.

This was to be Bhagwan's great all-out drive to realize his spiritual ambition, which specifically was 'to have a sight of the physical form of the Lord Dattātreya⋆ Himself and to get myself initiated into the realization of the Self'. He was determined to realize this or 'die in meditation while sitting in Yogic posture'. All of which is strikingly reminiscent of that stage in the Buddha's spiritual quest when he placed himself on the 'immovable spot' beneath the Bo tree at Budh Gaya, equally determined to achieve his goal – which was to find a way to overcome suffering – or perish in the undertaking. By that time he had tried all the conventional religious paths and found them unable to provide a fully satisfying answer. He had also abandoned home, family, fortune, social rôle – in fact all material and emotional supports. He was in short a man *in extremis*; all that remained was his determination to find an answer to his spiritual problem.

In a similar way, Bhagwan had run the whole gamut of mental and physical sufferings. He had pushed himself far from home to an outlandishly remote and inhospitable place. All he had too was 'the intensity of my longing to realize my

---

⋆ According to Alain Daniélou (*Hindu Polytheism*, New York, 1964) Dattātreya is said to have been born of an emanantion of Vishnu which impregnated the wife of the sage Devourer (Atri). Dattātreya protects men from evil influences; he was the originator of Tantras and Tantric rites; he liked women, drink, songs, music and the company of those of low birth. Yet he was greatly praised by the gods, who he saved from demons. He had numerous other distinctions as well. J. Dowson (*Hindu Classical Dictionary*, London, 1928), on the other hand, maintains that Dattātreya is, 'A Brahmin Saint in whom a portion of Brahma, Vishnu and Shiva, more particularly Vishnu, was incarnate.'

goal'. And realize it he did. First, he heard the voice of his Lord. This was not enough, however: he had to see the physical form. Accordingly, after continued meditation, the mental form which he had kept fixed between his eyebrows disappeared and, when he opened his eyes, his Master, Lord Dattātreya, was standing before him. Bhagwan prostrated himself at his Master's feet immediately; then Lord Dattātreya lifted him up, embraced and caressed him. He then gave him a *mantra* (sacred formula) and initiated him into the Realization of the Self:

> Here my Manas [mind] merged into Antahkarana [heart]; the Antahkarana with the Manas merged into Chitta [mind-stuff]; the Chitta along with Antahkarana and Manas merged into Buddhi [intellect]; the Buddhi with Chitta, Antahkarana and Manas merged into Ahankar [egoism]; and the Ahankar along with Buddhi, Chitta, Antahkarana and Manas – all merged into Absolute Brahma! I found myself reflected everywhere in the whole Universe! It was all one harmony – full of Wisdom, Infinite Love Perennial and Bliss Eternal! Where was the body, its tenements and the 'I'! It was all Satchidānanda [Truth, Wisdom, Bliss].
>
> (*Ibid.*)

It was an overpoweringly blissful event; words could not adequately describe the joy which Bhagwan felt. In default of description, he proffers his reader two lines of poetry translated from the Sanskrit:

> The Master preaches through his silence,
> And all the doubts of the disciple are solved.
>
> (*Ibid.*)

Afterwards, Lord Dattātreya blessed him and, lighting a sacred fire, asked Bhagwan to perform the sacrificial ceremonies. This having been done, the Master initiated his devotee into the *Giri* order of *Sanyasins** and gave him the name, 'Hamsa'. In return, Bhagwan offered his Master all he had – a single biscuit. Lord Dattātreya ate half and returned

---

* The order of holy men who pursue the religious life in the mountains.

the other half as *prasad* (a sacred food offering). Finally, he told Bhagwan to request a boon. Bhagwan hesitated. . . .

'Let my heart always feel the same attachment towards Thee, though divested of its harm, that the undiscriminating soul feels in worldly objects,' Bhagwan requested after a second bidding.

'*Let it be so!*' his Master replied, blessing his devotee and smiling.

Together, the two of them journeyed back to Bhagwan's camp. Although the outward journey had taken fifteen hours, in the company of his Lord the return journey was accomplished in a mere fifteen minutes.

After leaving Kailas and the Lord Dattātreya, Bhagwan visited Tirthapuri, where he met another *Mahatma* mentioned to him by the one he had met in the cave on the sacred mountain. This second *Mahatma*:

> . . . seemed a little older, but in other respects [was] much like the Mahatma on Kailas. He had the same sweet voice, the same peace and serenity beaming on his face, the same Light of the Absolute radiating from his eyes, the same full yet graceful stature. The Mahatma asked me to close my eyes and sit in meditation, saying he would do likewise. He asked me what more I had to gain. I made no reply.
>
> (*Ibid.*)

Having lived in the company of this holy man for three days, Bhagwan set out on his return journey to India. Six months and seven days after setting off on his pilgrimage, he was back in Bombay. Alighting from the train at V.T. (Victoria Terminus), he was met by three or four friends. He was justifiably proud to have attained his spiritual goal, but also rather pleased that in all the whole undertaking had cost him only 175 rupees – a mere £13. Indeed, not much to have had to pay for a glimpse of the Absolute!

EDWIN GILBERT SCHARY

In the summer of 1918, a group of Indians were standing on the summit of a low-lying hill about half a mile from the bazaar in Gyanima. They were staring intently at something on the distant horizon. This aroused the curiosity of a travel-worn pilgrim who had arrived there three days before, and he asked a young Indian with whom he had struck up a friendship what these people found so interesting. The young Indian said nothing, merely took his friend by the hand, led him to the summit of the hill and pointed.

About fifty miles away, standing alone and isolated upon the plain, was a tremendous mountain peak of startling beauty. Its symmetrical contours were clearly defined in the rarefied atmosphere, and the late afternoon sunshine dappled its snows with subtle hues – pink, rose, purple. This was Kailas Parbat, the young Indian said: the Mecca of all the Hindus and Buddhists of the world; the sacred dwelling place of their highest gods. Moreover, this year was a year of special pilgrimage to it.

The following day the pilgrim traded a robe that he had been given by a lama at Hanle *gompa* and set off in the direction of Tarchan with warnings against the dangers of the local *dacoits* ringing in his ears. On the afternoon of the second day, having passed no streams and consequently beginning to feel the effects of thirst, he was beguiled by a mirage into thinking that a large lake lay ahead. Finding only an expanse of desert sage and by then being too exhausted to continue, he threw a blanket over himself and fell asleep.

Continuing his journey next day, he found a stream near a nomad camp at about noon, and slaked his thirst; then he followed the trail on into Tarchan, where he found several hundred pilgrims encamped. While walking through Tarchan, this indigent pilgrim met his young Indian friend again by chance. The Indian was delighted to see him, but told him that his sudden disappearance from Gyanima had aroused suspicions in the local lamas that he was some kind of devil. He then gave the pilgrim a few *tankas* – Tibetan coins – and took him to the adjacent *gompa*, where he instructed the attendant lama to give his friend food and shelter.

The lama took the pilgrim into a large, corridor-like room, where he left him. Time passed and the promised food did not arrive. However, whenever the lama passed the pilgrim in company with other lamas, he would make faces. The pilgrim eventually grew disgusted at this neglect and derision, and left the *gompa* to wander among the tents pitched on the plain.

Whatever his ragged, vermin-infested clothing might suggest, this penniless pilgrim did not hail from Ladakh; nor, as his disintegrating looks might lead one to believe, was he a native Tibetan. Despite his command of Hindustani, he was not from the plains of India either. He was, in fact, a citizen of San Francisco, California. His name was Edwin Gilbert Schary. He was just twenty-three years old and this was his second journey to Tibet.

Schary does not appear to have had any clear notion of what precipitated him into the life of a spiritual searcher: the life that eventually brought him to Mount Kailas in the abject state described above. There does not, as in the case of the Buddha, seem to have been any precipitating crisis. It may have been that the surroundings of his early youth 'wove the spell of romance and adventure into my life', or 'the fact that I was born with an intense imagination and the power to crystallize into fact those imaginary pictures'. His 'early longing to see what lay beyond the Farallones' led him at the age of twelve to embark upon a life of wandering. His distracted parents were even driven to employing detectives to keep track of this footloose son of theirs. All to no avail. As he grew older the propensity merely intensified itself and became directed towards ever more exotic locations, especially when he came in contact with Oriental philosophical and religious ideas. His particular obsession became to make contact with the so-called Mahatmas of Tibet,* the notion of whose existence was propagated in the latter part of the last century by Madame Helena Blavatsky's Theosophical movement. The Mahatmas were exalted beings versed in the ancient esoteric wisdom: the profound hidden teachings that underlie the more or less superficial exoteric doctrines that the religions of the world retail to the uninitiated masses. Portions of this ancient wisdom were communicated to Madame Blavatsky and other of the early Theosophists, either directly or by occult means. Perhaps Schary himself hoped to be similarly enlightened – or at least to have the veils of mystery drawn slightly aside.

* See also pp. 157 ff.

Schary set off on his first trip to Tibet on 18th December 1912, travelling first to Hawaii and then on to Australia before finally taking ship for Ceylon. He took odd jobs wherever he landed up and in this respect there is something of the classic hobo about him – something out of Jack London, perhaps, though his interest in Oriental philosophy gives him closer affinities with the hippies who were to emerge in his own native city half a century later. The experience of being down and out in many parts of the world seems to have humbled Schary, and the fact that he had as a result to live alongside the native people in the Asiatic countries he visited stripped him of that uncongenial arrogance that afflicted so many white men who lived or travelled in the East. He also learned to bear the vicissitudes of fortune with equanimity and to take abuse without rancour – all very useful spiritual lessons.

An interview with a Buddhist monk in Ceylon resulted in Schary's being advised to continue his search but to look for wisdom in the life of the peoples of the East rather than among priests. He journeyed on to Madras, where he tried but failed to get an interview with Annie Besant, one of the luminaries of the Theosophical Society, which had – and indeed continues to have – its headquarters at Adyar on the outskirts of Madras. After travelling and working in many parts of India, Schary eventually arrived in Kashmir on a bicycle, worked there as a schoolmaster for a short time and then proceeded to Ladakh with the intention of entering Tibet in search of the Mahatmas. He crossed the Tungi La and arrived on the great plateau: alone, equipped only with the barest supplies and riding a horse that was totally unacclimatized to the rigours of travelling at altitudes in excess of 13,000 feet. In short, Schary was as thoroughly unprepared practically as he was psychologically for the terrible experiences that were about to beset him.

He travelled as far as Pooga before finally admitting to himself that it would be madness to continue. He turned back, but the return journey was a nightmare of thirst and fatigue that reached a horrific culmination in the sudden death of his horse. This experience had an inordinate effect upon his mind, became charged with deep symbolic significance, and haunted his nights with awful nightmares for long afterwards. He managed to stagger back over the Tungi La on foot but was only saved from almost certain death by the timely arrival of a caravan belonging to two American missionaries who happened to be on a trek up in the mountains.

Schary returned to San Francisco, but three years later he was crossing the Tungi La again. This time he had decided that he would not take a horse, or indeed any equipment or supplies beyond what he could carry on his own back. He would 'show a larger faith than I had on the first journey' by eschewing money and heavy sleeping robes, and instead beg for simple food from the nomads he would meet, and generally live off the natural resources of the land. With formidable courage and resolution, accepting with equanimity the appalling hardships that inevitably beset him in that most inhospitable of lands, he proceeded in a generally easterly direction across Western Tibet (Ngari), passing through Pooga, Hanle, Chimurti, Tashigong and Gyanima until he finally arrived at Tarchan at the foot of Mount Kailas.

Later at Tarchan he bought and ate several large strips of cooked yak meat; then a sudden and violent hail storm drove him along with three or four hundred Hindu men, women and children to take shelter in a room in the *gompa*. While the storm raged all night long, Schary cradled two children in his arms while their mother told him with joy that she had accomplished the deepest wish of her heart in making this journey to the sacred mountain.

Next day, Schary went on to Barkha, where he struck a deal with a Tibetan caravan master to give him food and guidance for the next two days. As they passed Lake Manasarovar, he saw pilgrims making the *parikrama* of the sacred lake. He did not join them, as he had not joined those making the Kailas *parikrama*. The goal and object of his own pilgrimage lay elsewhere: not too far ahead now.

It had all fixed itself some time before. While asleep one night in a bungalow in which he had lived while working on a rubber plantation in the Malay Peninsula during the outward journey, Schary had had a prophetic dream:

Across my vision was portrayed a map of India and the Himalayas, also including the Bay of Bengal and the Malay

Peninsula and the plantation. As I looked, I saw a finger pointing. The finger followed from the plantation across the Bay of Bengal to Calcutta, on to the north-west frontier of India, up into Kashmir, and thence over the Himalayan passes, following the trail I had previously taken into Tibet itself. The moving finger continued across the place on the map representing the Tibetan Highland and stopped half-way across. Then the map disappeared from my vision and I beheld a narrow canyon through which ran a tiny stream over a terribly rocky course and walled high on each side by decaying mountains of shale and rock. On the left-hand side, about 300 feet above the stream, was a cave. Above the cave I saw the figures 9–5.

I received the impression when beholding these numerals, that they represented September 5, and on awakening that morning I felt that I had been given direct guidance by which to reach the Mahatmas.

> (Edwin Schary, *In Search of the Mahatmas of Tibet*)

September 5th was now rapidly approaching.

On 3rd September, Schary arrived at Todom. He was travelling faster than ordinarily. He promptly left Todom and ascended a high pass where he met an Indian trader travelling on foot. They crossed the pass together but the Indian would not let Schary stay at his campfire that night for reasons of caste propriety and so the American burrowed into a huge mound of wool and there slept the night of 4th September. His sleep was terribly troubled:

> I seemed to be overcoming terrible obstacles, crossing high passes below which I could see great banks of clouds, and staggering over trails which led across endless desolation.
>
> (*Ibid.*)

When he awoke the next morning, he felt totally unrefreshed by his night's sleep. Nevertheless, he got up and started on down the trail through a valley under the pall of a tremendous sense of apprehension. Nothing about his present surroundings suggested the terrain he had seen in his dream. When the sun was well up, he rested for about an hour beside a small stream; then, continuing for about two miles, the stream turned into a desolate canyon:

The stream ran over a jagged and rocky course between high banks of sand and shale; the ground sloped away on both sides and upward into strata of rock which seemed part of an ancient and decaying mountain range. As I entered this canyon, I suddenly looked up and beheld the vision of my dream.

(*Ibid.*)

He found the cave. After a difficult climb, he reached its mouth and entered.

At this point – the very climax of his journey – Schary refuses to indulge his reader in any dramatics. This is simply because there was no drama. He is utterly and confoundingly honest. The cave –

. . . was just a cave – no more, no less – and no one within. . . .

(*Ibid.*)

Within this cave, I sank down on my blanket and, with a feeling of utter despondency, I suddenly realized that all my expectations of finding the Mahatmas of the East in this cave, living their life of seclusion, was now brought to naught. My dream came true in its physical aspect but that was all.

(*Ibid.*)

For what purpose then had the dream been visited upon him? He could only conclude that its purpose was to lead him to Tibet in order that he might have the strange experiences of that pilgrim journey. But the anti-climax and the disappointment were shattering; he lay for three days in a state of total prostration, mentally undergoing many strange experiences, and finally coming to this conclusion:

If I learned anything at any time in all my travels, I learnt this lesson in that cave – a lesson read somewhere before in one of the writings of an Eastern sage but never until that time wholly understood:

'Within thyself deliverance must be sought. Each man his prison makes; each hath such lordship as the loftiest one. Nay, for with powers above, around, below, as with all flesh and whatsoever lives, Act maketh joy and woe.'

(*Ibid.*)

There remained nothing now but to quit the cave and push on to the British trading post at Gyangtse. Schary accomplished this in a spirit of utter hopelessness, with 'an emotional indifference which to this day, many years later, has remained with me in part'.

Mr. David MacDonald, sometime British Trade Agent in Gyangtse, recalls in his book, *Twenty Years in Tibet*, a strange incident that took place there in October 1918. He was in Yatung at the time, but had the story from the Gyangtse men:

> One evening, at dusk, a begrimed and filthily clad figure, covered with festering sores, crawled to the main gate of Gyangtse Fort. In Hindustani he asked the sepoy sentry to let him in, but the latter, taking him for a Tibetan beggar, refused and ordered him away from the post. Sinking down on a stone nearby, the man said 'I am a white man, you must let me in.' The sepoy was sceptical but the matter was taken out of his hands by an Indian officer of the Detachment, who realized after a few inquiries that the wanderer was really a white man in distress. Eventually, Schary wrote a note to Mr. Martin, my head clerk at Gyangtse, to the effect that he was sick and starving, and asking for help. As soon as Mr. Martin read this letter, he of course had Schary brought in, and given food and attention. He was in a terrible condition, verminous, ill-nourished and really very ill. . . .
>
> (*Ibid.*)

Thus Schary was saved for a second time by a fortunate fall into the hands of sympathetic Westerners. Having recruited his strength at Gyangtse, he returned to India by way of the Chumbi valley, Sikkim and Darjeeling. Arriving eventually at Calcutta, he took ship for Singapore and thence sailed via Yokohama back home to San Francisco.

This harrowing ordeal in Tibet, together with the crushing disappointment in the cave, did not put end to Schary's ambition of meeting the Mahatmas. He concluded, after lengthy consideration, that he simply did not yet merit the honour of such a meeting. He had therefore still to go through some 'very severe course of penance and personal sacrifice' to arrive at the required state of fitness. He also decided that he had probably failed during his second journey because he had been too indulgent with himself. The next time, he determined, he would take absolutely no provisions or equipment whatsoever but rely entirely on faith for everything. He would also consciously abstain from food and drink, 'feeling that one who wished to become a disciple of these Great Ones must show the greatest manner of personal sacrifice and indifference to physical needs. . . .' He was, in short, preparing to go back to Tibet and submit himself to a more extreme programme of self-mortification. If he met the required standards, however, he expected that someone would meet him along the trail of that 'forbidding plateau' and take him to the Mahatmas.

Unfortunately – or perhaps, fortunately – the British were now alerted to the fact that Schary was endowed with a marked propensity for slipping into Tibet without authorization. Consequently, they were on the lookout for him, and when he tried to reach the high passes for the third time, he was caught and taken back to Kashmir, where he was imprisoned for a while before being packed off out of the country.

This was still not the end. He returned to India for a fourth time, and gained employment in a caustic soda plant on the Hooghly River below Calcutta. He then wrote to his old employer in Kashmir asking for a job but promising not to enter Tibet. He had made many such promises in the past and broken just about all of them, so to anyone who knew him they could not have meant much. His old employer wrote back that the officials would never countenance Schary's return to Kashmir.

Quite suddenly and calmly a few days after receiving this letter, this strange, obsessed man Schary decided that he must put all further notion of meeting the Mahatmas of Tibet out of his mind, for 'to find them was not for me'. He promptly secured a berth for himself on a Standard Oil tanker sailing from Calcutta to San Francisco.

Between September and December, 1924, Schary completed a circuit of the world in ninety-five days. Returning to the East Coast of the United States, he bought a transcontinental railway ticket from New York to San Francisco. He only had enough money for about two days' food. Therefore it Cheyenne, Wyoming he dismounted from the train, hoping to sell or pawn some of his clothes, buy something to eat with the proceeds, and then resume his journey. He found everything closed up in Cheyenne, however, and had to spend the night in a Salvation Army hostel; then he sold a shirt and a sweater for two dollars. He eventually arrived back in San Francisco with only five cents in his pocket.

'Thus did I consummate a 12-year cycle of pilgrimage and quest over the world's open spaces.'

And promptly the man vanishes into the mists of anonymity.

What is particularly striking about Schary's spiritual search is that – unlike Hamsa's, or Kawaguchi's, for instance – it did not take place within the matrix of an established spiritual tradition. The ambitions and objectives that he was contemplating 'had possibly never before been thought of by a Westerner.* I had nothing upon which to lend me comfort, but had simply to pursue my journey with nothing but very great faith together with absolute resolve.' He was in short a total loner: not sure of what he was seeking, nor how to get it, not even of the significance of the experiences that came to him in his quest – but driven by a tremendously powerful force nevertheless; a force he could not resist.

Modern psychologists would probably diagnose Schary as some kind of neurotic as he was prone to fits of depression, panic and nerves, and could moreover not hold down a steady job or even stay put in one place for any length of time. On the other hand, the reader of his narrative cannot help being at times awed by the sheer persistence and courage of the man. Yet the fact that these qualities were not informed by a clear sense of direction and a solid understanding of what he was about leaves one ultimately with the sad impression of a person afflicted with a desperate foolhardiness that might well have brought him to disaster. If he survived at all, it was by the skin of his teeth. Perhaps his humility and the engaging kind of innocence with which he seems to have been endowed may also have helped bring him through his terrible trials. All in all, however, Schary's story is an object lesson in the danger

---

* They in fact had – by the great Christian mystics, for instance.

of embarking upon the spiritual quest without proper preparation, a tried and tested tradition in which to work, and a teacher who has trodden the way himself and can guide the seeker.

CHAPTER EIGHT

Pilgrims to the Sacred Mountain – 2

SWAMI PRANAVANANDA OF THE HOLY KAILAS AND MANASAROVAR

One man deserves special homage as the Kailas pilgrim *par excellence* and unrivalled authority on all matters relating to the sacred mountain, its lakes and general environs. This is Shri Swami 108 Pranavananda Maharaj (of the Holy Kailas and Manasarovar), to give him his full religious title. In the frontispieces of his books he appears as a rather splendid Shaivite *sanyasin* or holy man, with thick beard, shoulder-length hair (parted in the middle) and large, inspired eyes.

Swami Pranavananda first visited Kailas in 1928, travelling there from Srinagar in Kashmir via Ladakh and Gartok, and returning to India by way of the Niti pass. From 1935, he visited the sacred region almost yearly, travelling by a variety of routes and staying for periods ranging from two to six months on the shores of Lake Manasarovar. In 1936–7 and again in 1943–4, he stayed for periods of twelve and sixteen months respectively at Thugolho (Thokar, Trugo) *gompa*. In the last published account of his achievements (1950), he claimed to have made in all some twenty-three circumambulation circuits of Mount Kailas, and twenty-five of Lake Manasarovar; he had also made one circuit of Rakshas Tal.

The main purpose of these visits was spiritual, for at the time the Swami belonged to that particular fraternity of the devotees of Lord Shiva who pursue their *sādhanā* or spiritual training in the mountains – and where better than in the vicinity of the Throne of Lord Shiva itself? Swami Pranavananda was, however, very much more than just a religious ascetic. In his spare time he conducted extensive scientific researches in a variety of fields and was as a result able to amass an encyclopaedic amount of information about the sacred region, upon which he subsequently lectured to learned bodies, and published articles and books, both in English and the native Indian languages. His *Exploration in Tibet* ran to two editions (1939 and 1950), and he also produced an invaluable baedeker for Kailas pilgrims: *The Pilgrim's Companion to the Holy Kailas and Manasarovar*, published in Allahabad in 1938. The discovery of an aged and battered copy of this venerable work in one of the learned libraries of London was one of the sweetest finds during the research for the present book.

For anyone with an interest in Mount Kailas and environs, the *Pilgrim's Companion* is a truly 'sumptuous feast' of useful information and timely advice, liberally endowed with maps and photographs, and garnished with passages of magnificently purple prose:

The perpetual snow-clad peak of the HOLY KAILAS (styled 'Kang Rinpochhe' in the Tibetan language) of hoary antiquity and celebrity, the spotless design of Nature's art, of the most bewitching and overpowering beauty, has a vibration of the supreme order from the spiritual point of view. It is like an immediate revelation of the Almighty, which makes man bend his knees and lower his head. Its gorgeous silvery summit, resplendent with the lustre of spiritual aura, with awe-inspiring solemnity and weird grandeur, pierces the heavenly height of 22,028 feet above the even bosom of the sea.

(*Ibid.*)

As any good guide-book should, the *Pilgrim's Companion* analyses some of the more-frequented routes to Kailas and Manasarovar, and both the circumambulation routes of the sacred mountain and the sacred lake, stage-by-stage, giving exact specifications of distances and times of travel between the various stages. It also provides copious ancilliary notes on places of interest or of special religious significance that the pilgrim will encounter either along the way or by making side-trips. That the Swami has so much information to impart bears able testimony to his close acquaintance with the various routes as well as with the sacred region itself. It moreover demonstrates the high degree of development which the great Hindu institution of pilgrimage to Mount Kailas had attained over the centuries.

Arguably most interesting to the general reader is the mass of general information which the *Pilgrim's Companion* contains. Right at the beginning, for instance, Swami Pranavananda discusses the significance of *tirthas* or places of pilgrimage. These, he maintains, are pervaded by 'magnificent spiritual vibrations' as a result of various kinds of highly-evolved holy men having lived and performed *tapas* (spiritual practices) in them. Subsequently aspirants are drawn to the great *tirthas* precisely because they hope, by exposing themselves to these subtle vibrations, to gain spiritual enrichment. There are many *tirthas* in the Himalayas, but almost undoubtedly the holiest are Kailas and Manasarovar:

In the surroundings of the Holy Kailas and Manasarovar, even the most wandering mind – to whatever religion he may belong . . . becomes concentrated and irresistibly, unknowingly and unconsciously feels the Divine Presence that seems hidden behind the apparently vast universe, as if propelled by some one from behind, and a good *sadhaka* may even enter into sublime ecstacies involuntarily. But, just as a man, the mucous membrane of whose nose has become dull, cannot perceive the scent of an article, so it is no wonder if a person devoid of any spiritual tendencies cannot perceive or feel the effect of the spiritual vibrations existing in a particular place.

(*Ibid.*)

A little further on, in a section designed to orientate the would-be pilgrim to conditions generally prevailing in Tibet at the time, he deals with the evocative matter of *mahatmas* and *mystics*:

Several sensational articles are freely published both here and in the west about the Mahatmas and *Siddhas*★ in this little seen and less studied part of the world. Most of these stories, gaining currency here, are more of the nature of stunts than anything else. I may mention that I visited altogether about 50 Monasteries and not less than 1500 monks. During these visits I came across a Lama (from Lhassa) in the year 1936, and attended some *tantric* rites he conducted in the Similing Monastery [in Taklakot] for three days; and another *Tulku*† Lama aged sixteen in the year 1928 whom I felt to be an elevated soul. These are the only notables who I happened to meet. This is not to say, however, that really great Mahatmas and yogis do not exist. . . . The simple fact remains that really spiritually advanced Yogis or Lamas are as rare a phenomenon here as everywhere else. . . . *There is no doubt however that the surroundings of the Holy Kailas and Manasarovar are surcharged with spiritual vibrations of the supreme order which make one exhilarated and elevated.*

(*Ibid.*)

As regards who is capable of undertaking the rigours of a pilgrimage to Kailas, Swami Pranavananda maintains that 'any person who had not got very weak lungs or affected heart' could go. If he were an Indian, he would need no passport, but he would be well advised to take with him a fair amount of clothing, a stock of medicines and a number of miscellaneous other items, all of which the Swami is kind enough to list. That the list of medicines runs to some twenty-one items is explained a little later when the Swami discourses upon the 'general ailments of the way':

★ Perfected sages.
† Incarnate Lama.

Dysentery, diarrhoea, cold, cough, fatigue and feverishness due to tiresome ascents [*sic*] and descents . . . and reeling sensation or headache during high ascents. . . .'

(*Ibid.*)

Among the other exigencies of pilgrimage are the ruthless *dacoit* bandits that infest the areas about a day's travel beyond Taklakot. For protection against these desperadoes, the good Swami advises the pilgrim to travel within a group, which should also be armed. Guns or armed guards could be hired from the Bhotia traders in Taklakot. If guards were hired, they would also act as guides and interpreters. One final stratagem that the Swami urges as beneficial for deterring *dacoits* is to fire two or three warning shots into the air about an hour or two after sunset when stopping at places known to be prone to *dacoit* attack.

The pilgrim should also be prepared to meet with all the extremes of weather known to meteorology:

During the pilgrim season – July and August, very often, the Holy Kailas and Mandhata peaks would be under cloud and be playing hide-and-seek with the visitors. When the sky is clear the sun is scorching. During the cloudy part of a day and during nights it would be very cold. The weather changes like the weathercock. Now you will be perspiring profusely in the scorching sun; in a few minutes a cool breeze gently blows; the next moment you will have clouds with terrific thunders and lightnings followed by drizzling rain or downpours of water in torrents; sometimes you will see a rainbow, shortly after, you may have a hailstorm followed by showers of snowfall. . . . Here is perfect calmness, the next moment there break out whizzing, tempestuous winds. . . . Here on a conical peak the ice is glittering in the sun like a silver bar, there on a dome-like peak are hanging golden canopies, the far-off mountain ranges are enveloped in thick wreaths of inky black clouds, there a belt of amber clouds or the seven-coloured semicircular rainbow encircles the Kailas dome, or the nearby Mandhata's giant heads are ablaze in scarlet flames when the sun begins to dip in the west or the meagre snow-capped Punri peak raises its head into the pitch-black messengers of Indra. . . . Sometimes it seems that day and night, morning, noon and evening and all the six seasons of the year have their sway simultaneously.

(Ibid.)

Against all these exigencies, the pilgrim would not be without the benefit of what Swami Pranavananda calls 'help and popular persons'. He reports on the noble efforts of the 'Shri Kailas-Manasarovar Kshetras Committee, newly constituted in Almora and Provincial Branches at Lahore, Rawalpindi, etc.' to provide food, blankets and accommodation for pilgrims and to generally look after their 'comforts and conveniences'. On the whole it would seem that there were numerous *dharmasalas* (rest-houses) and other places where the pilgrim could find lodging on the Indian side of the passes. Once across into Tibet, however, they were virtually non-existent and Swami Pranavananda therefore recommends the pilgrim to hire himself a tent or to bring one with him from the Plains. He also gives the names of various people – Bhotia traders, post masters, schoolmasters – to whom the pilgrim may apply personally for help at various specific places. Mail could also be forwarded via Bhotia traders from the final post office on Indian territory: at Garbyang.

Regarding the best time for commencing a pilgrimage, Swami Pranavananda is of the opinion that one should start from Almora around the middle of June if one wishes to avoid the rains, though most pilgrims in fact set off at the end of that month. The full round trip via Almora may be accomplished in some fifty days, though an extra three or four days should be allowed if the pilgrim wishes to make a circumambulation of Lake Manasarovar, and a further week if he wishes to visit Tirthapuri and Gyanima. The largest *mandi* (market) in Western Tibet is to be found at the latter place; others at Tarchen, Taklakot and Thugolho on Lake Manasarovar. Food might be bought at these places, though 'articles of any special liking' should be brought from Almora. The Swami enumerates the various kinds of food that might be obtained along the route, but warns that in Tibet it becomes less plentiful, and the pilgrim is well-advised to stock up at Taklakot with enough provisions to last both the outward and return journeys from Kailas. In Tibet, transactions might be made either in Indian rupees or Tibetan *tongas* (see *Fig. 17*), though Tibetans preferred the former.

17. Tibetan coins (tongas)

Finally, the brave pilgrim having, with the noble Swami's advice and the guidance of his itineraries, successfully negotiated the fraught route to the Holy Kailas and duly made the prescribed circumambulation of the sacred peak, he is sent on his way home with the following inspiring remarks:

Return journey should be done, taking proper rest wherever needed, following the route of the outward journey. As this pilgrimage cannot be undertaken easily, or often, one should spend some days leisurely in quiet meditation either at Kailas or preferably on the shores of the Manasarovar, where one can enjoy the *darsan* [sight] of the Holy Kailas and a bath in the Manas. Whether one be a pilgrim or tourist one should not fail to derive full benefit of these holy and grand places by staying there at least for a few days, but not run on in indecent haste. Pilgrims should make it a point to devote sometime daily for peaceful meditation and contemplation, by the side of the turquoise-blue surface of the charming lake. One breathes more happily and with greater ease; one feels a real pleasure in life, and yearns to remain sailing indefinitely on the fascinating blue depths and the sacred waves . . . (T)he inner joy which one feels when one is faced with an object of superhuman beauty and eternal charm, such as is presented by this summit under a cupola of perpetual snow . . . is certainly better described by one more gifted poetically and aesthetically disposed than myself. How can Manasarovar and Kailas be the objects of divine honour from two religions so different as Hinduism and Buddhism unless it be that their overpowering beauty has not only appealed to, but made an indelible impression on, the human mind, that they seemed to belong rather to Heaven than to Earth? Even the first view from the hills on the shore causes one to burst into tears of joy at the magnificent landscape; and a more intimate association undoubtedly throws one into a deeper mystic trance wherein one feels nearer the Divine Presence than anywhere else. The author feels that if he has stimulated interest in any of the numerous prospective readers of his book, to undertake this very whole-some journey to this Abode of Bliss in the Abode of Snow and to feel that inner joy and enjoy that peace of mind which he is sure every mortal is bound to share with himself, his labours will have been more than amply rewarded. If in addition any one devotee, having been inspired by the August Presence himself, can hand on this torch of Illumination to his fellow brethren, the gratifying reflection of having originated and perpetuated this chain of inspiration will fill the author with that supreme satisfaction, which the fulfilment of a noble and self-imposed mission of serving humanity naturally yields as its most legitimate consequence.

(*Ibid.*)

The writer of that fine panegyric was born Kanakadandi Venkata Somayajulu in East Godavari District in south India in 1896. After graduating from the D.A.V. College in Lahore in 1919, he worked in the Railway Accounts Office in the same city for a short period before resigning and becoming a political activist. He joined the non-Cooperation movement and between 1920 and 1926 was an active Congress worker in West Godavari district. Then he 'had a call from the heights of the Himalayas in consequence of an internal urge for search after Truth'. In plain language, he took to the religious life.

Swami Pranavananda's *guru* or spiritual mentor was H.H. Shri 1108 Dr. Swami Jnanananda, D.Sc., Ph.D., F.Inst.P., M.S. Sigma Xl, who 'after attaining Realization took to Scientific Research with the aid of his intuitional knowledge'. Swami Jnanananda's scientific research took him to places as far afield as Dresden, Ann Arbor (Michigan) and Liverpool, and ranged from the study of X-rays to that of nuclear physics. According to Dr. Paul Brunton, who met Swami

Pranavananda in the 1930s, it was the fact that Swami Jnanananda had already made a Kailas pilgrimage, and whetted his disciple's appetite with vivid descriptions of the journey and its goal, that prompted Swami Pranavananda to make his own initial Kailas journey, along with an unnamed companion, in 1928. His *guru*, the great 'Swami-Scientist', also whetted his appetite for things scientific.

Among his own scientific achievements (mainly attained in the Kailas region), Swami Pranavananda lists the following:

> I discovered the sources of the Four Great Rivers of this region from all points of view, namely tradition, quantity of water, length and glacier. I negotiated four new passes . . . reached the northern, southern and eastern bases of the Kailas peak; ascertained the number of islands in the Rakshas lake (two); discovered Tso Kapala; studied the lakes cursorily when they were frozen in winter; sounded Gouri kund and Manasarovar; collected some fossils; and undertook some minor expeditions to the 'Deserted Cave City'* and other places.
>
> (Swami Pranavananda, *Exploration In Tibet*, 2nd Edition)

In claiming to have discovered the true sources of the 'Four Great Rivers' he is, of course, challenging the claims of Sven Hedin, the Swedish explorer. Naturally, any great river will have many tributary streams at its headwaters, and it will be a matter of debate as to which can with most justice be cited as the true source. Various criteria may be invoked: local tradition, for instance, or length, or volume of water. Pranavananda contends that Sven Hedin's sources for the Sutlej, Indus and Brahmaputra 'would not satisfy any one of the above three criteria . . . in its entirety; and as such he cannot claim to be "the first white man and European" to discover the sources of these rivers finally, unless one accepts his fixing of the sources at random, applying different criteria for different rivers, to suit his own convenience, whim and taste.' (*Ibid.*)

(Incidentally, there is a slight whiff of contentious nationalism about both this and about Swami Pranavananda's chal-

* Pangtha.

lenges of other European commentators, Charles Sherring, for instance – residues, perhaps, of the old political activism. Nevertheless, he must also have been deeply fascinated by things European to have dabbled so deeply in scientific research, though he subsequently seemed obliged to prove that native Indians could outdo the Europeans at their own games.)

The Swami's researches at the sacred lakes apparently began during his twelve-month sojourn at Thugolho in 1936–7, when he studied their freezing and thawing. It must have been exceedingly chilly work, for at one time the thermometer sank to 50.5° below the Fahrenheit freezing point. He was able to use the ice, however, to cross to the two islands of Rakshas Tal and survey them both. Later, in more benign weather conditions, he continued his researches with the aid of two boats. The first, a three-seater rubber boat called *Janma Bhoomi*, was presented to him by a Bombay well-wisher; he sailed it on Manasarovar in 1946 and also used it to take soundings of the Gauri Kund lake. Meanwhile, the Maharaja of Bhavnagar, Sir Krishna Kumar Sinha, had presented him with a four-seater sailing-cum-motor-boat called *Jnan Nauka*. This was made of galvanized steel and had airtight compartments fore and aft to make it unsinkable. It

18. *Diagram of Swami Pranavananda's soundings of the Gauri Kund Lake*

was not, however, a simple matter to have this craft transported across the Himalayas for, although he had got it as far as Almora by 1942, he had to wait until mid-1947 before he had mustered sufficient funds to have it taken to its destination. It was eventually launched upon the sacred Manasarovar on 17th August 1947, with, so far as can be judged from his own account, no sense of sacrilege on either Swami Pranavananda's part or on that of the spectators watching the event from the shore:

> With the 🕉 and Tri-coloured Cakra and Charkha flags proudly fluttering side by side on the deck, the 'Jnan Nauka' rushed into the turquoise-blues of the celebrated celestial Lake amidst deafening cheers of pilgrims, Tibetans and Bhotia traders. A few soundings were formally taken.
>
> (*Ibid.*)

Times must indeed have changed. A century earlier, heads would surely have rolled!

In 1948–9, the Government of U.P.* made a special grant towards an outboard motor. The Swami's main ambitions with these boats was not only to take soundings but also to locate the thermal springs situated in the bed of Lake Manasarovar and to reach the centre of the lake, said by Tibetans to be inaccessible. When his work was done, Swami Pranavananda planned to leave *Jnan Nauka* at Manasarovar 'for the benefit of future pilgrims and tourists'. In a similarly public-spirited way, he is reputed to have donated many of the Tibetan curios and other items from his 'Kailas-Manasarovar Museum' to the Provincial Museum at Lucknow.

Swami Pranavananda must indeed have been a unique individual, apparently able to combine Eastern Spirituality and the Western Scientific Outlook without experiencing any kind of internal conflict. One moment he is detailing cold, empirical data or giving precise numerical specifications, the next he is quoting Walter Bagehot or soaring off into a giddy effusion about the aesthetic delights or the mystical power of the landscape. Then he can abruptly come down to earth again

* Uttar Pradesh.

and dispassionately debate the possibilities for the future commercial development and exploitation of the sacred region. He can look forward with equanimity to a day when a 'Kailas-Manasarovar Air Company' begins operating flights from airfields on the plains of Barkha, and when an 'All-India Kailas-Manasarovar Club' inaugurates boat and launch trips on the sacred lakes. He can even go so far as to moot a mountaineering expedition to the Holy Kailas itself – 'if such a venture be at all allowed by the conservative, superstitious and suspicious Tibetans'.

Although those who kindly write in his favour in the introductions and forewords to his books naturally claim that Swami Pranavananda was well-known and even loved in the sacred region – on account of his high spirituality and the fact that he also maintained a 'Free Travelling Dispensary' through which he gave medical aid to rich and poor alike – it may well be that he was not in fact without his critics, as Lama Govinda suggests in the following letter to the author, dated 11th January 1981:

I met Swami Pranavananda in Almora and Calcutta, but he refused to come to my camp, though we sent a messenger to him. But he did not dare leave the monastery, because he was afraid of robbers. He was not much appreciated by the Tibetans, for whose religion and tradition he had not much understanding. He even planned to make the holy-Manasarovar-lake into a pleasure resort with motorboats and the like. The Tibetans regarded this as a desecration and his discovery of the sources of the Brahmaputra, Indus and Sutlej were already forestalled by Sven Hedin, who described the Manasarovar in glowing terms.

Swami Pranavananda may still be alive today, though advanced in years – around eighty-five years old. Shri Uma Prasad Mookerjee of Calcutta, who himself made a Kailas pilgrimage in 1935, met him in the same year and used to meet him often for several years thereafter. In a letter to the author of February, 1981, he says that he has not heard of him for the last two or three years. He was able, however, to provide the Swami's last known postal address – in the Kumaon district of

northern India, in the Himalayan foothills – but a letter sent
there evinced no reply.

Dr. Sálim Ali,* the noted ornithologist of Bombay, who
made an 'ornithological pilgrimage' to the Kailas region in
1945, meanwhile writes:

> I met Swami Pranavananda for the first time since 1945 at an
> official ceremony in New Delhi in 1976, where both he and I
> were receiving civil awards from the President of India. Unfortu-
> nately, there was little time to talk, and I don't know where he is
> now. In all my travels in Western Tibet, he was the only rational
> and science-orientated man I came across!
>
> (Letter to the author; March 1981.)

The rest is silence – the vast silence of the desolate wastes of
the Tibetan plateau, where, unseen by Western eyes, the
silvery dome of Mount Kailas still rises from beyond the
turquoise waters of Lake Manasarovar: a scene which Swami
Pranavananda knew and wrote about so lengthily and
lovingly. Wherever he is, what ever has become of him – *Peace
be unto him!*

PROFESSOR GIUSEPPE TUCCI

In the summer of 1935, the distinguished Italian scholar,
Professor Giuseppe Tucci, visited the sacred mountain during
an expedition to Western Tibet; he was accompanied by Navy
Medical Captain Eugenio Ghersi.

Tucci, arguably the foremost Tibetologist of modern
times, is a man whose deep knowledge of the history and

---

* Dr. Sálim Ali, a self-confessed materialist, sceptical of all religion,
writes in the same letter of his own reasons for travelling to the Kailas
region and his responses to the sacred mountain: 'My chief motive for
visiting Mt. Kailas and Lake Manasarovar was to study the ecology,
behaviour, breeding and biology of the birds of that high elevation, many
of which we know only as winter migrants in the Indian subcontinent. I
must confess that the sight of Mt. Kailas produced no different spiritual
response to what I feel at the sight of any other, maybe less holy,
Himalayan giants – for example, Nanda Devi or Kanchenjunga – a mixed
feeling of ecstasy at their supreme majesty and indescribable grandeur.'

prehistory of the land, its art, culture and languages, is informed by an equally deep sympathy with the spiritual life of the place. According to the distinguished Anglo-German scholar, Dr. Edward Conze, who worked with him, Tucci was 'also a believing and to some extent even practising Buddhist'. Dr. Conze adds that Tucci believed that he had been a Tibetan in a former incarnation, and that this fact accounted for his friendly reception by the 'normally suspicious Tibetans'. Whatever the substance of these matters, it is certain that Tucci came to Kailas as something very much more than a mere scholar. The fact that there was spiritual sympathy and sensitivity there too enabled him to accumulate invaluable information about the sacred mountain during the latter phase of its religious heyday, information which no other Kailas pilgrim or traveller with the possible exception of Lama Govinda could have acquired. Tucci understood the iconography he encountered; he knew what ascetics were trying to achieve in their particular practices; he could read sacred texts; he could detect in remains and ruins the residues of political and religious traditions that were current long before the Lhasa authorities brought this corner of Western Tibet under their control, or even before Buddhism became the prevalent religion – residues, in fact, of the times when this part of the world fell within the domains of independent kings and when Bon shamans and the luminaries of the folk religion were the arbiters in matters spiritual.

Just how Tucci managed to make himself *persona grata* with the Lamaist authorities it has not been possible to find out, but evidently, between 1927 and 1949, he did travel extensively in Tibet with their cognisance and even their co-operation, and was able to bring away large quantities of texts, art objects and artefacts for later study. Sherpa Tensing, the conqueror of Everest, who was with Tucci on a later expedition to Lhasa and central Tibet, maintained that he had purchased 'whole libraries' and altogether came away with a total haul amounting to some 40 *maunds* – 3,300 lb. – of books. Clearly expeditions on this scale were a costly proposition, but then Tucci was a very rich man – 'a man of outstanding wealth, social position and power' (Conze). His work was also generously financed during this period by the Mussolini government, though beyond photographing his porters making the Roman salute, Conze does not believe that Tucci helped to forward the cause of Fascism to any extent.

Tucci's party reached the shores of Rakshas Tal on 7th July, having set off from Almora on 6th June and travelled by way of the Lipu Lekh, Kojarnath and Taklakot. He duly noted the characteristic atmosphere of depression haunting the western lake, and did not prolong his stay there, but was soon travelling over hillocks and ridges in the direction of Manasarovar. The sight of the rippling turquoise waters of the eastern lake formed a contrast and relief to the unremitting desolation prevailing all around. He observed, however, that few Tibetan and Indian pilgrims were still prepared to undertake the lengthy and difficult business of a Manasarovar *parikrama*, most being satisfied to take a brief dip and leave the matter at that. This struck Tucci as highly significant. It indicated to him a shift of pre-eminence away from the Lake of Brahma, the Creator, to the Mountain of Shiva, who is many things in Hindu mythology: Destroyer, Great Ascetic, and the Lord of the Dance. Esoterically this shift signified a move away from preoccupation with the creative energies of the universe to one with death and the cycles of continual renewal. Indians and, apparently a little less so, Tibetans had come to despise rebirth in the Paradise of Brahma – or indeed in any heaven or hell, because like all other forms of existence they are subject to the Law of Impermanence and must pass. Peace, ultimate peace, could only be found in the deathless: in *Nirvana*.

Tucci decided to resist latterday laxness, however, and to make a Manasarovar *parikrama*. Arriving at Giu *gompa*, which he found to be built over a cave associated with the great guru Padmasambhava, he left the bulk of his baggage there before setting off. He visited all eight of Manasarovar's *gompa* but found their contents and inmates unimpressive in the main, and the *gompa* themselves of unexpectedly recent provenance. None seemed more than two or three hundred years old, indicating that Buddhists had not long to come to live on these shores permanently. Indeed, it was probably the fact that the sacred lake had for so long been venerated by Hindus that had ultimately prompted Buddhists to add it to their roster of sacred places. Certainly pilgrims from India had been making their way to Manasarovar at least since the Heroic Age, for the great epic, the *Mahabharata*, repeatedly sings in praise of its sanctity.

But Tucci's *parikrama* was not a sedate spiritual-scholarly progress. For two days his party was attacked by violent storms that delayed its progress. Mighty winds brought monsoon rains lashing down upon their heads; the waters of the sacred lake were whipped up into violent waves, and the summit of Kailas was shrouded in thundercloud, while deep, ominous rumbles broke constantly near its southern side and resounded along the valleys and ravines of the Gurla range.

And then *dacoits*. They had first been reported at Bunti, and then confirmed at Seralung. The band, reputedly led by a man of noble birth, had been raiding extensively in the vicinity. A little perversely, Tucci found the prospect of an encounter exciting: offering a welcome relief to the boredom that had set in as he had travelled in the monotony and silence of that lakeside wasteland. The herders, merchants and pilgrims camped around Trugo (*lit*: 'door to the bath') *gompa* were not so unperturbed, however. They spirited all their possessions inside the *gompa*, confident that the *dacoits* would not wish to invoke the wrath of the unseen powers by violating that sanctuary. Even a high official retired inside the monastery walls for protection. As confrontation-hour inexorably approached, preparations were made. Tucci's party had a number of weapons but only Tucci and Ghersi knew how to use them.

At six o'clock on 17th July, the *dacoits* appeared over the horizon. There were about thirty of them, wearing sheepskin coats and long pointed hats. Mounted, they drove before them the herds of yak, sheep and horses they had seized during their recent depradations. They were armed with the usual long muzzle-loaders that are fired by lighting a fuse and retiring.

At the crucial moment, it was the expedition's cine camera that proved to be their decisive weapon. When Ghersi mounted it upon its tripod, took aim and began to turn the handle, the hearts of those formidable desperadoes were filled with abject terror and they took to headlong flight. Tucci put this down to the same superstitiousness that would have prevented the *dacoits* from invading a *gompa*. Indeed, to any ordinary Tibetan of this and earlier periods, the world was suffused with demonaic, divine and semi-divine powers in which they lived in fear and awe. The advent of Buddhism did little to change this disposition; indeed, in Tibet as elsewhere, Buddhism accommodated itself very largely to such beliefs and the practices of exorcism, divination, and propitiation that they spawned, and absorbed many of them. There was a similar complementary process on the other side: Buddhist elements entered and modified the other, older religious traditions of Tibet. Thus in his definitive work, *The Religions of Tibet*, Tucci is able to identify three separate living religious traditions, all fruitfully interacting: Buddhism, the Bon religion, and also a *folk religion* practised very largely by the ordinary people, varying from place to place, and liberally endowed with 'multifarious and all encompassing pre-Buddhist beliefs'. It was undoubtedly the deep-seated fears rooted in the superstitious pre-Buddhist folk religion that manifested themselves when the *dacoits* saw Ghersi's cine camera. Here was probably a piece of magical apparatus capable of enslaving the vital spirit – thus exit the *dacoits*, frantically pummelling their horses' flanks.

The *dacoits* were not the only ones to be impressed by the quasi-magical 'powers' apparently possessed by the Europeans. Thereafter, Tucci's party attracted numerous timid souls from among the ranks of the Indian pilgrims, some of whom had already suffered at the hands of the *dacoits*. Subsequently, he was never without an entourage craving protection.

One Indian who did not lose his nerve was the celebrated *sadhu* (holy man), Bhumananda, who instead of bolting into a *gompa* had sedately retired to a grotto on the shores of Manasarovar, where Tucci later encountered him, seated on the vocational tiger-skin and attended by two devotees. Instantly on meeting, the Italian became aware of a deep affinity: a sympathy emanating from the subconscious level – far more than ordinary friendship. Thereafter they would travel together, and Tucci looked forward to learning a great deal from this living repository of the ancient spiritual traditions of India.

Back at Giu to recover his baggage, Tucci witnessed the cremation of a Nepalese pilgrim woman who had just died. There were no tears, no lamentations; she had merely quit one life for another and had been fortunate to do so on this most auspicious of grounds. The sounds of sacred songs filled the silence of the infinite wastes: the reflection of red flames glimmered on the sacred waters.

Tucci's Manasarovar *parikrama* had taken him ten days to complete, though he noted ruefully in his journal that practitioners of *lung gom*, an esoteric yoga endowing its adepts with the power to cover enormous distances by means of long, floating strides while in a state of trance, could accomplish as much within a single day.

Thereafter the Italian turned northwards and began to traverse the great grasslands beyond the sacred lakes. Increasingly he was made aware of the vast spiritual resonance of the place. Here surely the Divine – call it by what name you will – had left its signature. The prevailing desolation and immensity somehow had a unique capacity to put man in contact with the eternal. The earth was an altar, the sky a vault, and the pillar of the sacred mountain joined them. It was not hard for him to appreciate on this evidence why so many great mystics had been produced from among the

19. Brónton (or Bromston)

nomadic herders who grazed their beasts on these grassy plains. Notable among them had been Brónton (alternatively Bromston, A.D. 1005–64; see *Fig. 19*), the pupil of the Indian master, Atiśa, who had played such a large part in the second diffusion of Buddhism in Tibet. Traditions maintain that Buddhism was originally introduced to Tibet around the seventh century A.D., simultaneously from Nepal and China, during the reign of King Songtsen gampo. However, in the ninth century it was all but obliterated during a savage persecution waged by one Glangdarma, and it was not until the eleventh century that a new generation of teachers, translators and proselytizers appeared to restore and reform what had in the interim fallen into decadence as well as decline. This decadence, Professor Tucci maintains, set in due to the teachings of the Tantras having been 'taken in a grossly exoteric and literal sense, not according to the esoteric interpretation'. Atiśa, along with Rinchen zangpo and Marpa (Milarepa's teacher) were of this new generation, and indeed the Kailas area was the scene of great activity during this period of Buddhist regeneration.

At Darchan, the general spiritual fervour began to intensify. There were all manner of people here: folk from India and the foothills, nomads from distant provinces of Tibet, rich merchants from Lhasa, ascetics, brigands, Bon-po, Hindus and Buddhists of every school. Equal faith and devotion had brought them thither and united them in a single spirit that transcended all divergences and controversies.

Having called on the local Bhutanese official, Tucci pitched camp near the Hindus. Their numbers were growing all the time, and although they looked undernourished, poorly dressed and emaciated, Tucci clearly saw the power of their faith in their eyes, which had obviously fortified them against all hardships. The need for sleep also seemed to have left them, for they chanted together until the early hours of the morning. All seemed to have a guide – not a guide to show them the geographical route but one conversant with the uncharted depths of inner space. These were not the phoney, degenerate *sadhus* so often encountered on the plains, but men of genuine spirituality. Each was the spiritual centre of the small group with which he travelled and by his devotees was regarded as an embodiment of spiritual truth – in a sense, as cosmic consciousness itself. Such men knew the true significance of the sacred mountain – as Bhumananda explained to Tucci:

> God is here within us . . . and not there on the mountain: the mountain is no more than a heap of stones. But people cannot raise themselves instantly to the heights of our contemplation: the life of the spirit is an ascent – some begin from a long way off, some from nearby; but though the paths are various – and must of necessity be various, since men think, understand and feel in varying ways – though the paths are various, the point of arrival is one alone.
>
> (G. Tucci, *Santi e Briganti nel Tibet Ignoto*)

Each evening, dressed in orange, Bhumananda would sit on his tiger skin before his devotees as they sang their sacred songs to accordion accompaniment and recited repetitious litanies in which the name of a god was repeated over and over again with accumulating exaltation until all were intoxicated with religious feeling. By contrast, Bhumananda would remain immobile, eyes focussed inwards in meditation, breath almost imperceptible. He seemed to have passed out of his body into another world. Tucci realized that for him the spiritual world was as real as the material world is for other people, and just as they would think him mad to throw away what small time is allowed him on earth in pursuit of spiritual goals, the ascetic would equally pity those who trade their chance of the bliss that can only be attained by following the spiritual life for the vain pursuit of worldly desires.

And so to his own Kailas *parikrama*, during which Tucci visited all of the *gompa* of the sacred mountain, catalogued their libraries, studied their statuary and pictures and himself collected a large number of Buddhist and Bon-po artefacts and manuscripts.

His first port of call was Gyangtrag (Gengta), one of the two *gompa* on the southern side of Kailas. Cloud obscured the surrounding mountain heights and snow fell as he climbed the steep ridge to the *gompa*, which was set in a spectacular amphitheatre of rock and seemed part of the single upthrust of the earth that had produced the eminence upon which it was situated. Within, amid the usual Tibetan artefacts and arms and armour said to have been taken from Zorawar Singh's Dogra soldiers, he found memorabilia of Indian *sadhus* who, apparently, had a special predilection for the place. The keepers spoke with deep respect of two in particular: Ananda Singh, who had for many years lived there, like the guru-poet Milarepa, taking no other food than herbs and nettles; and a nameless ascetic who had lived entirely naked at the foot of the *gompa* practising *tumo*, the yoga of the psychic heat. This produces great inner warmth in the practitioner, even in the coldest of climates, and may be tested by placing wet cloths on the body and noting how long it takes for them to dry through.

Tucci's second *gompa* was Nyandi (Chocu); the weather was freezing and cloud again obscured the surrounding mountain heights, though just before midday the wind tore a rent in them through which the sacred cone of Kailas was momentarily visible, sparkling in sunlight in the upper air. The library and paintings at Nyandi Tucci found to be of little significance, and only one lama was in attendance, his confrères having descended to Darchan. Tucci reflected that with the onset of the bitter Tibetan winter, the lamas would have to shut themselves off within the well-protected walls of the *gompa* and hug closely to the fire till summer. They might do nothing or study the life of a great saint . . . or just while away the long hours of boring solitude with dice. Clearly many of them were lesser men, not capable of maintaining the high standards of religious practice set by their ancient mentors.

Diraphuk (Tithipu) Tucci found to have been built over a cave where Coxampa, one of the masters of the Drugpa school, had pursued his austerities, in which he had been initiated by Naropa, the teacher of Marpa – who in turn was the teacher of Milarepa. At one time this *gompa* had been the seat of an incarnate lama as well. In ancient Tibet, certain distinguished lamas, including the Dalai Lama, were thought to be *bodhisattvas* – highly evolved spiritual beings who had elected to forgo their own spiritual realization in order to work for the good of other beings. Thus they would return time and time again to the world of suffering to continue their altruistic and compassionate endeavours. Continuous lineages from one birth to another could be traced, and special oracles and divinations had been developed to help locate each new incarnation. Those seeking a reborn *tulku* (incarnation) might, for instance, go to a place indicated by the oracle priests and there begin to look for particular signs. Finally, when they had located the possible new incarnation, they could apply tests – such as showing the baby personal objects used by the previous incarnation. Often children would select the correct objects and discard spurious ones introduced to try to trick them. They might even recognize old acquaintances and begin to behave generally as though they knew who they were and what was expected of them. The *tulku* of Diraphuk had, however, apparently become tired of the endless cycle of incarnations in which he had found himself locked and, renouncing his *Bodhisattva* Vow, had eventually failed to return. A substitute had therefore been sent from Lhasa: a very humble and devout man who received Tucci in his cell and spoke with him.

Tucci also found a printing shop at Diraphuk. Tibetan books consist of long unbound sheets of coarse paper printed by means of wood blocks and retained within heavy wooden boards, the whole being finally wrapped in silk. The Italian scholar was particularly delighted to locate the blocks from which a guide to the sacred region could be printed. This outlined the history, geography, religious and mythological associations of the sacred region, and was obviously a kind of spiritual baedeker. He carried paper with him and so was able to commission a copy for his own study purposes.

The final *gompa* which Tucci visited during his *parikrama* was Zunthulphuk (Zuprul), which he found to be also attached to the Drugpa sect. It was a modest building of comparatively recent origin and owed its importance to the association with Milarepa. It contained a stucco statue of the great *guru*, who was posed in characteristic fashion, hand to ear, singing one of his myriad songs. Silver lamps and votive objects had been placed upon the adjacent altar; also copper and bronze goblets, which the monks changed religiously every day. These lamas were not, in Tucci's view, men of the same spiritual calibre as their mentor; the Italian noted that their religious ardour had atrophied to the cold conventionality of monastic life – and they eyed his money offering with unseemly keenness.

Tucci entered fully into the spirit of the *parikrama* and was clearly moved by it. He noted the places of auspicious association and also observed the palpable piety of his fellow circumambulators, Buddhist, Hindu and Bon-po alike. Even the dogs, regarded as spiritually-endowed beings themselves, followed their masters around. The whole landscape around the sacred mountain was clearly not of this world but a thoroughly spiritualized landscape: an earthly projection of the cosmic mandala, no less. As he stood in the blast of the wind at the Dolma La, amid the great rock and the various prayer-flags and relics, he reflected upon the truth of Radhakrishna's dictum that it is good to kneel where others have knelt before because the Divine is present in those places. Academically, his tour drew him to the conclusion that Kailas must have been a sacred mountain since the dawn of history. Long before the advent of Buddhism, it had been venerated by the Bon-po, but its importance in more recent times was certainly due to the influence of the Kargyu school and the association with Milarepa, who had succeeded to the leadership of the school, after the death of his own teacher – Marpa – the founder of the school. As regards its Tibetan name, *Tise*, he was of the opinion that this derived from an ethnic substratum of great antiquity, possibly from the ancient languages of Guge, a vanished independent kingdom which had once had its capital at Tsaparang in the Upper Sutlej valley to the south-west of the Kailas region.

A fresh influx of pilgrims arrived in Tarchan from India on the night that Tucci completed his circuit. The echoes of their ecstatic hymns to Lord Shiva filtered through the canvas of his tent. Rising to the sky in one concerted sound, they seemed to express the universal cry of an anguished humanity: a cry of pain and dissatisfaction with this impermanent life, and a consequent longing for the eternal. Of course, by and large ordinary religious are not able to grasp the notion of a purely formless Absolute so they need the tangible symbol of the god with his topknot, trident and ash-smeared body. Behind the symbolic form, however, lurks that great formless reality:

> I bow to the most exalted Lord, God made manifest, the total cessation of all activity, who is everywhere, who pervades all things. He is Brahma, he is the sacred revelation. Hail to Him, the essence of the Absolute, free of attributes, beyond imagination, beyond all desire; pure mind, filling infinte space.
>
> Hail to him who is without form, but who is the source of all that has form, the fourth dimension of the Spiritual. Hail to the King of the mountain, who transcends speech, understanding and the senses. In his fearful aspect he spells death to the king of death; in his merciful aspect, by making himself accessible to us through his attributes, He takes us beyond Phenomenal existence.
>
> (*Ibid.*)

On 26th July, Tucci's party left Tarchan to pursue its journey to Ladakh by way of Dulchu and Tirthapuri. They were in Gartok on 1st September and reached Leh just over a month later.

At the time of writing, Professor Tucci is still alive and is head of I.S.M.E.O. – the Instituto Italiano per il Medio Estremo Oriente – which has its headquarters in the Palazzo Brancaccio in Rome.

LAMA ANAGARIKA GOVINDA

Our last Kailas pilgrim is also, so far as is known, the last westerner to have personally visited the sacred region. He is (for at the time of writing he is still alive, though in poor health, for which he is receiving medical attention in California), a very cosmopolitan character: born in the former kingdom of Saxony in 1898 of a German father and a Bolivian mother; a writer, artist and spiritual seeker; widely travelled and eventually, in Burma in 1928, an *anagarika* – literally, a 'homeless one' – a Buddhist monk eschewing both the security of the monastic life and the comforts of that of the householder in order to seek truth in his own way:

Mine was the way of the Siddhas: the way of individual

experience and responsibility, inspired by the living contact between Guru [teacher] and Chela [disciple] through the direct transference of power in the act of initiation.

(Lama Anagarika Govinda, *The Way of the White Clouds*)

In 1931, he also became a lama.

His unattached spiritual wanderings took Lama Govinda several times to Central, Southern and Western Tibet. He was able to convince the authorities of the sincerity of his wish to study Tibetan Buddhism, for he was not a covert traveller but carried proper authorization papers (*lamyiks*). He regards all his Tibetan journeys explicitly as *pilgrimages* rather than ordinary travels, for a pilgrimage –

> does not follow a laid-out plan or itinerary . . . does not have a fixed inner or outer purpose, but . . . carries its meaning in itself, by relying on an outer urge which operates on two planes: on the physical as well as on the spiritual plane. [It is] a movement not only in the outer, but equally in inner space, a movement whose spontaneity is that of the nature of all life, i.e. of all that grows continually beyond its momentary form, a movement that always starts from an invisible inner core.
>
> (*Ibid.*)

A great expositor of Tibetan Buddhism to the West, Lama Govinda's special interest to our present field of study lies in his capacity to trace the underlying esoteric aspects of the sacred mountain and its lakes, and of his pilgrimage to them. He visited Mount Kailas in September 1948 in company with his wife, Li Gotami. The principal objective of that journey was, however, to visit the abandoned city of Tsaparang in the Upper Sutlej valley, once the capital of the Kings of Guge, and study the remains of the temples and monasteries founded there by Rinchen Zangpo.

In the account of his pilgrimages to Tibet, *The Way of the White Clouds*, Lama Govinda splendidly elucidates the special qualities of sacred mountains in general. Some mountains are just mountains, he maintains, but others are more: they have personality, and hence the power to influence people. *Personality* in mountains consists in the qualities of consistency, harmony and one-pointedness of character. When personality occurs in a human being it can result in his becoming a great ruler or sage, like the Buddha; when it occurs in a mountain, then it is recognized as a vessel of cosmic power and elevated to the status of a sacred mountain. There is never any need to point this out or argue the case; it is usually quite obvious, and the sole response available is one of worship. To the truly spiritual man, the whole notion of climbing a sacred mountain would be utterly unthinkable. He would want to be conquered *by* the mountain rather than conquer the mountain himself. To achieve his goal he will open himself to the mountain, contemplate it from every point of view and in all its moods and aspects, and thereby approach the very life of the mountain – 'a life that is as intense and varied as that of a human being. Mountains grow and decay, they breathe and pulsate with life. They attract and collect invisible energies from their surroundings.'

But even among these spiritually-charged colossi there are some that soar even higher than the rest to become symbols of the highest aspirations of humanity. They are 'milestones' in the 'eternal quest for perfection and ultimate realization'; 'signposts that point beyond our earthly concerns towards the infinity of a universe from which we have originated and to which we belong. . .'. And the greatest of them all, since the very dawn of time, has been Mount Kailas.

Why has Kailas attained this position of pre-eminence among the world's sacred peaks? For one thing, it lies at the intersection of two of the most important cultures of the world: those of China and of India. It is also the highest point on the great Tibetan plateau: a kind of spire to the Roof of the World. There too arise the four great rivers that, flowing off in the four directions, symbolize the cultural and religious links between India and Tibet. Moreover, two of them – the Indus and the Brahmaputra – clasp northern India like great embracing arms. Then there is the noble isolation of Kailas in the sequestered Transhimalayan range: and finally the regular, architectural quality of its form that irresistibly reminds the beholder of a great temple.

Govinda does not fail to remind us of the spiritual associations of Kailas to both Hindus and Buddhists. To the latter it is the gigantic mandala of the Dhyani Buddhas and

Bodhisattvas 'as described in the famous Demchog Tantra:
the "Mandala of Highest Bliss"'. He also equates Lake
Manasarovar with the Anotatta (or Anavatapta) lake of
Buddhist mythology. Finally, just as every Indian temple has
its water tank in which the pious may bathe, so also Kailas has
its pair of lakes. Govinda ascribes solar and lunar symbolism
to these respectively: Manasarovar is solar, light and masculine; Rakshas Tal is lunar, dark and feminine.

When he deals with the significance of the Kailas pilgrimage, Lama Govinda clearly shows how the trials of the
outward trek across the Himalayas and the crossing of the
high passes into Tibet all represent a kind of chastening
preparation for the ultimate experience of Kailas itself: a kind
of grinding down of the pilgrim's ego – his sense of separate
(and special) individual identity; his sense of 'I' – so that he is
brought to a state of sufficient receptivity. There is an initial
visionary glimpse when at last the high passes are crossed: a
look into a 'country of eternal sunshine' where everything is
totally different from that which the pilgrim has so far
experienced. Then comes the actual descent into Tibet itself,
where 'the vivid colours and chiselled forms of rocks and
mountains stand out in brilliant clearness, divested of any
trace of vegetation, like the world on the first day of creation,
when only heaven and earth were facing each other in primal
unity'. Indeed, the journey through Tibet could actually be
seen as a recapitulation of earlier phases in the evolution of the
world: after bare but beautiful desolation, the pilgrim encounters small patches of green pasture and small fields of yellow
barley, followed by the first simple habitations of primitive
men – cubiform and cave dwellings. A great obstacle then
stands in the pilgrim's way in the shape of the great swastika
massif of Gurla Mandhata. He must cross a high pass
surmounting one of its arms, and thereby go beyond the zone
administered by the *Dzongpon* of Taklakot into the lawless
zone of *dacoits*. The pilgrim may well begin to feel apprehensive at this stage – and with good reason – but as though to
dispel his anxieties and send him forward with refurbished
faith and confidence, he is given a second visionary glimpse:
this time of the shining ice-cone of the sacred mountain itself
'like the full moon in the dark blue sky'. This is just a prelude,

a foretaste of greater things yet to come. When he actually reaches the summit of the Gurla pass all his expectations are exceeded.

> Who can put into words the immensity of space? Who can put into words a landscape that breathes this immensity? – where vast blue lakes set in emerald-green pastures and golden foothills, are seen against a distant range of snow mountains, in the centre of which rises the dazzling dome of Kailas, the "Jewel of the Snows" . . .
> It certainly is one of the most inspiring views of this earth, a view, indeed, which makes the beholder wonder whether it is of this world or a dreamlike vision of the next. An immense peace lies over this landscape and fills the heart of the pilgrim, making him immune to all personal concerns, because, as in a dream, he feels one with his vision. He has gained the equanimity of one who knows that nothing can happen to him other than what belongs to him already from eternity.
>
> *(Ibid.)*

A deep bond of brotherhood unites all those who have been fortunate enough to have these experiences. It is the brotherhood of Kailas pilgrims, and in Lama Govinda's description it almost amounts to a religious order, though one devoid of vows, rituals, dogma and the like. It is shared experience that bonds them; experience that they will carry back with them when they return to the ordinary world and which will be a source of strength and inspiration to them throughout the remainder of their lives, 'because they have been face to face with the eternal, they have seen the Land of the Gods'.

Initial excitement gives place to 'exalted serenity' as the pilgrim proceeds to the shores of Lake Manasarovar. The waters of the sacred lake grade from emerald blue near the shore, through deep blue to purest ultramarine at the centre. Wonderful sunsets take place here when the world is aflame 'with all the colours of fire'. Indeed, everything is bewitchingly beautiful and awe-inspiring, animals know no fear because men do not commit the sacrilege of killing them, and health-giving herbs as well as other salubrious gifts of the gods abound, also precious metals.

By contrast to the benign Manasarovar, which is endowed

with many temples, none have been built on the shores of the neighbouring Rakshas Tal. (According to Swami Pranavananda, Rakshas Tal has one *gompa*: Tsepgye, situated near its north-west corner.) Evidently, the uncannily sombre, even sinister atmosphere that haunts the dark lake has deterred people from building them.

Then Lama Govinda describes how the subtle but irresistible force draws the pilgrim on towards the goal of his pilgrimage: the sacred mountain itself. At most times during the day its ice-dome is obscured by cloud, but it is usually clearly visible in early morning and in the evening, and at those times the pilgrim will reverently bow down to it and repeat his sacred *mantras*. He keeps both eye and mind fixed one-pointedly upon it as he approaches it across the wide, grassy plain that occupies the space between sacred mountain and sacred lakes. When at last he reaches Tarchan, the last outpost of civilization and the place where he will begin his *parikrama*, he begins to feel a joyful tension brewing up inside him. Will he, he wonders, be up to the tremendous mental and physical demands of the great circumambulation?

> Nobody can approach the Throne of the Gods, or penetrate the *mandala* of Shiva or Demchog, or whatever name he likes to give the mystery of ultimate reality, without risking his life – or perhaps even the sanity of his mind. He who performs the *Parikrama* . . . with a perfectly devoted and concentrated mind goes through a full cycle of life and death.
>
> (*Ibid.*)

So the pilgrim knows that during the course of his *parikrama* he will have to confront death. In Zen Buddhism there are traditionally two deaths: ordinary death and the Great Death. The latter is by far the more significant from the spiritual point of view. It is the death of the 'I': the individual ego consciousness, the root of all our delusions and consequent woe and loss of Eden. The pilgrim experiences the 'joyous tension' of which Lama Govinda speaks precisely because it is quite on the cards that he may encounter either or both of these forms of death during the course of his circumambulation.

Ekai Kawaguchi referred to Kailas as a 'natural mandala';

Lama Govinda talks of it in similar vein: as the 'Mandala of Highest Bliss according to the teachings of the Demchog Tantra'. He expounds the mandalic significance of the sacred mountain in wonderful detail, elucidating the esoteric import of the landscape and its colours, and the mythological and religious associations attendant at every stage. As a whole, the *parikrama* represents one turn of the Wheel of Life (see back cover) during which symbolic death and rebirth will be experienced.

The pilgrim sets off from the golden plains of the south in the prime of life. He proceeds into the red western valley, the Valley of Amitabha (the fourth of the Dhyani Buddhas, the Buddha of Infinite Light, personification of Compassion), where the sun is setting. Here the architectural quality of the ruddy rocks makes him feel as if he is passing between rows of gigantic temples adorned with all manner of wonderfully carved ornaments. From above, the ice-dome of Kailas seems to look down upon him from two deep hollows reminiscent of the empty eye-sockets of a skull – and skulls, Lama Govinda reminds us, adorn the terrible aspects of both Shiva and Demchog, reminding us of the transiency of all things.

The northern valley of Kailas is dark and full of intimations of mortality. Here, however, the pilgrim is presented with a magnificent view of the great northern face of the sacred mountain: a sheer rock wall five thousand feet high and flanked by attendant peaks symbolic of Manjushri, Vajrapani and Avalokitesvara.* Here:

> The mountain is so near that it seems to the pilgrim as if he could just walk over and touch it – and at the same time it is intangible in its ethereal beauty, as if it were beyond the realm of matter, a celestial temple with a dome of crystal or diamond. And indeed, to the devotee, it is a celestial temple, the throne of the gods, the

---

* *Manjushri*: one of the Dhyani Bodhisattvas associated with Wisdom; he is often shown carrying the Sword of Wisdom in his right hand, and a volume of the Prajnaparamita literature in his left. (see *Fig. 20*) *Vajrapani*: another of the Dhyani Bodhisattvas, the Wielder of the Diamond Sceptre. *Avalokitesvara, Tib*: Chenresi; *Chin*: Kwan Yin (female aspect), 'the greatly compassionate', a Bodhisattva who became the chief Protector and Patron Deity of Tibet and who manifests in the Dalai Lama.

seat and centre of cosmic power, the axis which connects the earth with the universe, the super-antenna for the influx and outflow of the spiritual energies of the planet. . . .

What the pilgrim sees with the naked eye is only the substructure and emanation of something much more grand and far-reaching. To the Tibetans the mountain is inhabited and surrounded by thousands of meditating Buddhas and Bodhisattvas, radiating peace and bliss, and sowing the seeds of light into the hearts of those who want to liberate themselves from the darkness of greed, hatred and ignorance.

(*Ibid.*)

The pilgrim passes through the portals of death when he crosses the Dolma La pass: the highest point on the *parikrama* and dedicated to Dolma (*Skt*: Tara, the Goddess of Mercy). The ascent to the pass is, according to Lama Govinda, the greatest trial that the pilgrim has to undergo. Here he must shed his 'I', his ego; here too he will encounter the Mirror of Yama, the Lord of Death, in which all his past deeds are reflected. Here too are a couple of rocks between which he must lie in the posture of a dead man to receive the judgement of Yama. He should also think with gratitude of all who have helped him in life but who are now dead, and leave some relic of them behind him before he proceeds on his way towards rebirth.

The new man who proceeds down the other side of the Dolma La into the green valley of Aksobhya can celebrate his resurrection from the dead by bathing in the Gauri Kund Lake – the 'Lake of Mercy', as it is known to the Tibetans. The eastern valley is redolent with associations of the *guru*, Milarepa, who composed at least some of his hundred thousand songs while he was pursuing his religious practices there. The place most strongly connected with him, according to Lama Govinda, is the cave at Zunthulphuk, where there is what is reputed to be a print of his foot in the rock of the roof. Legend has it that when he first went to live in the cave, he found it too low and cramped, so he used his occult power to raise the ceiling. Not knowing the full extent of that power, he pushed too hard and in consequence made the cave too large and draughty, so he had to go above and press it down again – presumably with rather more closely regulated force – until it was just right for comfort.

The rocks in the eastern valley are a 'fairyland of colours', a recapitulation of all the other rocks encountered during the circular route: flaming red, dark blue, vivid orange, bright yellow. Having run the chromatic gamut, the pilgrim finally returns to his starting point, Tarchan, on the margin of the open, sunny plains of the south. The symbolic colour of these plains is gold and their association is with Ratnasambhava, another of the Dhyani Buddhas, known as 'The Jewel Born' or 'The Compassionate Giver'. Here too there are many *mani* walls, which are composed of stone tablets upon which the sacred *mantra*, *Om mani padme hum*, has been carved. The pilgrim should rightly add a tablet of his own to one of these, as a token of his gratitude for the blessings conferred upon him during his *parikrama*. If he has been especially fortunate, he may not only have seen the various aspects of the sacred mountain itself, all of them stunningly beautiful in their various ways, but he may also have been treated to a splendid vision of the deity or ideal of his heart, 'be it in the divine forms of Shiva and Parvati, or of Buddhas and Bodhisattvas, or any other significant symbol connected with this place and its compelling atmosphere'. He also adds a stone for the benefit of those who will come after him.

Finally, Lama Govinda concludes (a little strongly, some might say):

> Only he who has contemplated the divine in its most awe-inspiring form, who has dared to look into the unveiled face of truth without being overwhelmed or frightened – only such a person will be able to bear the powerful silence and solitude of Kailas and its sacred lakes, and endure the hardships and dangers which are the price one has to pay for being admitted to the divine presence on the most sacred spot on earth. . . . It is as if their individual consciousness, which obscured or distorted their views or their conception of the world, were receding and giving place to an all-embracing cosmic-consciousness.
>
> (*Ibid.*)

When, many months after setting off on their final pilgrimage to Tibet, of which their visit to Mount Kailas formed part,

Lama Govinda and Li Gotami crossed the high passes back into India and so 'returned to the world', they did not realize that 'Tibet's hour of fate had struck' and that, except in their dreams, they would never see that magical land again.

'Tibet's hour of fate' is an apt description of the culminating events of the progressive Chinese encroachment, which resulted in the flight of the Dalai Lama from Lhasa in 1959 and with that the effective termination of the old Lamaist régime. During the last thirty years, Tibet has been more effectively sealed off from the outside world than it was even in the old days. No Westerner has set eyes on the sacred mountain and its attendant lakes during the intervening period, and indeed, since the Sino-Indian agreement allowing for the passage of pilgrim traffic across the border lapsed in 1962, it seems unlikely that any Hindus or Buddhists from the south have seen them either. Whether Tibetan Buddhist or Bon-po pilgrims continue to make the sacred *parikrama* must remain purely a matter for speculation due to insufficiency of information, as must whether the *gompa* of Kailas and Manasarovar continue to operate, or even exist. One would imagine that a vigorously anti-religious but materialistically very energetic communist régime would have effected great changes in the sacred region. . . . Perhaps now that China seems to be relaxing her hitherto xenophobic attitude, Western visitors may again be allowed to travel to Mount Kailas and bring us news of its present condition and circumstances – and especially, whether during the last thirty years it has lost any of its old power and magic. Somehow one doubts that it has: after all, mountains possess the capacity to survive, unscathed, even the most convulsive events of human history; and thirty years in the life of a mountain, especially that of a sacred mountain, is an insignificant flicker of time.

CHAPTER NINE

The Heart of the Matter

Of course, the world knows many other sacred mountains besides Kailas, and indeed there is a whole panorama of religious and semi-religious associations that may become attached to mountains. As J. A. MacCulloch writes: 'There are few peoples who have not looked upon mountains with awe and reverence, or have not paid worship to them or to gods or spirits associated with them in various ways.' And he concludes: 'Sporadically we find no cult of mountains or mountain-spirits, but that is generally where no cult of nature exists, or, of course, where no mountains exist.'

This powerful capacity to sound the deepest resonances in the heart of man must in part at least stem from the large and imposing qualities that mountains possess. 'Their height, their vastness, the mystery of their recesses, the veil of mist or cloud now shrouding them, now dispersed from them, the strange noises which the wind makes in their gorges, the crash of a fall of rock, or the effect of the echo, their suggestion of power, their appearance of watching the intruder upon their solitude – all give them an air of personality, and easily inspire an attitude of reverence and eventually of worship. . .' – MacCulloch again. In short, mountains may impress themselves upon the human imagination as *beings*, necessarily great beings at that, with spiritual properties akin to or even greater than those of man. They may come to be regarded, in fact, as *gods*.

An outstanding example of such a mountain is *Fuji*, that beautifully balanced volcanic cone rising from sea level to rather over 12,000 feet, which has become the symbol of Japan. The subtle and various moods of Fuji have inspired many Japanese artists. The *haiku* poet, Basho, for instance:

> A day when Fuji is unseen
> Veiled in misty winter showers –
> That day, too, is a joy.

And Mushinaro:

> Lo! There towers the lofty peak of Fuji
> From between Kai and wave-washed Saruga.
> The clouds of heaven dare not cross it,
> Nor the birds of the air soar above it.
> The snows quench the burning fires,
> The fires consume the falling snow.
> It baffles the tongue; it cannot be named.
> It is a mysterious god.

Arguably most evocative of Fuji's visual moods is the way it sometimes appears to hover suspended in the middle air, severed from the earth by engirdling mists.

Although declared as a god by Mushinaro, Fuji is also looked upon as the abode of a god (*kami*), to whom there is a shrine on the summit where Shinto priests annually hold religious rites connected with the opening and closing of the mountain. This may exemplify a shift or development that may take place in the religious connotations of mountains, whereby the divinity of the mountain somehow becomes detached from the mountain proper and takes on a connected, but partially autonomous, life of its own. Thus a mountain may cease to be regarded as a god but as the abode of a mountain god.

Mountains may also be seen as the dwelling places of sky or rain gods, or of the great gods in general. Their height and consequent proximity to the skies or heavens, traditionally the dwelling places of 'higher' spiritual beings, naturally invites this kind of role. The most famous example of this to be found within our European heritage is *Mount Olympus*, a 9,551 foot peak spanning the borders of Thessally and Macedonia which, so classical Greek mythology informs us, was set aside to be held in common by the gods when the sons of Cronos drew lots for the partition of the empire of the world. And on Olympus the immortals passed their days in merrymaking and laughter, feasting, supping ambrosia, serenaded by Apollo and the Muses, savouring the aromas wafted upwards from the altars of the world below . . . and eventually, at the end of each day when the torch of sun was doused, retiring for repose in houses built for them with wondrous craft by Hephaestus. Olympus soars in a single sweep above a deeply-flanked plateau. Below, fall wooded slopes furrowed by many torrents – hence 'Olympus of the thousand folds'; above, meanwhile, the main line of the peak is curved in the form of a kind of amphitheatre, the upper tiers of which, often hung with shreds of cloud, have the appearance of gigantic seats set out to accommodate the gods in council under the presidency of great Zeus. When thunder and lightning were loosed about the summit, mortals in the world below knew that the gods were wrathful.

Marco Pallis, however, argues that such classical Greek fancies were strictly for exoteric consumption only. The relationship between the gods and Olympus, he maintains, was essentially symbolic: 'The true Olympus is only discernible by those "who have eyes to see".'

Their capacity to bridge the gulf between the twin spheres of earth and heaven also makes mountains convenient half-way stations where men and gods may meet. Numerous such vital encounters are reputed to have taken place and been duly recorded in the annals of the world's great religions:

And the Lord said unto Moses, Come up to me into the Mount

and be there and I will give thee tablets of stone, and a law and commandments which I have written, that thou mayst teach them. . . . And Moses went up into the Mount and a cloud covered the Mount. And the glory of the Lord was upon *Mount Sinai* and cloud covered it six days; and the seventh day the Lord called Moses out of the midst of the cloud. And the glory of the Lord was alike a devouring fire on the top of the Mount in the eyes of the Children of Israel. And Moses went into the midst of the cloud and gat him into the Mount; and Moses was in the mountain forty days and forty nights. . . .

(Exodus, 24)

Indeed, the Jews of old seem to have been highly impressed with the spiritual power of mountains. 'I will lift up my eyes to the hills, from whence cometh my help,' sang the Psalmist, David, who himself spent a lot of time at the heights, at first as a shepherd boy and later when he was on the run from King Saul. *Horeb*, *Nebo*, *Zion*, *Carmel* and *Moriah* are other mountains accorded religious veneration in the Bible; *Jerusalem*, meanwhile, is '*God's Hill*' and the *Dome of the Rock* is venerated by Jews and Muslims alike.

Christians, on the other hand, venerate their 'Skull Hill', *Golgotha*, where Christ was crucified; esoterically it is to them the spiritually 'highest' place on earth and hence by virtue of the homology of the material and the spiritual must logically also be the physically highest one. A similar status, backed up by similar thinking, is accorded by the followers of Islam to the black rock known as the *Ka'ba* in the city of Mecca, which is kissed as part of the orthodox *Hajj*, the great pilgrimage that every true Muslim is required to make to the holy city. Another *Hajj* rite involves circling two small mountains or beacons of God called *Safa* and *Marwah*, upon which heathen idols were situated until dethroned by the prophet Mohammed. It was to the mountains adjacent to Mecca that Mohammed began to withdraw for meditation and prayer around the year 610 A.D., the direct result of which was his fateful encounter with the Angel Gabriel in a cave upon *Mount Hira*, when he felt himself seized by the neck by an overpowering force, and given dictation of the *suras* of the Holy *Koran*. Finally, mention should be made of a popular Muslim belief that the world is bounded by an outer range of curtain mountains: the *Qāf*.

Somewhat further east, the *Elburz Mountains*, which rise in Iran just north of the capital, Teheran, and run for some 600 miles in extent, have long been spiritually significant for local peoples. They were identified with *Haraberezaiti*, an axial mountain lying at the centre of the world and linking earth and sky. 'The sun and stars revolved around it; light came from it and returned there; on it, was no light or darkness, no cold, no wind, no sickness; on it, Amesha Spentas built a dwelling for Mithra, and he looks upon all the material world from it; below it was the Chinvat bridge. . . . 'According to Zoroastrian belief, on the other hand, all the mountains of the world sprouted from the Elburz – rather like runners, one presumes. It was on one of their peaks that the avatar Ahura Mazda revealed the law; indeed, Ahura is 'him who goes to the lofty mountains', and the mountains vivify his creation and oppose the antithetical forces of Ahriman ranged against him. The highest peak of the Elburz is the 18,600 foot *Demavend*, itself liberally endowed with all manner of religious and mythological associations. The epic writer of the *Shahnama* records how the tyrant Zohak was overthrown by Feridun and allowed to die in chains in a cavern on the slopes of the mountain. The heroes Jemshid and Rustem are also reputed to have been habitués of Demavend, and legend even associates the mountain with the final settling of Noah's Ark after the subsidence of the waters of the Great Flood – though this claim would be challenged by the partisans of the none-too-distant *Mount Ararat*, a fine, symmetrical peak rising gracefully from the arid floor of the earth in the north-east corner of Turkey, not far from where the border converges with those of Iran and the USSR.

The capacity of mountains to link earth and heavens, the twin spheres of men and gods, also serves to make their summits ideal situations for altars, shrines and temples. Many a mountain-top monastery in modern Greece, for example, stands where once an old mountain-shrine was located. Indeed, in places where suitable eminences do not naturally occur, man has repaired the deficiency himself – with his own hands. The *ziggurats* of ancient Babylon were nothing less than man-made mountains seven storeys high, with an apartment on the summit reserved for the local deity. On festive occasions the god might descend from here to his city to receive worship and petitions and to dispense benefits. The *teocalli* of ancient central America are another example of the same sort of phenomenon, and we have already elsewhere mentioned the great *stūpa*-temple at Borobodur, which was a man-made Mount Meru. Many another – and far less spectacular – mound or tump may have been created for similar purposes, perhaps even our own enigmatic Silbury Hill. Mention has also been made elsewhere of the fact that certain buildings (as opposed to solid constructions like pyramids or mounds) are endowed with mountain symbolism: the Hindu temple, for example.

Mountains are also universally associated with the dead – again perhaps in the first instance because they were buried upon their slopes and summits, from where it was thought they might most directly rise to world above. In time, however, negative associations might set in: fear of the presence of ghosts or of monsters, or even of the forces of the powers of evil – responses that the ominous moods of mountains and their darker, heavier characteristics might well tend to compound. Many a European mountain is disgraced with a diabolical name – *Eiger* (Ogre), *Teufelsberg, Monte Disgrazia, Les Diablerets* – and there was once a time when the regular falls of rock from the summit of the *Matterhorn* were thought to be direct action by the Devil himself. A sinister 'Grey Man' haunts the mists of the Scottish *Ben McDhui*, while the *Himalayas* will never again be free of the unsettling presence of the vast-footed *yeti*,* which at any time may come charging from the snowy heights to carry off some forlorn Sherpa maiden in its great hairy arms, or beat to death some hapless traveller caught out at the heights with no means of escape.

The dead need not always arouse the fears of the living, however. Indeed, in the noblest of them the deepest hopes and aspirations of a people may reside. In many traditions – the

---

* There are, apparently, two types of yeti: the larger yak-eating variety, and the smaller man-eater.

Celtic, Teutonic, Slavic – a great hero like Arthur, Fionn, Merlin or Bruce, lies asleep in the heart of some hill or mountain, whence to re-emerge sometime in the future to 'renew all things sublunar'. In Hindu tradition, on the other hand, the souls of the sainted dead are thought to go and live on *Himavat*, while ancient Chinese Taoist mythology maintained that they repaired to the dwelling place of the immortals, one of two Chinese heavens, which was situated in the *Kunlun Mountains*. Here the Lady Queen of the West held court in a fabulous nine-storey palace of jade, around which were magnificent gardens in which the peaches of immortality took their 3,000 years to ripen. Needless to say, these were totally forbidden fruit to any but those who had lived thoroughly virtuous lives. As on Olympus, the denizens of this Chinese heaven enjoyed a continual round of banqueting and pleasure.

The Chinese have traditionally displayed themselves highly sensitive to the natural world and keenly aware of the deeper qualities and dispositions inherent in natural phenomena like features of landscape and climate. The accumulation of their wisdom in such matters is systematized in their geomantic doctrines (*feng shui*), where the special effects of the presence or absence of a mountain in a landscape are delineated, and in the *I Ching* or *Book of Changes*, where the hexagram associated with *Mountain* is *Kên*, alternatively called *Keeping Still*. The symbolism of *Kên* is full of intimations of meditation. It is a state of strong immoveability; of perfect balance, male above and female below; a state in which all motion hangs suspended, not in death or inertia but in that great stillness that is the origin and resolution of all things. Like a great meditating sage, a mountain sits with strong solidity upon the surface of the earth, quietly accumulating massive protean energies. Within the context of the old Chinese state, furthermore, the Emperor was seen as discharging a function analagous to that of the *axis mundi* or world mountain. He mediated with Heaven on behalf of his people. Not surprisingly, therefore, the axial mountain formed an essential decorative feature of the border of the robe he wore on ritual occasions.

Old China abounded with sacred mountains and every year

hordes of pilgrims resorted to them, often journeying together down the pilgrim roads in groups under the banner of the pilgrim club.to which they belonged. In their hands they clutched little bundles and ritual bags; also the obligatory thermos flasks and umbrellas. The old Chinese term for pilgrimage was in fact 'journeying to a mountain and offering incense'. The hallowed slopes and cloud-hidden summits of the sacred peaks were liberally endowed with wonderful temples and shrines, guest halls, pagodas, and rock-cut statues and inscriptions, which the pilgrims toured in appropriate order, mounting the particularly steep places perhaps by means of specially-cut stairs or chainways. The poor travelled under their own devices; the better off might be carried in slings or *palanquins*, or borne in the arms of stout-hearted bearers. Their motivation for making these pilgrimages might not seem very high-minded to us: to gain good luck, or secure an improvement in health or fortune, or to discharge an old penance. A genuine religious element was rarely lacking, however; and the practical disposition of the Chinese enables them to mingle the mundane and the spiritual with greater flexibility than westerners.

Among the Taoists, five 'official' peaks were venerated in particular: *Tai shan, Wu yueh, Hua shan, Heng shan* and *Sung shan*. They were guarded by five Taoist emperors, the most exalted of which was the Great Emperor of the Eastern Peak (Tai-yueh ta-ti), who resided upon *Tai shan* in Shantung province. He was a manifestation or appointee of the Jade Emperor, with special powers over the lives and deaths of mortals, the dispensation of fate and fortune and so forth. In these onerous functions he was assisted by a sizeable and complicated spiritual bureaucracy. The great German Sino-logist, Richard Wilhelm, was deeply impressed by a visit to Tai Shan that took place earlier this century:

It spreads itself with majestic calm over the region, and at its foot springs flow together from various directions. The clouds brood about its summit and it dispenses rain and sunshine over a wide area, because when its head is covered with clouds, which brood above it, then it draws more fog towards itself and the humid winds drive the clouds into cracks and hollows and rain descends upon the land. When it disperses the mists again, exhaling them, in tiny delicate clouds, so that they float gently away and disappear in the blue, the people know the grey days are over. The sun shines again over the fields and at night the great stars flicker in the deep black sky. . . . The vital forces innate in these proceedings, the mysterious clarity of these powers, have always attracted me. . . .

(Richard Wilhelm, The Soul of China)

Chinese Buddhists, on the other hand, bowed their heads in special awe to four 'famous' mountains, each of which was associated with a particular *bodhisattva*: *Omei* in Szechuan (Samantabhadra), *Wu tai* in Shansi (Manjushri), *Chiu-hua* in Anhwei (Kshitigarbha) and *P'u-t'o* (really an island) in Chekiang (Avalokitesvara). Legends and stories flourished in all these places of the presiding *bodhisattva* presenting himself in some unlikely guise to a pilgrim or visitor, so pilgrims tended to be on their guard and to treat all whom they encountered from the most elevated down to the most lowly with special care. Indeed, in all these places, a vivid atmosphere of wonder and magic must have asserted itself in the popular imagination, and in consequence it is not surprising to find reports of all kinds of marvels. John Blofeld, in a captivating account of a visit to *Wu tai shan*, records seeing 'fluffy balls of orange coloured fire, moving through space, unhurried and majestic – truly a fitting manifestation of the divinity!' The *bodhisattva* associated with Wu tai shan was Manjushri, he who wields the sword that slices away delusion; he had often appeared on the sacred mountain in the guise of a monk. Many of these marvels would today of course be accountable in terms of natural phenomena, however. Beyond the great precipice at *Mount Omei*, for instance, a figure might appear in the golden mists of sunrise which the ardent would take to be an apparition of the *bodhisattva* Samantabhadra. Moving forward to meet the *bodhisattva* in a state of exaltation, however, they would plunge into the awful abyss below with fatal results. What they had in fact witnessed was their own shadow, projected with subtle atmospheric trickery.

The religious associations of at least some of the spiritually significant peaks of the world must derive, not so much from the qualities of the mountains themselves, as from the fact that they are associated with particular and noteworthy mystics. In this connexion, one thinks especially of *Arunachala*, a hill near the town of Tiruvannamalai in southern India which in modern times was the home of the great Ramana Maharshi. Maharshi seems to have identified the mountain with the Highest Principle:

> Nandi Said: 'That is the holy place! Of all, Arunachala is the most sacred! It is the heart of the world! Know it to be the secret Heart-centre of Shiva! In that place He always abides as the glorious Aruna Hill!'
>
> (A. Osborn (ed.), The Teachings of Ramana Maharshi, London, 1962)

In fact, mountains have always and everywhere been regarded as ideal places for religious retreats. There, at least, far from the hurly-burly of the everyday world, the solitude necessary for the cultivation of the contemplative life may be found. Thus not only have hermits and *yogis* retired to lonely caves and cells in high fastnesses, but the members of great orders have also gone there to found secluded monasteries. We have already in this book encountered innumerable Asian instances of such things, but they are not lacking elsewhere – even here in homely Europe. We have our *Mount Athos*, our *Monte Cassino*, the high *Mount St. Bernard* monastery, the lofty retreats of the beleaguered Cathar heretics in southern France, *Mont St. Michel* and *St. Michael's Mount* – and a great many others besides.

Moreover, mystical experience is not necessarily the monopoly of dedicated mystics. Even modern-day mountaineers, as a breed not particularly noted for their spirituality, have reported all kinds of mystical or semi-mystical encounters on the heights. These may be incidences of what might be called Nature Mysticism, where exalted states are encountered amid sublime natural surroundings, in situations of great solitude, often when in a hyper-oxygenated or physically stressed condition. Or they may be incidences of Danger Mysticism, where it is the imminent possibility of sudden death that serves to trigger off heightened states. Perhaps indeed, subconsciously, many mountaineers venture into the hills half in search of such experiences. It is at least comforting to know that, even in our spiritually barren age, the mountains are still there, still endowed with a capacity to free the spirit. When in his baleful *Waste Land* Eliot intones, '*In the mountains, there you feel free*' – it is as though he is appealing to a last hope.

Mention of Eliot brings us into the ambit of literature, and here we also find testimony to the spiritual power of mountains. The ominous presences of *Popocatepetl* and its 'wife' *Ixtaccihuatl*, both spiritually resonant peaks in Mexico, loom over the pages of Malcolm Lowry's anguished religious novel, *Under the Volcano*. There the connotations are distinctly hellish, redolent with forebodings of death and damnation, but literature also has its great redemptive peaks. The *Montsalvat* of the Grail literature, for instance, where the golden chalice that is the end and object of the heroic spiritual quest is guarded by dedicated knights. And in Dante's *Divine Comedy*, after the terrible descent into the pits of Hell, spiritual regeneration begins with an ascent of the *Mountain of Purgatory*, upwards, cornice by cornice from the nether realms of the excommunicate and the late repentant via St. Peter's Gate to the Earthly Paradise itself, situated, most significantly, upon the summit.

This is not the first time that we have encountered the graduated stages in the development of the spiritual life likened to the stages of an ascent of a great mountain; in Mount Meru there is another. It is in many ways a natural metaphor. Lost amid the open places of the world, buried in minutiae, unable to see further ahead than our own noses, we are tossed hither and thither by every random event and can attain no lasting sense of who we really are or where we are going. When we begin to climb a mountain, however, things become clearer. Then we disengage from the pressures and pulls of the world, which recedes below us, becoming smaller and hence less threatening. We then reach a stage where we have a clearer perspective: when the full scope and scheme of things can be grasped as a whole and our own place therein identified. Finally, there is a growing sense of having triumphed over confusion, of the possibility of real growth and transcendence.

But is this really the case? There are in fact objections that may be levelled against the vertical model of spiritual development. To rise to the heights is certainly to reach a privileged position and there one may feel suitably superior to those caught up in the turmoil of the world. The vital question, however, is whether we are truly transformed, whether our passions have been properly changed into true wisdom and compassion or whether they are merely resting in abeyance, temporarily out of play but essentially still very much there. In orthodox Buddhist mythology, the fortunate denizens of the cloud palaces of Mount Meru may enjoy great pleasure and freedom from pain for a very long time, but inevitably the sad day must come when the beautiful flowers in their hands begin to wither and their armpits begin to give off odours that make them uncongenial to their *deva* play-mates. Then the bitter season will soon arrive when they too must die. A true leap from the Wheel of Life may not in fact be made from the heights of Meru but only from a human situation, down upon the terrestrial plane, where the passions may be properly encountered, engaged and transformed.

The theme which we have undertaken to investigate here is one of truly vast proportions, and we could range on expansively over the whole surface of the earth accumulating fresh evidences. We could trace the significances of *Adam's Peak* for the people of Sri Lanka, investigate why *Mount Abu* has become such a great place of pilgrimage in Rajasthan, note how the Masai of Africa regard *Mount Kilimanjaro* or the North American Indians *Mount Shasta*; we could unravel the mysteries of the volcanoes of the Hawaiian isles, travel on to the Antipodes, the islands of south-east Asia. . . .

All of which would ultimately serve to so disperse and break up the theme rather than bring it together in final focus for an attempt at a solution of the problem posed in the beginning: namely, what in its highest, fullest manifestations does the great universal symbol of the sacred mountain represent; what great mystery does its heart enshrine. . . ?

★   ★   ★

The matter of the sacred mountain reaches its consummation in the concept of the *axis mundi* or world mountain – a great manifestation of which was *Mount Meru* or *Sumeru*, the linch-pin of the Hindu, Jain and Buddhist world-views, which in past centuries held currency extensively in Asia. The axial mountain crops up in other traditions too: there is the *Haraberezaiti* of the Iranians, the *Himingbjör* of the Germans, the *Tabor* of the Israelites and the *Golgotha* of the Christians. In fact, according to the great historian of religion, Mircea Eliade: 'it is even found among such "primitives" as the Pygmies of Malacca and seems also to be part of the symbolism of prehistoric monuments.' In other traditions again the axis is not represented by a mountain but by a great tree, such as the Sacred Oak of the Druids, the World-Ash of the Scandinavians and the Lime-tree of the Germans. Or by a navel or *omphalos*, as at Delphi in ancient Greece . . . and indeed as is indicated in the etymology of Tabor, *tabbur* meaning 'navel'. All in fact are representations of that profound and potent reality which may be called *The Centre*.

When initially discussing the significance of the Centre, it is useful to distinguish an outward, *exterior* or macrocosmic aspect (the way it occurs in a cosmos or cosmic system) from an *interior*, microcosmic aspect (the way it occurs in man). The old traditions were able to identify fine correspondences or homologies between the microcosmic and the macroscosmic, between man and the universe: 'as above, so below'. As we shall see, however, this is really an artificial distinction, at worst downright misleading, at best merely pragmatic, but useful insofar as it allows us to approach the heart of the matter, where ultimately we will find all distinction and dichotomy resolved – for in essence the Centre is the place of unity *par excellence*.

Externally, in any world system, the Centre represents that one great fixed point against which all measures may be taken and relations drawn. It is like a great surveyor's rod at the heart of things, by its very presence giving coherence and form to that which would otherwise be incoherent and formless. It has the power, in short, to make cosmos out of chaos. It is also the most *spiritual* of places: indeed it is here that divine or spiritual reality impinges upon profane or mundane reality. This being so, it is the 'place' where the gods or higher spiritual realities may be most readily encountered.

Finally, it is the place where creation began – as is suggested by the navel associations. In Tibetan depictions of the cosmos, Mount Meru appears to be the spearhead of what looks like a massive downward thrust of spiritual power or energy. This congeals into matter at the summit of the mountain, and thence proceeds downwards, diminishing as it goes, until it hits the terrestrial level, where it suddenly spins outwards, whirling a vortex of oceans and continents as far as the outer limits.

Paradoxically, while there is and can be only one Centre, there may also be innumerable other 'centres'. This is possible by virtue of its essentially spiritual nature. Being omnipotent, the spirit is splendidly free to manifest itself as and where it wills, even in apparent defiance of normal laws. As Mircea Eliade points out, any vital location may be a 'centre': a temple, a shrine, a palace, a city, the place where some crucial event took place. It is easy to see why this should be so in the case of temples and shrines. Earlier we discussed how the Hindu temple was built upon the model of Mount Meru and hence penetrated by the *axis mundi*, thus spiritual 'power' being drawn into the place and concentrated at its heart. Mircea Eliade extends the argument still more widely and asserts that any construction – not just the palace of a great World Emperor or *Chakravartin* but even the simple *yurt* of a humble Mongolian nomad – insofar as it imitates the created world, is theoretically penetrated by the *axis mundi* and constitutes a 'centre.'

Internally, in man, on the other hand, the Centre represents the spiritual essence, which goes by many names in the various traditions. Hindus call it simply *That* or *Ātman*. In Buddhism it is the Buddha Nature, the Heart; 'the Unborn, Unoriginated, Uncreated, Unformed'. Christians might call it the Christ Nature. To the great German mystic, Meister Eckhart, it was 'the little point' – an apt term, for the Centre is emphatically not a thing, a place, a substance, or indeed anything that may be grasped in a concrete way at all. It is essentially conceptual – Eliot's *still point of the turning world*. Yet for all its elusiveness, it is the origin and goal of all our life and energy; 'the place of creative change', in Jung's account; the great home in which we all dwelt before self-conscious-ness drove us out of Eden and set us ranging through the ten thousand things on our desperate search for that lasting rest and resolution that can only be attained by returning whence we have come.

Nostalgia for the lost Centre initiates the heroic spiritual quest – and here the threads begin to draw together, paths to converge and run increasingly in parallel. The way that the aspirant must travel is notoriously difficult, fraught with all manner of difficulty and danger up to the most extreme. Death is always very much on the cards. And casualties are legion: the margins of the path are said to be lined with the bleached bones of those who have fallen by the wayside. But this is all necessarily so; only the most intense of pressures can secure the most exacting of transformations: initiation from the profane into the spiritual. Finally, for the few who penetrate that far, all paths coalesce in a single goal and realization. He who reaches the Centre of the World reaches his own Centre and finds them one.

Pilgrimages in general, and pilgrimages to sacred Moun-tains like Kailas in particular, might be fairly regarded as, to a greater or lesser extent, representing conventionalized re-enactments of the heroic spiritual quest. As such they combine an outward physical journey through concrete space to a geographically-defined centre, with a concomitant inward spiritual progress. The goal itself – in our case, Kailas – is of little real importance in itself. It may at first *seem* charged with vast significance, be overwhelmingly beautiful, endowed with wonderful supernatural energies and generally replete with all manner of exotic association, but all these qualities merely help serve its essentially pragmatic function of providing a focus for the spiritual aspirations of the pilgrim. As Bhumananda told Professor Tucci, Kailas is really just a heap of stones. What is really important from the spiritual point of view is the journey itself. With its inevitable exposure to hunger, the exigencies of climate, its very palpable dangers (*dacoits*, wild animals, precipitous falls), its constant demands to endure the unendurable with patience and to accept the unacceptable, to curb self-indulgence and face the hazards with equanimity, its all-pervading insecurity – with all this, and with its mitigating joys and diversions, it no doubt amounted to a very effective course of spiritual training such as might elsewhere be applied in a monastery, though there less dramatically and intensively, and thus taking rather longer to achieve similar results.

In her book, *The Catalpa Bow*, Dr. Carmen Blacker describes elaborate mountain pilgrimages to peaks named Haguro and Ōmine in Japan. They are still enacted each year, though nowadays with considerably less rigour than in times past. Here pilgrims are put through what is clearly a carefully worked out programme of spiritual training, being deliberately subjected to a succession of ordeals and endurance tests in a context replete with esoteric Buddhist symbolism and ritual. Unrelenting discipline is applied, and the threat of death is exploited extensively and deliberately. Pilgrims are, for instance, dangled head downwards over yawning precipices; and in the past they were left in no doubt that if they fell by the wayside they would be left to die. Clearly, the ultimate fears need to be invoked in order to bring about that pitch of seriousness that spiritual change requires. Only the man who has been driven to an extreme, in fact, who has lost everything and has nothing left to lose, is ready for the final awakening.

There is no doubt that, if fully realizing its potential, pilgrimage to Kailas could result in a full spiritual awakening. On the other hand, it would be naïve to suppose that anything like a constant procession of enlightened beings came tripping back over the Himalayas from there. The failure rate among those undertaking the spiritual life is notoriously high: 'Many are called, few are chosen'. Nevertheless, it is also inexorably the case that in the spiritual life nothing short of the ideal is really good enough – or in fact amounts to anything at all. One cannot be partially enlightened: it is one thing or the other.

Finally, may we hazard a guess at what lay at journey's end for the rare few among Kailas pilgrims who achieved some sort of spiritual illumination at the sacred mountain?

Here we tread upon especially treacherous ground. The nature of that which lies at the end of the spiritual quest is, in all traditions, said to be beyond the power of words to convey. Indeed, even to attempt to do so is to run the risk of throwing up new proliferations of misleading pictures and ideas, thereby obscuring rather than clarifying the matter. What confronts us here is, in fact, a great mystery that cannot be grasped by the mind – and thereby appropriated to the province of 'I': of the self-aggrandizing ego. The best that we can do therefore is to attempt some general indications – and then chop them ruthlessly away. . . .

The most complete account of an actual spiritual event of some considerable profundity is given us by Bhagwan Shri Hamsa. He describes encountering the physical form of his spiritual master, Lord Dattātreya, on the Gauri Kund lake, and receiving initiation into the Realization of the Self. Although he maintains that words are inadequate to describe the joy he experienced, he is in fact quite specific as to what happened technically. His various faculties merged one with another until finally all merged with Absolute Brahman:

> It was all one harmony – full of Wisdom, Infinite Love Perrennial and Bliss Eternal! Where was the body, its tenements and the 'I' It was all Satchidānanda (Truth, Wisdom, and Bliss).
> (Bhagwan Shri Hamsa, *The Holy Mountain*)

This is clearly a description of a state of consciousness from which all sense of a separate, individual 'I' had vanished, leaving nothing less than – Totality.

Bhagwan was, of course, an orthodox Hindu. Orthodox Buddhists might well aspire to something similar.

Many who pursue the spiritual life do so in despair of the sufferings of *samsara*, the world of illusion, aspiring instead towards some kind of transcendence. And indeed, by the practice of spiritual techniques, it is possible to attain certain spiritual states in which both personal suffering and the suffering of the creation as a whole seem safely transcended. The problem with such beguiling states is that they are, like everything else, subject to the law of impermanence. They must pass, and in consequence cannot constitute a complete and lasting solution to the problem of suffering, which in Buddhism is axiomatic.

Buddhist practice is in fact centrally concerned with *clear-seeing*: with seeing things *as they really are*. The chief impediment to clear seeing is the delusory notion of 'I' that seeks to establish itself in the temporary and unstable combination of elements that comprise what we know as a human being. These elements are undergoing changes all the time, though the greatest and most dramatic is their dispersal at death. Fuelled by the energy of the passions, 'I' is forever devising new schemes for securing and substantiating itself upon the shifting sands of the ever-changing patterns of existence. Thus when Manjushri, the *Bodhisattva* of Wisdom (see *Fig. 20*), wields his enlightening sword, he summarily slices away the encrustations of self-promoting pictures and notions that 'I' has thrown up against its own eclipse, and reveals the true face of things. Nothing at all is added; in fact, a great deal is taken away. What remains is true *wisdom*, which in basic Buddhist thought is invariably accompanied by

20. Manjushri, Bodhisattva *of Wisdom*

compassion – and therein lies an end of suffering. As the great Sixth Patriarch of the Zen school, Hui Neng, said:

> The idea of a self and of a being is Mount Meru. . . . When you get rid of the idea of a self and of a being, Mount Meru will topple. . . .
>
> (trans. Wong Mou Lam, *The Sutra Of Hui Neng*)

Or equally, Mount Kailas will topple. . . .

And what remains after that mighty falling: after the thunder has reverberated away and the dust begins to settle?

Just a heap of stones – a mere mountain, in fact: nothing more or less than that. The great miracle is our ordinary, everyday lives – as Layman P'ang, the great Chinese Zen man, says:

> How wonderful, how miraculous!
> I fetch wood; I carry water.

The writing – and perhaps also the reading – of this book has been a kind of literary pilgrimage to the sacred mountain, pursued in studies, in correspondence, in the learned libraries of London, with here and there the vivid high-point of an actual meeting with a real-life Kailas traveller. There has been the commercial side too: the meetings and negotiations with producers and publishers. There has been the endless accumulation of papers: notes, photocopies, drafts. . . . And the writing itself: the conjuring of veritable mountains of words and then the honing and fining. . . .

Just a heap of stones – just a heap of papers. . . .

This is in fact what seems to lie at the heart of all matters, not merely the matter of the sacred mountain: the simple reality of the here and now, so basic and yet so very hard to face, accept and fully grasp. There never was anything particularly special about that silver mountain shining against the indigo sky up on the dizzy heights of Tibet. . . . Nothing more special in fact than anything I encounter on the way to work each morning through remorselessly unromantic London N.W.10: down past the council flats; on by the crash repair garage with its acrid fumes of paint spray. . . .

All that remains for us unenlightened beings is our practice . . . and the hope that we too may see our sacred mountains topple. Then, finding ourselves at last disencumbered of the burdensome sense of 'I', we may look squarely into the reality of things. . . . Indeed, how wonderful, how miraculous!

AFTERWORD

Since the foregoing was written there has been a dramatic thaw in mainland China's relations with the rest of the world and many new developments have taken place with a bearing on our subject. Most significantly, the pilgrim route from India to Mount Kailas, closed since 1962, was reopened in 1981. In August that year it was announced that three groups of pilgrims would be leaving for the sacred mountain in September and October. Applications had to be in within a week. They poured in – over a thousand – so that lots had to be drawn to decide who should go. The first party of twenty pilgrims was, according to Charles Allan, led by Pundit Kishen Singh's grandson, S. C. Rawat.

Raghubir Singh, who was a member of one of these first pilgrim parties, reports (*Smithsonian*, Vol. 13, No. 2, pp. 94 ff.) that while there has been damage to the religious buildings in the sacred area, spiritual life does at present go on to a degree and pilgrims still circle the Kailas *parikrama* route. Throughout the time Singh's party was in Tibet it was accompanied by members of the militia that patrols the Tibetan borderland. The pilgrims were driven in Chinese jeeps to the sacred lakes via the Gurla Pass, and so on to Tarchen – 'the much-damaged Buddhist monastery near the southern base of Kailas'. A photograph of two young nomads accompanies the report; they stand amid the ruins of the *gompa* wearing traditional dress save for incongruous American-style sneakers. Singh goes on: 'At the monastery we conversed with four monks in halting Hindi . . . The herders, other lamas and devout Tibetans came daily through Tarchen to walk round Kailas.'

BIBLIOGRAPHY

PRIMARY SOURCES

Books

Chang, Garma C., *The Hundred Thousand Songs of Milarepa*, New York, 1962

Gansser, A., *The Throne of the Gods* (With Heim, A.), London, 1939

— *Geology of the Himalayas*, London, 1964

Govinda, Lama Anagarika, *Bilder Aus Indien Und Tibet*, Haldenwang, 1978

— *Psycho-Cosmic Symbolism of the Buddhist Stūpa*, Emeryville, 1976

— *The Way of the White Clouds*, Berkeley, 1962

Govinda, Li Gotami, *Tibet in Pictures*, Emeryville, 1979

Harrer, Heinrich, *Seven Years in Tibet*, London, 1953

Hamsa, Bhagwan Shri, *The Holy Mountain*, London, 1934

Hedin, Sven, *Transhimalaya*, 3 vols, London, 1910

— *Southern Tibet*, 9 vols, Stockholm, 1917

Kawaguchi, Ekai, *Three Years in Tibet*, Adyar, 1910

Landor, Arnold Henry Savage, *In the Forbidden Land*, 2 vols., London, 1898

Longstaff, Dr. Tom, *This My Voyage*, London, 1950

Pranavananda, Swami, *Pilgrim's Companion to the Holy Kailas and Manasarovar*, Allahabad, 1938

— *Exploration in Tibet*, 1st ed., Calcutta, 1939; 2nd ed., Calcutta, 1951

Rawling, Capt. C. G., *The Great Plateau*, London, 1905

Schary, Edwin, *In Search of the Mahatmas of Tibet*, London, 1937

Sherring, Charles A., *Western Tibet and the British Borderland*, London, 1906

Tichy, Herbert, *Tibetan Adventure*, London, 1938

Tucci, Giuseppe, *Santi e Briganti nel Tibet Ignoto*, Milan, 1937

— *The Religions of Tibet*, London, 1980

The Sacred Mountain

Tucci, Giuseppe, *Transhimalaya*, London, 1973
— *The Theory and Practice of the Mandala*, London, 1969
— *Tibet*, London, 1967
Webber, Thomas W., *In the Forests of Upper India*, London, 1902

Articles

Blakeney, Major T. S., *Approach to Kailas*, in *Alpine Journal*, Vol. 55, 1945–6, pp. 316–7

Hedin, Sven, *Journeys in Tibet, 1906–8*, in *Geographical Journal*, Vol. XXXIII, April 1909

Kapur, Chatter Bhuj, *A Pilgrimage to Mount Kailas*, in *The Modern Review* (India), Vol. LX No. 2, August 1936

Longstaff, T. G., *Notes on a Journey through the Western Himalaya* in *Geographical Journal*, Vol. XXIX, Feb. 1907, pp. 201 ff.

Moorcroft, William, *A Journey to Lake Manasarovar in Undes, a Province of Little Tibet*, in *Asiatick Researches*, Vol. 12, 1818 pp. 375 ff. (see also *Geographical Journal*, August 1905, pp. 180 ff.)

Ruttledge, Hugh, *Notes on a Visit to Western Tibet in 1926*, in *Geographical Journal*, Vol. LXXI, May 1928, pp. 431 ff.

Ryder, Capt. C. H. D., *Exploration and Survey with the Tibet Frontier Commission and from Gyangtse to Simla vîa Gartok*, in *Geographical Journal*, Vol. XXVI, Oct. 1905, pp. 369 ff.

— *Sven Hedin's Expedition in Tibet*, in *Geographical Journal*, Vol. XXXII, Oct. 1908, pp. 585 ff.

Smith, Capt. H. U., *A Trip to Thibet, Kylas, Source of the Sutlej and the Manasurwur and Rakhas Lakes*, in *Proceedings of the Royal Geographical Society*, Vol. XI, 1866–7, pp. 119 ff.

Stoll, Eva, *TISE – der Heilige Berg im Tibet*, in *Geographica Helvetica*, Bd. 4, Berne, 1966

Strachey, Lieut. Henry, 66th Bengal N.I., *Narrative of a Journey to the Cho Lagan (Rakas Tal), Cho Mapam (Manasarovar) and the Valley or Purang etc.*, in *Journal of the Asiatic Society of Bengal*, July, August and September 1948

Strachey, Lieut.-Gen. Sir Richard, *Narrative of a Journey to the Lakes Rakas-Tal and Manasarovar in Western Tibet, Undertaken in September 1848*, in *Geographical Journal*, Vol. XV, February 1900 (pp. 150 ff.), March 1900 (pp. 248 ff.), April 1900 (pp. 394 ff.) and *On the Physical Geography of the Provinces of Kumaon and Garhwal in the Himalaya Mountains, and the Adjoining Parts of Tibet*, in the Journal of the *Royal Geographical Society*, Vol. XXI, 1851, pp. 57 ff.

Wilson, R. C. *Kailas Parbat and Two Passes of the Kumaon Himalaya* in *Alpine Journal*, Vol. 40, 1928, pp. 23 ff.

Archives
The India Office Library and Records lodges much material of interest. The records of the Political and Secret Department contain the following in particular:

Report by *W. S. Cassels*, Assistant Commissioner, Almora, on a visit to Western Tibet in July 1907 (L/P&S/7/207/No. 1873)

Report by *N. C. Stiffe*, Deputy Commissioner of Almora, on his visit to Tibet of July 1911. (L/P&S/11/21/No. 2476)

Narrative of Personal Experiences in Western Tibet in 1929 by *E. B. Wakefield*. (L/P&S/12/4163)

Report on a visit to Western Tibet in October 1932 by *F. Williamson*, Officer on Special Duty in Sikkim. (L/P&S/12/4163)

Original Texts
i. Dewang, N. Norbu, *mTsho Mapham dKarchag* – 'History of the Sacred Mountain Tise and Blue Lake Mapham'. Cited by B. Olschak in Mystic Art of Ancient Tibet, London 1973 – credited to ISMEO, Rome – who disclaim all knowledge, a copy of this text never tracked to ground.
ii. *Two Rare Bonpo Dkar-chag of the Sacred Kailash and Manasarowar written by Ye-ses-rgyal-mtshan and Dkarru Grubdban Bstan-'dzin-rin-chen, reproduced from rare manuscripts preserved at Baam-glin Monastery in Dolpo by Tshi Dorji* – Tibet House, New Delhi (1979)
iii. Professor G. Tucci claims to have collected a copy of a guide book to Mount Kailas which he found at the Dindipu monastery in 1935.

SECONDARY SOURCES

Ali, S. M., *The Geography of the Purānas*, New Delhi, 1966
Avalon, Arthur (Sir John Woodroffe) (trans.), *The Tantra of the Great Liberation*, London, 1913
Beal, Samuel, *A Catena of Buddhist Scriptures from the Chinese*, London, 1871
Blacker, Carmen, *The Catalpa Bow*, London, 1975
Blofeld, John, *The Wheel of Life*, London, 1959
— *The Tantric Mysticism of Tibet*, New York, 1970
Brunton, Dr. Paul, *A Hermit in the Himalayas*, London, 1975
Burckhardt, Titus, *Sacred Art in East and West*, London, 1967
Daniélou, Alain, *Hindu Polytheism* New York, 1964

de Filippi, Filippo (ed), *An Account of Tibet: The Travels of Ippolito Desideri of Pistoia, S.J., 1712–21*, London, 1937

Ekvall, Robert B., *Religious Observances in Tibet*, Chicago, 1964

Eliade, Mircea, *Patterns in Comparative Religion*, London, 1958

— *The Myth of the Eternal Return*, Princeton, 1974

Gombrich, Richard, *Ancient Indian Cosmology*, in Blacker, C. and Loewe, M. (ed.) *Ancient Cosmologies*, London, 1975

Hardy, Spence, *Manual of Buddhism*, London, 1860

— *Legends and Theories of the Buddhists*, London, 1881

Hastings, James (ed), *The Encyclopaedia of Religion and Ethics*, Edinburgh 1921 – articles by L. de la Vallée Poussin, *Buddhist Cosmogony and Cosmology*; by H. Jacobi, *Hindu Cosmogony and Cosmology*; and J. A. MacCullock, *Mountains and Mountain Gods.*

Havell, E. B., *The Himalayas in Indian Art*, London, 1924

Hoffmann, Helmut, *The Religions of Tibet*, London, 1961

Hori, Ichiro, *Folk Religion in Japan*, Tokyo, 1968

Huc, M., *Travels in Tartary, Thibet and China*, Chicago, 1900

Keay, John, *Where Men and Mountains Meet*, London, 1977

Lauf, D. I., *Tibetan Sacred Art*, Berkeley and London, 1976

MacGregor, John A., *Tibet – A Chronicle of Exploration*, London, 1970

de Nebesky–Wojkovitz, R., *Oracles and Demons of Tibet*, The Hague, 1956

Olschak, B. and Wangyal, G. T., *Mystic Art of Ancient Tibet*, London, 1973

Osborn, Arthur (ed), *The Teachings of Ramana Maharshi*, London, 1971

Pallis, Marco, *The Way and the Mountain*, London, 1960

Rooke, G. H. (trans.), *The Meghadūta of Kalidasa*, Oxford, 1935

Sandberg, Graham, *Exploration in Tibet*, Calcutta and London, 1904

Schmid, Toni, *The Cotton Clad Mila. The Tibetan Poet-Saint's Life in Pictures*, Stockholm, 1952

Sircar, D. C., *Cosmography and Cosmology in Early Indian Literature*, Calcutta, 1967

Snellgrove, D., and Richardson, H., *A Cultural History of Tibet*, Boulder, 1980

Stevenson, Mrs. Sinclair, *The Heart of Jainism*, Oxford, 1915

Takakusu, J., *Essentials of Buddhist Philosophy*, Delhi, 1975

Tripathi, Maya Prasad, *The Development of Geographical Knowledge in Ancient India*, Benares, 1969

Bibliography

Waddell, L. A., *Lamaism or the Buddhism of Tibet*, Cambridge, 1967
Ward, Michael (ed), *The Mountaineer's Companion*, London, 1966
Warren, H. C., *Buddhism in Translations*, Cambridge, Mass., 1896
Welch, Holmes, *The Practice of Chinese Buddhism*, Harvard, 1967
Wilford, F., *The Sacred Isles of the West*, in *Asiatick Researches*, Vols. VIII, IX and X, Calcutta, 1808
Wilhelm, Richard, *The Soul of China*, London, 1928
— *I Ching*, London, 1975
Zimmer, Heinrich, *Myths & Symbols in Indian Art & Religion*, Princeton, 1974

ADDENDA

Allen, Charles, *A Mountain in Tibet (The Search for Mount Kailas and the Sources of the Great Rivers of India)*, London, 1982
Conze, Edward, *Memoirs of a Modern Gnostic*, Parts 1 and 2, Sherborne, 1979
Singh, Raghubir, *Pilgrims Return to Kailas, Tibet's Sacred Mountain*, in *Smithsonian* magazine, Vol. 13, No. 2, May 1982, pp. 94 ff.

INDEX

NOTE ON SPELLING: There are no standard transliterations for many of the Tibetan names and words used in this book. Different writers use different spellings, and thus variations occur in the narrative and in the quotations introduced into it. Cross-references, however, are given in the Index.

Index

Index

Index

Index